AZURE CLOUD COMPUTING
AZ-900 EXAM STUDY GUIDE

4 IN 1
MICROSOFT AZURE CLOUD DEPLOYMENT, SECURITY, PRIVACY & PRICING CONCEPTS

BOOK 1
CLOUD COMPUTING FUNDAMENTALS
INTRODUCTION TO MICROSOFT AZURE AZ-900 EXAM

BOOK 2
MICROSOFT AZURE SECURITY AND PRIVACY CONCEPTS
CLOUD DEPLOYMENT TOOLS AND TECHNIQUES, SECURITY & COMPLIANCE

BOOK 3
MICROSOFT AZURE PRICING & SUPPORT OPTIONS
AZURE SUBSCRIPTIONS, MANAGEMENT GROUPS & COST MANAGEMENT

BOOK 4
MICROSOFT AZURE AZ-900 EXAM PREPARATION GUIDE
HOW TO PREPARE, REGISTER AND PASS YOUR EXAM

RICHIE MILLER

Disclaimer

Every effort was made to produce this book as truthful as possible, but no warranty is implied. The author shall have neither liability nor responsibility to any person or entity concerning any loss or damages ascending from the information contained in this book. The information in the following pages are broadly considered to be truthful and accurate of facts, and such any negligence, use or misuse of the information in question by the reader will render any resulting actions solely under their purview.

Table of Contents – Book 1

Table of Contents – Book 2

Table of Contents – Book 3

5

Table of Contents – Book 4

BOOK 1

CLOUD COMPUTING
FUNDAMENTALS

INTRODUCTION TO
MICROSOFT AZURE AZ-900 EXAM

RICHIE MILLER

Introduction

In the following chapters, we're going to talk about the AZ-900 exam and how to prepare for it. We will first cover the benefits of getting Azure certified and why you should consider getting the AZ-900 certification. We will then do an overview of the AZ-900 certification exam, what you will be evaluated on, as well as learn about the skills measured document. Finally, we will do an overview of our learning materials for this exam. By the end of this book, you will know what's needed to start studying for the AZ-900 Microsoft Certification exam. Let's start by learning what are the benefits of getting Azure certified and, more particular, why the AZ-900 exam. Let's start by asking, why do we even want to get a Microsoft certification? First of all, Microsoft certifications can really help give you a professional advantage by providing globally recognized and industry-endorsed evidence of mastering skills in a digital and cloud business. If we look at the numbers, according to multiple studies, 91% of certified IT professionals say that certification gives them more professional credibility, 93% of decision makers agree that certified employees provide more added value, and 52% of certified IT professionals say that their expertise is more sought after within the organization after getting certified. Honestly, certifications can also help you in the financial aspect of your career. 35% of technical professionals say that getting certified led to salary or wage increases, while 26% of technical professionals reported job promotions after getting certified. Now let's get a bit more Azure-specific and talk why we want to get Azure certified. Microsoft Azure is one of the top cloud providers in the world for Infrastructure and Platform as Service workloads. 63% of enterprises in the world are currently running apps on Microsoft Azure, second only to AWS. However, 19% of enterprises expect to invest significantly more on Azure in 2022, and this is leading all of the other cloud vendors this year, so Azure is still growing at an astonishing rate. Finally, 44.5% of enterprises say that Microsoft Azure is their preferred provider for cloud business intelligence. If we get more specific into our Azure certification, the Azure certification portfolio is actually the biggest certification portfolio at Microsoft, and it includes 3 fundamental-level certifications, 10 associate-level certifications, 2 expert-level certifications, and 3 specialty-level certifications. But what makes the AZ-900 unique? The AZ-900 Azure Fundamental Certification is an optional, but very highly recommended prerequisite for all of the other Azure certifications. It's the place you should start whether you have done a Microsoft certification before and now you want to specialize in Azure, or if this is your first ever Microsoft certification, the AZ-900 is where you should begin your Azure certification journey.

Chapter 1 AZ-900 Exam Summary

Now that we know why the AZ-900 is a very important and valuable exam, let's do an overview of the exam. The Azure Fundamental Certification is an opportunity to prove knowledge of cloud concepts, Azure services, Azure workloads, security and privacy in Azure, as well as Azure pricing and support. From an audience point of view, the AZ-900 is intended for candidates who are just beginning to work with cloud-based solutions and services or are new to Azure. Also, as this is a fundamentals exam, before starting to study, candidates should be familiar with general technology concepts, but really no other requirements as you will learn the fundamentals in the study material for this exam. If we take a look at the basics, the AZ-900 exam costs 99 USD; however, the price might vary depending on your region. Furthermore, I highly encourage you to check with your manager or HR person as organizations will often reimburse the cost for learning and certifications. The worst that they can say is no, so it's always worth to ask. Also, something that is really nice is that fundamental certifications do not expire. For example, associate and expert-level Microsoft certifications expire after one year, but because this is a fundamentals-level exam, it doesn't expire, so that is nice. Lastly, if you're a student, you can actually get college credit for passing Microsoft exams and earning Microsoft certifications. This works mostly in the United States, not internationally. If we take a look at the skills measured, it's split up into six categories, the first one being describe cloud concepts, which is 20 to 25% of the exam. We then have describe core Azure services, which is 15 to 20% of the exam. Third, we have to describe core solutions and management tools on Azure, which is 10 to

15% of the exam. Fourth, we have to describe general security and network security features, which is between 10 and 15% of the exam. Our fifth category is describing identity, governance, privacy, and compliance features, which is 20 to 25% of the exam. Finally, describe Azure cost management and service-level agreements, which is between 10 to 15% of the exam. There is one keyword that is repeated throughout each objective, and that is the verb describe. Verbs are very important in Microsoft certifications. So, what does the word describe mean? As we're talking about the fundamentals-level exam, the verb describe tells us that you do not need to know how to configure, manage or implement features. What you really need to know is what features are available and what business problems they solve. The goal of this exam is for you to be able to know what cloud computing challenges can be solved by what Azure solution. If you talk with someone and they say we have this business need for a workload, you need to be able to know, this Azure solution can help you with that. This is why the AZ-900 is an amazing exam for anyone working in the Microsoft ecosystem. Whether you're an IT pro, dev, project manager or business stakeholder, knowing what solutions Microsoft offers can really allow you to better understand the projects you're working on and to propose the right solution at the right time. Now that we have talked about the high-level objectives, Microsoft also provides a document called the skills outline, or the skills measured document, and it's important to review it before and after studying for this exam. The skills outlined are the full detailed list of everything that you need to know for the exam. We will review it later, but really this should be our checklist of things to study for the AZ-900 exams.

Chapter 2 Skills Measured Document

If you open up your browser and type AZ-900, this page will be one of the first choices.

This is the Microsoft Learning page for the AZ-900 Microsoft Azure Fundamentals exam. On the exam page at the top, you will see the description and audience for the exam, you will be able to schedule it, but what we want to talk about is the skills measured.

Skills measured

- The content of this exam was updated on November 9, 2020. Please download the exam skills outline below to see what changed.
- Describe cloud concepts (20-25%)
- Describe core Azure services (15-20%)
- Describe core solutions and management tools on Azure (10-15%)
- Describe general security and network security features (10-15%)
- Describe identity, governance, privacy, and compliance features (20-25%)
- Describe Azure cost management and Service Level Agreements (10-15%)

⤓ Download exam skills outline

You will see on the exam page, you only have the high-level skills; however, it's important that you click this link, Download exam skills outline. If you click on it, it will open up a PDF, either it will download it or open up directly in the browser depending on your settings.

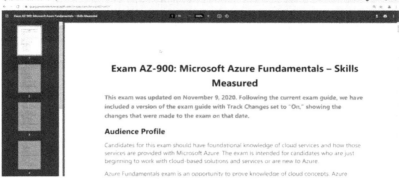

Something that is really important, because as the cloud always changes, so do Microsoft certification exams, so you might see at the top a warning like this one. This exam was updated on November 9, 2020, and if you go to the bottom, at the bottom you will have kind of a document with tracked changes on, so you can see what were the changes that were done on the date that it was changed.

NOTE: Most questions cover features that are General Availability (GA). The exam may contain questions on Preview features if those features are commonly used.

Describe Cloud Concepts (~~15~~ 2020-25%)

Identify ~~Describe~~ the benefits and considerations of using cloud services

- identify the benefits of cloud computing. ~~Describe terms~~ such as High Availability, Scalability, Elasticity, Agility, ~~Fault Tolerance,~~ and Disaster Recovery
- ~~describe the principles of economies of scale~~
- ~~describe~~ Identify the differences between Capital Expenditure (CapEx) and Operational Expenditure (OpEx)
- describe the consumption-based model

Describe the differences between categories of cloud services~~Infrastructure-as-a-Service (IaaS), Platform-as-a-Service (PaaS) and Software-as-a-Service (SaaS)~~

- describe the shared responsibility model
- describe Infrastructure-as-a-Service (IaaS),

And Microsoft generally also announces at least one or two months in advance if a change will happen, and it will be shown the exact same way, simply the date will be on the future so you can see if Microsoft will change the objectives. If you go to the top, you have the Audience Profile again, same thing, but what gets interesting is that for each exam objective, so let's say Describe Cloud Concepts, it's broken down into sub-objectives and details. Under Describe Cloud Concepts, we have Identify the benefits and considerations of using cloud services, identify the benefits of cloud computing such as high availability, scalability, elasticity, agility, and disaster recovery.

Describe Cloud Concepts (20-25%)

Identify the benefits and considerations of using cloud services

- identify the benefits of cloud computing, such as High Availability, Scalability, Elasticity, Agility, and Disaster Recovery
- identify the differences between Capital Expenditure (CapEx) and Operational Expenditure (OpEx)
- describe the consumption-based model

Describe the differences between categories of cloud services

- describe the shared responsibility model
- describe Infrastructure-as-a-Service (IaaS),
- describe Platform-as-a-Service (PaaS)

Then we have to describe the differences between the categories of cloud services.

Describe the differences between categories of cloud services

- describe the shared responsibility model
- describe Infrastructure-as-a-Service (IaaS),
- describe Platform-as-a-Service (PaaS)

- describe serverless computing
- describe Software-as-a-Service (SaaS)
- identify a service type based on a use case

Describe the differences between types of cloud computing

So you need to know what's the difference between Infrastructure as a Service and Platform as a Service and Software as a Service and then identify a service type based on a use case, so, you need to be able to know what workloads should go where. Then for each objective really, you have all of the details on what services do you need to know, what are the different things you should be able to describe. You can either save it locally or you can even print it and then use a highlighter, once you feel confident you learned something, highlight it, and this should be the checklist for your exam. You need to be able to go in the details in the skills measured document and then be able to say that all of the different tools, services, and concepts in here, I'm able to describe. It's an important tool for your study to pass the AZ-900 exam.

Chapter 3 Why Use Microsoft Azure

We're going to look at a lot of individual services within Azure throughout the book, but in this chapter, I want to give you a broad overview of what Azure can do and how it's structured. I'm going to demystify Azure for you and give you the bigger picture of the environment that all the individual services operate in before we go into many of those services later on. But first, I want to talk about the Azure Fundamentals certification. If you're studying for the AZ-900 exam, this book will definitely help you do that, but this book doesn't encompass all of the exam objectives. If you're studying for the exam, I encourage you to read the most up-to-date study guide provided by Microsoft because it does change from time to time and then map those objectives to the topics covered in this book. That way, you'll be able to see what else you need to learn outside of this book in order to pass the exam. That said, this is a book for people new to Azure, so we're going to start from the ground up by talking about why you would want to use Azure in the first place. Azure is a cloud platform with more than 200 products and services that help you create applications and solutions. The cloud platform part just means that Microsoft abstracts away all the underlying hosting infrastructure so you can rent basic things like web hosting, computing power, databases, and storage, as well as some really full-featured solutions, like business analytics tools, artificial intelligence services, and portals for managing devices for the Internet of Things. You might never use some of those advanced tools, but they give you options you probably didn't have on-premises, at least not without installing a bunch of software and services on your own servers to do those things. But even if you just host websites and file shares, traditional things that every organization does, why would you want to use Azure? Well, there's a lot that goes into managing your own servers and datacenter. There's buying the physical hardware, storing those servers in a secure place where nobody can tamper with them, there's cooling needed because servers generate a lot of heat, and there's electricity and of course backup electricity unless you don't mind your applications being unavailable during a power outage, plus all the networking components and monitoring for health, as well as to make sure that no one hacks your network and computers. But there's also less obvious things, like you might have a need for a lot of computing power at certain times of the day, week or year, so you need the servers to be able to handle that load. Let's say you're hosting an ecommerce application to sell your company's products and there's way more traffic around Christmas than during the rest of the year. You need your servers to be able to handle the load, but they sit underutilized the rest of the year. That's a waste of money and hard drives can fail or you might need to keep increasing your storage because the business groups keep generating more files. They tend to do that. Then they're storing backups of files and databases. What about disaster recovery? If there's a major outage at your datacenter, are you okay with the apps not being available or do you want to maintain another datacenter in another location that can take over that traffic? There's also the ongoing maintenance of the operating systems on those servers. They need to be patched and monitored for threats. Then every five years or so, you need to replace all that hardware, not to mention the networking components like routers, switches, and firewalls. Microsoft, Azure and cloud computing in general was created to address many of these issues. For the rest of this book, we'll look at services in Azure for hosting applications and data and all the virtual infrastructure that allows you to do that. You'll see how easy it is to create and configure that infrastructure in Azure without having to manage any physical hardware like you do on-premises. We'll start with signing up for a subscription in Azure. That'll give you a way to follow along and create your own Azure services. Then you'll start to learn how Azure is implemented using regions, how those regions are connected, and all about Azure datacenters in the regions. You'll learn about resource groups, which are the containers for holding multiple resources that make up a logical grouping, like for an application. Then we'll explore the Azure portal, which is the main way you'll be interacting with Azure and managing instances of services that you create. We'll create some resources in the portal, and I'll show you Azure Active Directory, which is the identity service in Azure for managing user accounts, and it provides the foundation for access control for managing Azure, as well as access control for the people using the applications that you deploy to Azure. Finally, we'll tie a lot of the Azure concepts together by discussing how Azure Active Directory and subscriptions are related. So let's get started by signing up for an Azure subscription next.

Chapter 4 How to Create an Azure Subscription

Let's create an Azure subscription we can use to explore the Azure portal. We're going to create a free trial account at azure.microsoft.com/free. For verification, we'll need three things, a Microsoft account, and I'll explain that more shortly, you'll need a phone number where a verification code can be sent, and you'll need a credit card. The card won't get charged, not unless you manually upgrade the account to a pay-as-you-go account. If you already have a pay-as-you-go account, you can just use that instead, but you will get charged for everything you create. Let's go to azure.microsoft.com/free.

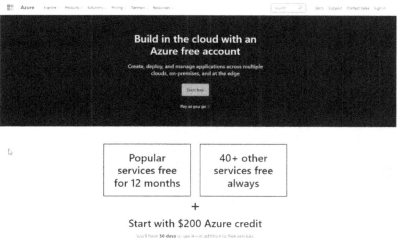

If you've never signed up for a free account, you can do that and get 200 USD credit for 30 days to use for creating resources in Azure. In addition to that, there are certain services that are free for 12 months and other services that are always free, but they're pretty limited in functionality. If we scroll down a bit, this page describes some of the things we can do in Azure, like hosting web applications using Azure App Services, using Azure Machine Learning, creating Azure Virtual Machines or containers, and serverless options like Azure Functions and Azure Logic Apps, which let you build workflows with tons of connectors to services inside and outside of Azure.

We'll talk about all these services later on. Further down, it says that if we upgrade this free trial to a pay-as-you-go account where our credit card can get billed for usage, we'll be entitled to some free services, like 750 hours of running a Linux or a Windows virtual machine, a 250-GB Azure SQL Database, and 5 GB of blob storage.

We'll talk about storage later on too. But now, let's scroll down and click Start free. The first thing we need is either a Microsoft email address or a GitHub account.

If you're not aware, Microsoft acquired GitHub in 2018, which is why you can use your GitHub identity to create an Azure account. If you're using an email address, it needs to be a Microsoft one, so usually an Outlook, Hotmail or a Live account, but you can even use a phone number now to create a Microsoft account. The point is that you need that Microsoft account already in order to create an Azure account, but you could create the account from this link. I already have a Microsoft account, so I'll enter that email address here and I'll enter my password. I don't have multifactor authentication set up for this Microsoft account, but you could do that in which case you'd need to provide another factor of authentication when logging in, like a code that's generated in the Microsoft Authenticator app on your phone or a temporary code that's sent to you by text or phone call. Now I'm brought to the screen where I can fill in my information. Since I'm logged in, it picks up my name and I need to enter a phone number. This can be a cellphone or a home phone because you can choose to have the code sent to you by text or through an automated voice call. I'll choose Text me and I get a text on my cell phone with a code. So I'll enter that code here and click Verify code. Now I need to enter my address.

Phone ⓘ

Address line 1

Address line 2 (Optional)

City

Province

--Select--

Postal Code

☐ I agree to the customer agreement and privacy agreement.

☐ I would like to receive information, tips, and offers from Microsoft about Azure and other Microsoft products and services, and for Microsoft to share my information with select Partners so I can receive relevant information about their products and services.

Next

Identity verification by card

Sign up

Now we need to agree to the customer agreement and privacy agreement. There are links here, of course, so feel free to read through those if you'd like before agreeing. I'll click Next and here's where you need to enter the credit card.

It says you won't be charged unless you move to pay-as-you-go pricing. You should use a credit card here that's never been used for a free trial account, otherwise you may get denied, which makes sense because you shouldn't be able to keep creating free trials in order to get credits to use Azure for free. So I'll enter my credit card info, and just click Sign up. Microsoft will verify your credit card, and once that's done you'll come to a screen that says you're approved and there's a link that will bring you to the Azure portal. So let's go to portal.azure.com, which is the administrative portal for Azure and the browser brings me into the portal.

Next, we'll explore the Azure portal a bit and see how to create a resource in Azure.

Chapter 5 How to Create Resources in Azure

I'm logged into the Azure portal at portal.azure.com. An Azure Active Directory instance gets created with this Azure trial, which means we can create individual users and assign them permissions, so you don't have to keep using this administrative account to log in and really you probably shouldn't because it has superuser privileges. It's a good idea to create an administrative account in Azure AD and use that instead. On this home page, you can access some Azure services, and there's a menu on the left that has shortcuts to some default services, like any Azure virtual machines you've created, SQL databases, and the Azure Active Directory associated with this subscription.

You can access the list of all services from this menu item. You'll see a tour of the Azure portal later, but let's just look at creating a resource. I'll choose the Virtual machines link here.

25

All services

That brings us to a page where all the virtual machines that were created in this subscription are listed, and of course there aren't any yet.

Let's select the drop-down list to create one, and at this point we haven't selected whether this will be a Linux or a Windows VM. That's fine. What I really want to show you here are some of the mandatory inputs.

Create a virtual machine

The first one is the subscription, and that's filled out automatically. And then there's the resource group that this virtual machine will belong to. Resource groups are basically a container that holds resources, and everything in Azure, including a virtual machine, is considered a resource. We'll talk about how resource groups are used for security and deployment purposes later on. The other thing is the region. You need to select the region that this virtual machine will be created in, which basically means the datacenter where it will exist. The list is pretty small, but that's because we're using a free trial account. Microsoft limits the datacenters available, so regions in high demand don't use too much capacity on free trials. But you could contact Microsoft support if you really want to create this VM in a region that's not listed here. I won't go through anything else on this page. We'll look at creating virtual machines in the next chapter. So, now you know that you'll need to choose a region when creating a resource. Let's talk about regions in Azure in more detail, next.

Chapter 6 What are Azure Regions & Availability Zones

Now let's talk about how Azure is physically implemented. You create services in Azure, like an Azure App Service for hosting a web app or a storage account for storing files. You can then deploy your applications and files to those services. That all gets hosted on Virtual Machines in Azure. Depending on the service you choose, you may have more or less access to those virtual servers for configuration. If you create a virtual machine, for example, you have full control. If you create an app service, you don't have direct access to the virtual machine. But the virtual servers in Azure are hosted on physical servers somewhere. That somewhere is an Azure datacenter. Azure datacenters are physical buildings located all around the world. At the time, there are over 200 Microsoft Azure datacenters worldwide. Each datacenter houses thousands of servers. There are about 4 million physical servers throughout the world. We're going to talk more about how datacenters are implemented later on too. Datacenters are located in regions. A region is a geographic location, often consisting of multiple datacenters. A region is what you choose when you create a resource. You decide which region you want your service created in. We'll talk about considerations in choosing a region in just a little bit. There are often multiple datacenters within a region, which helps in case a single datacenter becomes unavailable. But within certain regions, there's what's called availability zones. Availability zones are unique physical locations within a single region. There's a minimum of three separate availability zones in the region, and each availability zone is made up of one or more datacenters equipped with independent power, cooling, and networking. Some services like zone-redundant storage in Azure storage accounts will replicate your data automatically across all the zones in the region. Every region is located within a geography, which in Azure is a group of regions that define a boundary for data residency and disaster recovery. A geography is generally a single country, but it can be made up of multiple countries. Within a geography, there are region pairs available. Region pairs are datacenters that are generally at least 300 miles apart to reduce the impact on availability caused by a natural disaster or a major power outage. They're connected through a dedicated regional low-latency network. Regional pairs allow you to configure automatic replication and failover for certain Azure services, like when you choose georedundant storage for your Azure storage account. Azure automatically makes copies of your data across the regions in the region pair. For services that don't have built-in options for failover like that, you can design your own strategy for failing over to another region if your primary region isn't available. Virtual machines are an example of this. You have to deploy duplicate virtual machines in another region yourself if you want to have them available for failover. This is called the shared responsibility model in Azure. The services are there for you, you just have to design the solution to take advantage of them. This page in the Azure documentation shows you the regions that are available in the different Azure geographies.

Find the Azure geography that meets your needs

Get all the information you need to get started on Azure in the geography that best fits your needs, from compliance to residency features. Select an Azure geography using the drop-down menu and compare to other geographies nearby.

Discover more about our global infrastructure and how it all works

You can see some geographies have more regions than others.

And on this page in the docs, you can see the region pairs that are available.

They're generally located in the same country, but not always.

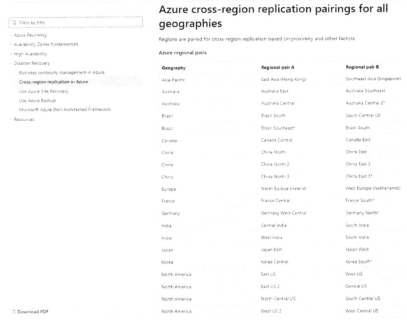

For example, at the bottom, it says that the Brazil South region is paired with the South Central US region.

ⓘ **Important**

- West India is paired in one direction only. West India's secondary region is South India, but South India's secondary region is Central India.
- Brazil South is unique because it's paired with a region outside of its geography. Brazil South's secondary region is South Central US. The secondary region of South Central US isn't Brazil South.

Next, let's talk about the factors that go into choosing an Azure region to deploy your resources to.

Chapter 7 How to Choose Azure Region for Deploying Resources

Now, let's talk about the factors that go into choosing an Azure region when you're creating resources in Azure. The first is proximity to users, and this has to do with performance. There are physical limitations to how fast data can travel around the world. If most of your users are located in Australia, for example, it doesn't make sense to host your website and database in a datacenter in the United States and have every request and response travel around the world, unless of course there are other reasons to choose that datacenter. One such consideration is that not all Azure services are available in all regions, especially when they're first released. You can go to this page in the Azure docs to see what services are available in which regions.

You can choose the regions and the service you're interested in or remove the filter and scroll through all the services to see what's available. Notice how there are services that are nonregional.

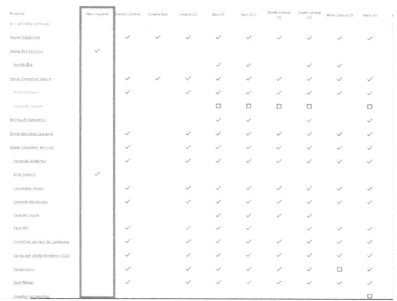

Products	Non regional	Canada Central	Canada East	Central US	East US	East US 2	North Central US	South Central US	West Central US	West US
AI + MACHINE LEARNING										
Azure Databricks		✓	✓	✓	✓	✓	✓	✓	✓	✓
Azure Bot Services	✓									
Health Bot					✓	✓		✓	✓	
Azure Cognitive Search		✓	✓	✓	✓	✓	✓	✓	✓	✓
AI Enrichment		✓		✓	✓	✓	✓	✓	✓	✓
Semantic Search					☐	☐	☐	☐		☐
Microsoft Genomics					✓	✓		✓		✓
Azure Machine Learning		✓		✓	✓	✓	✓	✓	✓	✓
Azure Cognitive Services		✓		✓	✓	✓	✓	✓	✓	✓
Anomaly Detector		✓		✓	✓	✓	✓	✓	✓	✓
Bing Speech	✓									
Computer Vision		✓		✓	✓	✓	✓	✓	✓	✓
Content Moderator		✓		✓	✓	✓	✓	✓	✓	✓
Custom Vision					✓	✓	✓	✓		
Face API		✓		✓	✓	✓		✓	✓	✓
Cognitive Service for Language		✓		✓	✓	✓	✓	✓	✓	✓
Language Understanding (LUIS)		✓		✓	✓	✓	✓	✓	✓	✓
Personalizer		✓		✓	✓	✓	✓	✓	☐	✓
QnA Maker		✓		✓	✓	✓	✓	✓	✓	✓
Speaker recognition										☐

These are ones that don't require you to choose a region when you create them, like the Azure Bot Services. It's also possible that within a specific service, some features might not be available in the region closest to you. A great example of this are different sizes for virtual machines. On the virtual machine pricing page, if I scroll down, the region is selected as East US.

Explore pricing options

Apply filters to customize pricing options to your needs.

General purpose

Balanced CPU-to-memory ratio. Ideal for testing and development, small to medium databases, and low to medium traffic web servers.

All the classes of VMs are shown below. The amount of cores, RAM, and temporary storage is shown for each.

Av2 Standard

Av2 Standard is the latest generation of A-series virtual machines with similar CPU performance and faster disk. These virtual machines are suitable for development workloads, build servers, code repositories, low-traffic websites and web applications, micro services, early product experiments, and small databases. Like the prior A Standard generation, Av2 virtual machines will include load balancing and auto-scaling at no additional charge.

Instance	Core(s)	RAM	Temporary storage	Pay as you go with AHB	1 year reserved with AHB	3 year reserved with AHB	Spot with AHB	Add to estimate
A1 v2	1	2 GiB	10 GiB	$31.3900/month	- -	- -	$12.5494/month ~60% savings	[+]
A2 v2	2	4 GiB	20 GiB	$66.4300/month	- -	- -	$26.5589/month ~60% savings	[+]
A2m v2	2	16 GiB	20 GiB	$86.8700/month	- -	- -	$34.7305/month ~60% savings	[+]
A4 v2	4	8 GiB	40 GiB	$139.4300/month	- -	- -	$55.7443/month ~60% savings	[+]
A4m v2	4	32 GiB	40 GiB	$173.7400/month	- -	- -	$69.4610/month ~60% savings	[+]

So, there are basic VMs and there are specialized ones for things like processor-intensive compute tasks. I'll just search for a certain class of VMs. And they're shown here for East US, but if I change the region to South Central US, pricing is not available for this region because you can't create this class of VM there.

| D64s v5 | 64 | 256 GiB | 0 GiB | $2,690.7800/month | $1,587.7500/month ~41% savings / ~40% savings | $1,022.6132/month ~62% savings / ~61% savings | $567.7546/month ~78% savings / ~78% savings | [+] |
| D96s v5 | 96 | 384 GiB | 0 GiB | $4,036.9000/month | $2,381.5812/month ~41% savings | $1,533.9198/month ~62% savings | $851.7859/month ~78% savings | [+] |

So that's a consideration when choosing a region if you have specific needs for certain services. Another reason you might choose one region over another is for regulatory or compliance reasons with regards to data residency. If you work in an industry that's highly regulated or your company has policies around where the data must reside, then you might need to choose your region based on that criteria.

Now let's talk about how datacenters are connected together, and for this I want to show you this awesome interactive page on microsoft.com. This lets you choose a geography which tells you how many regions are available, and then you can choose the regions and see details like where it's located, the year it opened, how many availability zones the region has, some of the products available, information on disaster recovery options like region pairing, and standards that the datacenter complies with.

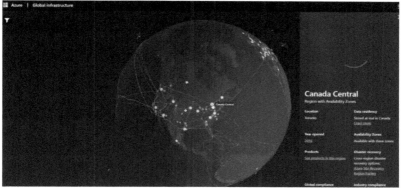

On this map, you can also see how the Microsoft global network is connected. There's over 165,000 miles of fiber optic and undersea cable systems that connect Azure datacenters around the world. When you access a resource in Azure, the traffic goes from your computer through your internet service provider to a point of presence, or PoP, that's managed by Microsoft where it enters into the Microsoft global network. Microsoft has over 185 of these PoPs around the world, so you get routed to the one closest to your location. You can click on these PoPs on the interactive map. PoPs are often placed within milliseconds of global population centers. Then, IP traffic stays on the Microsoft global network to access resources in Azure where it stays encrypted, flowing across the fiber and undersea cables to datacenter regions. You choose which regions to create your Azure resources in, so you can place your applications and data closest to where your users are, which helps keep the response time quick. Next, let's talk about Azure datacenters in more detail.

Chapter 8 Azure Data Centre Fundamentals

A Microsoft datacenter is a physical location that often looks like a bunch of warehouses. You can actually see a tour of a datacenter on microsoft.com. There's a virtual tour version as well that leads you through the areas of a datacenter. Each warehouse is big enough to store a commercial aircraft just to give you a sense of the size. Inside those warehouses are thousands of physical computers that host the virtual servers that you use when you create resources in Azure. The datacenter is built to withstand failures of individual components, so it has redundant networking, electricity, and cooling systems, as well as backup power sources. Because Microsoft hosts so many customers in their datacenters, you get the economy of scale of sharing those resources. Of course, your data is all separate from other customers and encrypted, and Azure datacenters undergo security reviews and have many industry certifications to ensure that your data is protected. Multilayered security is used to protect physical datacenters, infrastructure, and operations, and Microsoft has over 3500 cybersecurity experts monitoring activities in order to protect your business assets and data. So Microsoft is investing a lot more effort in security than any single customer could with their own on-premises datacenters. Microsoft used to be pretty secretive about their datacenters, but now they're more open about how their datacenters are structured and are working to standardize server and datacenter design through the Open Compute Project. Design specifications for server racks and server blades are being shared with the open source community through Project Olympus, similar to how software is made open source. Now let's talk about the energy needed to power a datacenter because this is a major consideration not only affecting cost, but affecting the environment, and that may be important to you when considering using Azure. Microsoft often chooses datacenter locations based on proximity to renewable energy sources. Microsoft enters into agreements with power companies to build wind and solar farms across thousands of acres of land. They build datacenters near hydroelectric dams and choose temperate locations so datacenters can be cooled by the outside air. There's even a project to convert waste heat from new datacenters in Finland into heating for cities. Heat is going to be transferred to customers through a system of insulated pipes for residential and commercial heating requirements. When it comes to backup power systems at datacenters, they are often powered by diesel fuel, but Microsoft is researching alternatives like synthetic fuels and hydrogen fuel cells. They plan to eliminate dependency on diesel by 2030. Let's look at the global infrastructure map again.

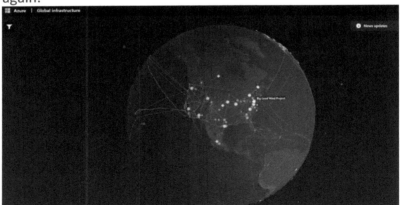

The yellow icons represent renewable energy projects that Microsoft is involved in for wind and solar. These are long-term purchase agreements with third parties. There's a lot of research and innovation going on into datacenter design, and especially cooling. One interesting development is Project Natick, which is an underwater datacenter that was operated for five years off the coast of Scotland where servers were housed in a sealed container at the bottom of the ocean floor. That allowed servers to be cooled using the temperature of the ocean. Another interesting development is the Azure Modular Datacenter. This is a shipping container that allows for setting up an Azure datacenter in a remote area where cloud computing wouldn't have been possible. They use Azure Stack to create a private cloud. These modular datacenters can be used as a mobile command center for humanitarian assistance, for military missions, and to set up wherever high performance computing is needed, and they can run connected to the internet or disconnected. So there's lots of interesting things happening with regards to Microsoft Azure datacenters, and you can read about it for hours online. But the important thing is that Microsoft spends a lot of effort on optimizing the design of their datacenters. Next, let's talk about the resources you create in Azure and how they're logically organized using resources groups

Chapter 9 Resources and Resource Group Basics

Now let's talk about resources and resource groups in Azure. A resource is just a manageable item in Azure. Let's take a look at the Azure portal. The All resources menu item shows all the resources that have been created in this subscription.

This includes things like App Services for web apps, Storage accounts, there's a Log Analytics workspace where logs are stored from the various services, a Key vault where encryption keys and certificates are securely stored, and there's a Virtual machine here. When you create a virtual machine, other resources are created too, like a public IP address for the VM so it can be reached over the internet, a disk to hold the operating system, a virtual network that the VM is connected to, and a network security group that's used to secure the network. We'll look at all these elements later on, but the point is pretty much anything that can be configured in Azure is considered a resource, even when you think it might just be part of another resource. Each of the resources in this list were created in a location, which is an Azure region, and each resources part of a subscription. A resource group is a container that holds a set of resources that share the same lifecycle. In other words, you deploy, update, and delete them together. You can add and remove individual resources to and from a resource group as your solution evolves, but the general guidance is that if a resource needs to exist on a different deployment cycle, then it should be in another resource group. Each resource you provision can only exist in one resource group. You can move a resource to another resource group if you need to, but it won't exist in both resource groups. Resources in different groups can communicate with each other. For example, you might have three different web applications being maintained by three different teams and they all exist in their own individual resource groups, but they all share a common database. That database can be in a completely different resource group and those web apps will still be able to use it. One of the main features of a resource group is that you can apply security controls to it for administrative actions, so you can assign reader roles to developers to be able to see what resources are in the resource group, but only administrators can make changes to the resource group. Resource groups allow you to leverage Resource Manager templates so you can deploy a set of resources using a JSON template and you can export a template from an existing resource group in order to deploy those resources in a repeatable way. This is great for moving a solution from a dev environment into a production environment, for example. When you create a resource group, you specify a region that it gets created in, but a resource group is just a container with metadata about the resources it contains, so the resource group can be created in a different region than the resources in the group. You can create a resource group during the creation of most resources, like when you're in the process of creating a new virtual machine. In that case, the resource group will get created in the same region that you specify for the virtual machine. You can also create the resource group by itself and then select it as the resource group to use when creating other resources. Next, let's explore the Azure portal, and in the process we'll create a resource group.

Chapter 10 How to Explore Azure Portal

Once you have an Azure account, you have access to the subscriptions associated with that account by going to portal.azure.com. I'll select the Microsoft account I used to create this Azure account. And I supplied my password earlier, so I'm already logged into my Microsoft account in this browser. That brings us into the Azure portal, and by default we're brought to the home page, which has some shortcuts, including shortcuts to create resources in Azure. Let's look at the menu across the top. At the top right is information about your logged-in account. There's a link to sign out, a link to go to the details of this Microsoft account, and the ability to switch directories. We'll talk about Azure Active Directory tenants later on, which is what this refers to. You can also access a link here to be taken to view your Azure bill if you have one.

Next across the top is the ability to send feedback to Microsoft. Then there's a link for Support + troubleshooting. Azure provides unlimited free support for subscription management, and for technical questions there are several support plans available which do have costs involved, but during a trial, you get the Developer support plan for free, which is normally a paid plan. Next is the Portal settings.

The first tab here has to do with directory management, which again involves Azure Active Directory, so I won't talk about that just yet. But this is the one I want to show you, Appearance + startup views.

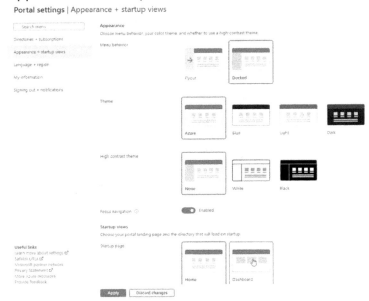

I personally like to see the left menu permanently docked and also prefer the first screen I see to be the dashboard. Let's apply these changes. Now that menu appears on the left.

We'll talk about this in a second, but first let's finish off with the menu at the top. The Notifications link shows anything that's in progress or has recently happened, like when you create a resource in Azure it will show here that it's in process and when it's finished being created. The next link is to change directories. So, this is just a shortcut to the first tab on the Portal settings. This farthest link on the left is for the Azure Cloud Shell.

This is basically a command line interface right within the Azure portal that lets you run PowerShell commands and commands for the Azure CLI, or command line interface. Those are powerful ways to manage Azure, and we'll take a look at them later on too, as well as using this Azure Cloud Shell. Now let's look at the menu on the left.

The Home link shows that screen we saw when we first logged into Azure, so that was the home screen. The dashboard is the screen that will get shown from now on when I log in because of the portal settings I changed. The dashboard is a focused view of your resources in Azure. You can visualize data from multiple resources here and pin charts and views to get a complete picture of the health and performance of applications you create in Azure. That'll make more sense as we go along. You can add and manage tiles, and they can be configured individually or you can modify the whole page by adding and removing tiles. There's some suggested ones here, but you can pin pretty much anything in Azure to your dashboard. You can create multiple dashboards, so you can have one for viewing the state of certain applications or one for viewing the state of all the virtual machines, basically whatever you want to see at a glance. Next, let's create a resource group in the Azure portal.

Chapter 11 How to Create Resource Groups in Azure

Since we talked about resource groups earlier, let's look at how to create one in the portal. You can do that from the existing list of resource groups. Along the left here are shortcuts to the various resource types in Azure.

You can modify this to list the types of resources you normally manage, but this is the default. So I don't have any resource groups yet, of course, but from the Create button we can create one. But before we do that, let's pretend we don't have a shortcut on the left menu for this type of resource. In that case, we can go to All services on the menu. From there, we could browse the categories or search for the name of the resource type we want to create or manage. If I click on the resource type, we get brought to the same screen as before. And this little pin beside the name of the resource type, this is how you would pin this view or list to the dashboard. The third way to create a resource is from the link, Create a resource.

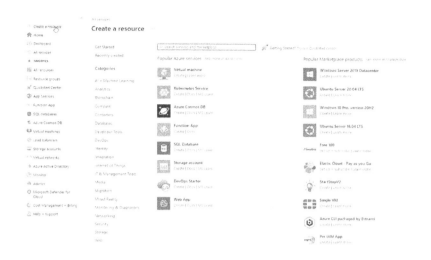

That opens the Azure Marketplace, which Microsoft calls its online store of IT software applications and services built by industry-leading companies. It looks similar to the All services screen you saw with categories of different types of services along the left, and you can use this to create basic Azure services, like a resource group. But the Azure Marketplace also contains add-ons you can install and sometimes purchase from other companies, like SendGrid is listed here, which is an online email service you can set up and use in your solutions. That's not a Microsoft service, so it's available here in the Marketplace, but not on the All services menu. Let's look at some of the categories here. Compute is where Azure services like virtual machines and function apps can be created, but also where preconfigured VMs can be chosen, like certain Linux distributions or a Windows Server VM with Visual Studio already installed. Storage has Azure storage accounts, but also offerings from other vendors that work in Azure on the right side. Same with Web. You can install plain Azure services or install a VM with WordPress already configured and ready to be used.

But let's just search for resource group from here, and it shows up in the results, so let's click this. Now, instead of being brought to the list of resource groups in our subscription, we're brought to the Marketplace view, which provides an overview of the service, information about plans that are available, and so on.

Of course, there's not much here because this is just a basic Azure service, so let's create this resource. We're brought to the create screen and our subscription is selected by default. I'm only logged into one subscription.

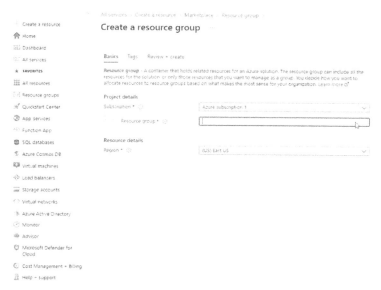

Create a resource group

Basics   Tags   Review + create

Resource group - A container that holds related resources for an Azure solution. The resource group can include all the resources for the solution, or only those resources that you want to manage as a group. You decide how you want to allocate resources to resource groups based on what makes the most sense for your organization. Learn more ☐

Project details

Subscription *   Azure Subscription 1

Resource group *

Resource details

Region *   (US) East US

We need to choose a name for this resource group, and this only needs to be unique within our subscription, not across all of Azure. You can name it whatever you want, it's just a string, but often companies come up with a naming convention for sorting and for searching. I like to end my resource names with an abbreviation of the resource type, so in this case I'll add an underscore and rg for resource group. Now you have to choose the region. A resource group is just metadata about all of the resources in the group, so this isn't where those resources will get created. You'll choose that separately for each individual resource that you create. This is just where the resource group or metadata itself will get created. I'll select the Azure region closest to me. Creating a resource in Azure is kind of like a wizard. You move through the tabs using the buttons at the bottom. The next page is Tags. Tags are key value pairs of metadata that you can add to resources, so they can be searched and grouped together.

You might use this to mark that a resource belongs to a certain application or a business group or an environment. Tags are helpful when it comes to billing too. There's a service in Azure for cost management, and you can filter resources by tags to see how much all the resources with a particular tag are costing you. You can also download a detailed spreadsheet of costs, and tags are included there for filtering purposes too. I've just added an environment tag. Let's move to the next screen. This is just a summary, so I'll click Create. We can see the new resource group by going to the Resource groups shortcut in the menu. Now we have one item listed.

I'll click the name, and that opens up the details for this resource group. The menu items are organized into groups, and this first group is common to all resources in Azure.

The Overview tab is where we can see all the resources included in this resource group. Of course there aren't any yet. We can also delete the resource group from the top menu. The Activity log is where any activity shows. I've already created and deleted a resource group with the exact same name, so it seems to be showing those activities on this resource group. The Access control tab is where you specify who can access the resource and what permissions they have. Of course there's only my account, and I'm the owner so I have full permissions, but you might want to grant someone read-only access so they can't modify resources here. Tags is where we can manage the tags for the resource. The next group of menu items are different depending on the type of resource you create, but you'll often see entries for monitoring metrics and logs for the particular resource. Now let's close out of these and go to All resources. We actually don't have anything here.

Resource groups don't show up in all resources; just resources contained in resource groups are listed here. that's a tour of the Azure portal and resource groups. Next, let's talk about Azure Active Directory.

Chapter 12 Azure Active Directory Basics

You probably don't plan on being the only person managing or using the resources in Azure. So now, let's talk about the directory in your subscription that stores user identities. That's called Azure Active Directory.

I've got a shortcut on the left menu, but let's go to All services, and Azure AD is right here at the top. This is called an Azure Active Directory tenant. When a subscription gets created, it gets its own tenant, so it's a place where the users for your organization only are managed. The Azure AD tenant is the container for users and groups that you want to give access to resources in Azure. That could be to administer things like deploying web apps or creating containers in Azure Blob storage, or it could be user identities for end users for accessing a web application or uploading data to that file storage. On the Users blade, and by the way, when you click a menu option, the panel that opens with the details is called a blade, so this is where all the users in this directory are listed. You can manually add users here, On-premises sync enabled. This means that you can actually synchronize your on-premises Active Directory with this Azure Active Directory tenant and then assign those on-premises users permissions in Azure. You do that by downloading and installing a tool on-premises called Azure AD sync. this identity is a Microsoft account. It has a really long identifier because it's an external entity. I'll show you shortly how you can use your own custom domain name for your company here, but let's create a new user first.

When you create a user, the first option you have is whether you want to create the user identity in this Azure AD tenant or you want to invite an external user. External users are part of something called Azure B2B collaboration, or business to business. That's for users outside your organization who aren't part of an Azure Active Directory tenant, and it lets you give them access to applications and services. They become an object in your Azure Active Directory that you can assign permissions to, but their sign-in process is handled by their own external identity provider. Let's create a generic account called administrator. I'll just give it a name, and we can create the password or let Azure do it. Just make sure you copy this somewhere. You won't see it again, but you can reset it. It says in the Notifications area that the user was created successfully. Let's drill into the details for this user. From here, we can add this user to groups. Groups let you create, well, groups of users, so you can then assign roles to either individual users or to groups.

Those roles are used to provide access to resources in the subscription. You don't have to use groups, but it makes management a lot easier. There are lots of roles in Azure, and they can get pretty granular in terms of what they allow. Let's just give this user the Global administrator role. That will allow them to perform pretty much any action in Azure. So I'll add this role and then refresh the view. It might take a few seconds for the portal to pick up the change. This user has the Global admin role now. Farther down the menu, you can assign licenses.

By default, your Azure AD tenant has the Azure Active Directory Free license, but there are other licenses that you can assign to individual users, like Azure AD Premium P1 or P2 licenses. These give users additional features, like being eligible for Conditional Access policies. I won't go into too much depth on Conditional Access policies, but basically they allow Azure to make authorization decisions based on things like the Azure AD groups that the user belongs to or the location the user is coming from and characteristics about the device they're using. Conditional Access policies can also work with Azure AD Identity Protection, which uses machine learning to identify risky sign-in behavior. If the user is approved to sign in after the Conditional Access policies are evaluated, you can also choose to enforce multi-factor authentication. That's where a user needs to provide a second factor of authentication after their username and password, and that's enabled by a service called Azure Multi-Factor Authentication, which can text a one-time passcode to the user's mobile device that they then enter into the browser to complete their login to applications in Azure. There's also an app the user can install on their device called the Microsoft Authenticator app. Azure can send push notifications to the app for the user to approve a sign in that was initiated in the browser. The app can also generate a rolling token code every 30 seconds that can be used when logging into Azure. That's just a quick introduction to Azure MFA. There's more to it than that, like being able to use the Microsoft Authenticator app for passwordless authentication. Let's go back to the Azure Active Directory tenant that we were looking at. You can use Azure MFA with Conditional Access policies if your users have at least an Azure AD Premium P1 license.

You can also enable it for individual users so they always have to use multi-factor authentication, and you do that from this screen. Let's go back up the hierarchy here to the root of this Azure Active Directory tenant.

Another thing you can create in Azure AD is app registrations, which represent an application, like a mobile app or a web app or a web API. It creates a trust relationship between your app and Azure AD, then those applications can use Azure AD to log in their users. Remember I mentioned that you can sync your on-premises Active Directory with this Azure AD tenant.

That's done using Azure AD Connect, and you can download the tool to install it on-premises from this blade. Then you have options on how to set up that connection, either directly or using federation with a tool like AD FS. I also mentioned earlier that you aren't restricted to the domain name that Azure creates for you.

You can add your company's own domain name to this Azure AD tenant. You need to own that domain name, though, just like you would have to own it when using it for a website. You can purchase a domain name from a domain name registrar. But let's create a new user and let's look at the domain drop-down list in the tenant. It shows both domain names, the default one that Azure created and the one I added, so I can create a user principal name. That's all for Azure Active Directory for now. You might have some questions still about subscriptions and directories and how they relate, so let's talk about that relationship in a little more detail next.

Chapter 13 Azure Directories & Subscriptions

Let's tie together some of the concepts you've learned about so far. Earlier when we created an Azure free trial, we used a Microsoft email account, and that created an Azure account. An Azure account is referred to as a billing account in the documentation. It's an entity that can have subscriptions. In other words, I can create multiple subscriptions and access all of them when I log in with my account. The documentation says there are several types of billing accounts. The Microsoft Online Services Program contains the Azure free account that we created. It also contains the pay-as-you-go accounts that charge our credit card for the resources consumed and the Visual Studio subscriber accounts that are basically pay-as-you-go accounts with some free credits. There are also enterprise agreements for organizations, Microsoft Customer Agreements also for organizations, and Microsoft Partner Agreements for cloud solution providers. Let's look at how these relate to subscriptions. For the type of account we created, we can have multiple subscriptions, so I could continue with my free trial subscription and also create a pay-as-you-go subscription, or I could upgrade the free trial subscription to a pay as you go.

Microsoft Online Services Program

Each of those subscriptions gets an invoice showing the resources that were consumed each month, and each subscription has a payment method, a credit card. Within a subscription, resources are created, and they're actually created within resource groups. We won't look at the other billing account types. They just add

63

some additional layers for management and accounting. When we signed up for the Azure free trial, a subscription was created, and there was an Azure Active directory tenant created too, so you might assume that this is a one-to-one relationship, but it doesn't have to be. Multiple subscriptions can have a trust relationship with the same Azure Active directory tenant, but each subscription can only be linked to one Azure Active Directory tenant, and you can change the tenant that the subscription trusts. To recap, an account can have multiple subscriptions. Subscriptions contain multiple resource groups, and resources groups contain resources. A resource can only belong to a single resource group, and a subscription has a trust relationship with an Azure Active Directory tenant. The subscription trusts Azure Active Directory to authenticate users, services, and devices. You can have multiple subscriptions trust the same Azure AD tenant, but each subscription can only trust a single directory, and all of the users have a single home directory for authentication, but each user can also be a guest in other directories. Okay, so you might be wondering why would you want to have multiple subscriptions? You might want individual subscriptions for different environments like dev and production and be able to apply separate access to manage each subscription using role-based access control, or you might want to keep resources separate in different subscriptions to make billing easier because each subscription can provide a bill for the resources that it uses, so maybe different business groups in your organization want that. Having multiple subscriptions might seem like it could be a management nightmare, but there's something called management groups that make this easier. Management groups can contain multiple subscriptions. They can also contain other management groups so you can create a hierarchy. Maybe you create management groups for different departments so they each have their own subscriptions or for different geo-regions, however your organization is structured. Then you can manage security for your subscriptions at the management group level. Permissions given at the management group level will get inherited by the management groups and subscriptions underneath. All of the subscriptions under the management group need to trust the same Azure Active Directory tenant, though. There's also something in Azure called Policies, and these allow you to set rules, like virtual machines can only get created in the East US region. Then you apply that policy to a subscription or at the management group level and it gets enforced and reported on. We won't get into Azure Policies in this book, but just know that you can use built-in ones, like requiring all resources to use certain tags or more complex policies like ones that enforce compliance to FedRAMP and HIPAA standards. You can browse all the built-in policies available in Azure on docs.microsoft.com, and you can also create your own custom policies and apply them to your management groups and subscriptions. In summary, so far you have learned how instances of services that you create are organized into subscriptions and resource groups, and you learned how the underlying physical Azure platform is implemented through regions and datacenters. You also saw how to create an Azure subscription, navigate the portal, and create resources, and you learned about how Azure Active Directory is used to manage identity and access for managing Azure, as well as being used as the foundation for access control by users of your applications. Next, we're going to look at some of the services in Azure used for compute, like virtual machines and app services.

Chapter 14 Azure Service Models

Let's talk about cloud computing service models. This might be a review for you, but it helps to put Azure compute options into perspective. These are categories that describe how much a resource is managed for you in the cloud. Another way to look at it is how much responsibility do you have with regards to managing the resource. Let's look at each of these. The on-premises model isn't a cloud model at all, it's just here to explain all the things that you're responsible for when you host your own infrastructure on-premises. This is what we talked about earlier, but besides all the physical infrastructure, if you're hosting your applications on virtual servers, then there's virtualization software that needs to be configured and managed. Then you're responsible to configure the virtual machines, which includes OS licensing and patching. You're responsible for installing the middleware on the servers and any runtimes, like the .NET Framework or Java, and then managing the data and applications that you host on those virtual servers. When you move to the cloud with the Infrastructure as a Service cloud service model, you can choose to provision resources like virtual servers. In Azure, you can create Windows or Linux VMs and everything below the OS layer of the VM is managed for you, so you don't have to worry about hardware refreshes or disks failing, you just choose the type of virtual machine you want and you pay for it. The cost includes the operating system license, but you can also leverage existing Windows Server licenses you might already own on-premises. You can install whatever you want on the VMs that you provision as Azure Virtual Machines. If you want to install a SQL Server database, for example, you can do that yourself. We'll look at some other options for SQL Server and Azure later on too. The next service model is Platform as a Service, or PaaS. Platform as a Service is a complete development and deployment environment in the cloud. Azure App Service is a compute service in Azure that allows you to host web applications and APIs in a preconfigured environment where all the runtimes are installed, like .NET Core,

Java or PHP. And those frameworks get updated along with the underlying virtual machines that they run on. You only need to manage the applications and services that you develop. Microsoft manages everything else. The third cloud service model is Software as a Service. This is actually the most popular use of cloud computing in terms of the number of users. These are fully functional cloud-based apps that users can connect to over the internet. Office 365 is the Microsoft solution for email, calendars, and office tools. Instead of buying software to install on the desktop and managing your own email servers, you can purchase Office 365 on a pay-as-you-go basis. You can still download and install Office tools like Word and Outlook, but they're also available in the browser. The central hosting of the Exchange Server is handled in the cloud and hosted by Microsoft. SharePoint is another Microsoft offering that falls under Software as a Service. As you can see with the Software as a Service model, you just use the software and you get a fully managed service that's available across devices and platforms. The services you'll be learning about throughout this book fall into the Infrastructure as a Service and Platform as a Service models. Now that you understand a bit about responsibilities with these service models, let's talk more about compute options in Azure next. Then we'll look at the major compute models individually, starting with virtual machines. Next, we'll talk about containers, which allow you to package applications and dependencies for deployment. After that, we'll look at Azure App Service. And finally, explore Azure Functions, which allow you to run small pieces of code without requiring a full-blown application.

Chapter 15 Azure Compute Options

Azure compute is really an overarching category for a bunch of services in Azure that provide on-demand computing power for running cloud-based applications. The main services in Azure compute are virtual machines, container instances, and there are a number of ways to host containers in Azure, Azure App Service and Azure Functions. Let's discuss each of these at a high level and then we'll get into more detail. Virtual machines are software emulations of physical computers. They run on physical computers in Azure, but multiple virtual machines, or VMs, can run on the same physical host and use the resources of that host. You connect to a virtual machine in Azure using a remote desktop client, and you can manage all aspects of the operating system, including installing whatever software on the VM that you want. It gives you the most control, but also requires the most management because you're responsible for all the configuration and security patches and updates required by the operating system on that virtual machine. But you'll see that Azure offers some services to make that easier. Let's talk about some of the benefits of choosing virtual machines in Azure. Virtual machines are probably the most familiar option for most IT pros because they're just like virtual servers that you would maintain on-premises. If you're planning on migrating to Azure from on-premises, virtual machines can provide a lift-and-shift approach by creating VMs in Azure similar to the physical or virtual servers you have on-premises. You might have applications that require operating system resources like registry access or that use authentication mechanisms like Windows Integrated Authentication and you don't want to rewrite those apps to run on cloud services like Azure App Service, or you might have older applications or custom off-the-shelf software that needs to be installed, VMs are the way to go. Besides having the ability to install whatever third-party software you want on the virtual machine, you can deploy your own applications and you can host multiple applications on the VM. So, virtual machines can have some cost savings versus deploying those apps to single instances of other services, but the applications share the resources on the VM, so you need to be aware of one application using too much CPU or memory and affecting the others. Or if multiple applications use a shared library, for example, updating that library to benefit one app could cause another app to break. That's an issue that containers are meant to solve. Containers are used to wrap up an application into its own isolated package. It's for server-based applications and services, so web apps are a typical example. When an app is deployed using a container, everything the application needs to run successfully is included in the container, like runtimes and library dependencies. This makes it easier to move the container around. Containers reduce problems with deploying applications. Containers are kind of like virtual machines, but they run on top of virtual or physical servers using a container runtime layer, similar to how virtual machines run on a virtualization layer. You can host multiple containers on a single virtual machine if you install a container runtime, and Docker is an example of one of those. In terms of the service models we discussed earlier, there are services in Azure that host containers on Platform as a Service offerings, like Azure Container Instances and Container Apps. The next Azure compute services fall under the Platform as a Service model. Azure App Service lets you quickly build and deploy web apps, mobile apps, and API apps that can be leveraged by other applications or accessed by client apps over HTTP using REST. They also allow you to run server-side apps and scripts, similar to how you would install a Windows service on your web servers to perform some task on a timer. You can choose your application runtime, like .NET, Node.js, and several others, and you can choose whether you want the underlying VMs to be Linux or Windows-based. Azure App Services takes care of managing those underlying VMs for you, which is the most obvious benefit, but you also get extra features like built-in integration with authentication providers like Azure Active Directory to handle authenticating users to your applications. You get something called deployment slots, so you can have multiple versions of your app for development and production and quickly swap those deployment slots to promote the apps. App Services also has built-in features to scale out the underlying VMs. You can add and remove virtual machines manually or Azure can autoscale the VMs based on metrics that you configure, like the amount of CPU being used. Azure App Services are great for running web apps and APIs that are used by mobile apps and client apps and other services, but sometimes you just need a piece of code to run in order to do some task like process a file or update a database table or send a message to another service, and that's what Azure Functions are for. It's a service to host small pieces of code, but you can chain functions together or use them as part of other solutions. Functions can run on a timer or in response to events like an HTTP call, and there are built-in triggers that you can use, like if a file changes in Azure Storage that can trigger an Azure Function to run. You only pay for the compute power that you use. For small tasks, Azure Functions are a great way to save effort and money. Azure Functions are often called serverless computing, although that's kind of a loose term. There are always servers involved, it's just how much you need to interact with them. There's another service in Azure that's often categorized as serverless compute also. It's called Azure Logic Apps. These allow you to configure workflows right in the browser and connect to various services inside and outside of Azure using built-in connectors. Logic Apps sometimes get discussed in the context of Azure compute, so we'll look at them later when we discuss Azure Functions. But next, let's look more closely at virtual machines in Azure.

Chapter 16 Azure Virtual Machine Basics

Using Azure Virtual Machines, you can set up servers in the cloud. You can basically recreate your on-premises environment in Azure if you choose. You could have an Active Directory server storing user accounts, a DNS server, web servers, file servers, and database servers. Using a virtual network in Azure, these VMs can all communicate and security can be enabled to restrict ports, all the same things as on-premises except they're in the cloud, so you can also enable access to the internet if you choose. There are additional features of Azure networking like load balancers and firewalls that allow you to secure your VM network. You can also extend your on-premises environment into the cloud by connecting your on-premises network to a VNet in Azure, then the VMs in Azure can essentially become part of your network. So if you're running out of capacity on-premises and don't want to buy new hardware, this is an option. There are several ways to deploy VMs to Azure. You can upload your own VM images into a storage account in Azure and use them as image templates to create instances of virtual machines. There are some steps involved to prepare your disk files, but there's a much easier way to create VMs in Azure by choosing from preconfigured VM images from the Azure Marketplace. Many of them are provided by Microsoft, but also by other third parties. When you create a VM from the Marketplace, the licensing costs for the operating system are included in the price. When you create a virtual machine in Azure, there are a lot of configuration options, but the three big decisions are the image you want to use, the size of the VM, and the availability options. You start by choosing a VM image.

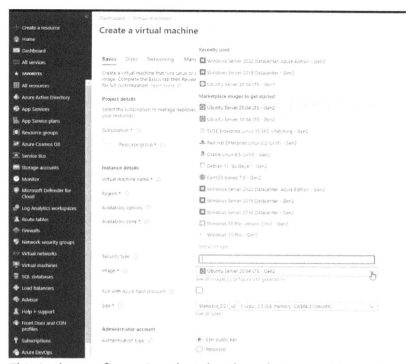

This is the configuration that decides what operating system is installed, and there are several available, like different versions of Windows Server and Windows desktop operating systems or different distributions of Linux. You can also choose images that are preconfigured with software. So you can create a VM image that has WordPress Server already installed or an SMTP server or development tools like Visual Studio. When you create a VM, you also choose the VM size.

Azure has predefined configurations that decide how many virtual CPUs are included and the amount of RAM. Different VM sizes are suitable for different workloads. By browsing the VM pricing page, you can see a description of each size of VM, and they're grouped into categories, series, and then the actual VM instance code that you choose when you create a VM. Under General purpose VMs are the B-series VMs.

It says here these are suitable for development workloads and low traffic web applications and small databases. Farther down, the D2-series VMs are for most production workloads. Within each series, you can choose an instance size with a specific configuration that you need.

74

D2as – D96as v5 (latest generation without local temporary storage)

The Dasv5-series virtual machines are based on the 3rd Generation AMD EPYC™ 7763v (Milan) processor. This processor's frequency can achieve up to 3.5GHz. The Das v5 VI offer a combination of vCPUs and memory able to meet the requirements associated with most production workloads.

The Das v5 virtual machine sizes do not have any temporary storage thus lowering the price of entry. You can attach Standard SSDs, Standard HDDs, and Premium SSDs disk to these VMs. You can also attach Ultra Disk storage based on its regional availability. Disk storage is billed separately from virtual machines. See pricing for disks

Instance	vCPU(s)	RAM	Temporary storage	Pay as you go with AHB	1 year reserved with AHB	3 year reserved with AHB	Spot with AHB	Add to estimat
D2as v5	2	8 GiB	0 GiB	$62.7800/month	$36.9964/month ~41% savings	$23.8637/month ~61% savings	$6.9124/month ~88% savings	+
D4as v5	4	16 GiB	0 GiB	$125.5600/month	$74.0804/month ~41% savings	$47.7201/month ~61% savings	$13.8240/month ~88% savings	+
D8as v5	8	32 GiB	0 GiB	$251.1200/month	$148.1681/month ~40% savings	$95.4183/month ~62% savings	$27.6480/month ~88% savings	+
D16as v5	16	64 GiB	0 GiB	$502.2400/month	$296.3362/month ~40% savings	$190.8585/month ~61% savings	$55.2968/month ~88% savings	+

Each size has a pay-as-you-go price and the price is listed per month, but you're actually charged at an hourly rate and you can deallocate a VM when it's not in use to save on compute charges. There are also options with some VM classes to reserve the VM for one or three years. If you expect to be using it for that long, you can get some significant cost savings with that commitment. There's also Spot VMs that allow you to use VMs that come from unused capacity in Azure. You can get them significantly cheaper, but you have to be able to tolerate Azure evicting the VM with only 30 seconds notice so Azure can recover the capacity. If you're just running a DevTest environment or a batch processing job, that might be fine. As you go farther down, the VM series gets more and more specialized.

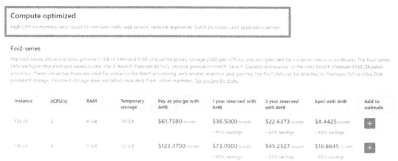

Compute optimized

High CPU-to-memory ratio. Good for medium traffic web servers, network appliances, batch processes, and application servers.

Fsv2-series

The Fsv2-series virtual machines provide 2 GiB of RAM and 8 GB of local temporary storage (SSD) per vCPU(s) and are optimized for compute intensive workloads. The Fsv2-series VMs are hyper-threaded and based on the Intel® Xeon® Platinum 8272CL (second generation Intel® Xeon® Scalable processors) or the Intel® Xeon® Platinum 8168 (Skylake) processor. These virtual machines are ideal for scenarios like batch processing, web servers, analytics and gaming. The Fsv2 VMs can be attached to Premium SSD or Ultra Disk persistent storage. Persistent storage disks are billed separately from virtual machines. See pricing for disks.

Instance	vCPU(s)	RAM	Temporary storage	Pay as you go with AHB	1 year reserved with AHB	3 year reserved with AHB	Spot with AHB	Add to estimate
F2s v2	2	4 GiB	16 GiB	$61.7580/month	$36.5000/month ~40% savings	$22.6373/month ~63% savings	$8.4425/month ~86% savings	+
F4s v2	4	8 GiB	32 GiB	$123.3700/month	$73.0000/month ~40% savings	$45.2527/month ~63% savings	$16.8645/month ~86% savings	+

There are compute optimized servers, which have a high CPU-to-memory ratio.

Memory optimized

High memory-to-core ratio. Great for relational database servers, medium to large caches, and in-memory analytics

E2as – E96as v5 (latest generation without temporary storage)

The Eas v5 series virtual machines are based on the 3rd Generation AMD EPYC™ 7763v (Milan) processor. This processor can achieve a boosted maximum frequency of 3.5GHz. The Eas v5 VM sizes feature up to 672 GiB of RAM, and do not have any temporary storage thus lowering the price of entry. These virtual machines are ideal for memory-intensive enterprise applications, relational database servers, and in-memory analytics workloads

You can attach Standard SSDs, Standard HDDs, and Premium SSDs disk storage to these VMs. You can also attach Ultra Disk storage based on its regional availability. Disk storage is billed separately from virtual machines. See pricing for disks.

Instance	vCPU(s)	RAM	Temporary storage	Pay as you go with AHB	1 year reserved with AHB	3 year reserved with AHB	Spot with AHB	Add to estimate
E2as v5	2	16 GiB	0 GiB	$82.4900/month	$48.6691/month −41% savings	$31.3316/month −62% savings	$11.0456/month −86% savings	[+]
E4as v5	4	32 GiB	0 GiB	$164.9800/month	$97.3309/month −41% savings	$62.6924/month −62% savings	$22.0905/month −86% savings	[+]

Memory-optimized series VMs have higher memory-to-CPU core ratio, so they're better for hosting database servers. You'll notice that some of the series aren't available in the region that's selected above. VMs get more specialized as we go farther down.

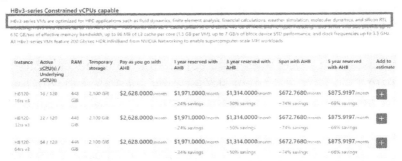

HBv3-series Constrained vCPUs capable

HBv3-series VMs are optimized for HPC applications such as fluid dynamics, finite element analysis, financial calculations, weather simulation, molecular dynamics, and silicon RTL

630 GB/sec of effective memory bandwidth, up to 96 MB of L3 cache per core (1.5 GB per VM), up to 7 GB/s of block device SSD performance, and clock frequencies up to 3.3 GHz. All HBv3-series VMs feature 200 Gb/sec HDR InfiniBand from NVIDIA Networking to enable supercomputer-scale MPI workloads

Instance	Active vCPU(s) / Underlying vCPU(s)	RAM	Temporary storage	Pay as you go with AHB	1 year reserved with AHB	3 year reserved with AHB	Spot with AHB	5 year reserved with AHB	Add to estimate
HB120-16rs v3	16 / 120	448 GiB	2,100 GiB	$2,628.0000/month	$1,971.0000/month −24% savings	$1,314.0000/month −50% savings	$672.7680/month −74% savings	$875.9197/month −66% savings	[+]
HB120-32rs v3	32 / 120	448 GiB	2,100 GiB	$2,628.0000/month	$1,971.0000/month −24% savings	$1,314.0000/month −50% savings	$672.7680/month −74% savings	$875.9197/month −66% savings	[+]
HB120-64rs v3	64 / 120	448 GiB	2,100 GiB	$2,628.0000/month	$1,971.0000/month −24% savings	$1,314.0000/month −50% savings	$672.7680/month −74% savings	$875.9197/month −66% savings	[+]

It says these HBv3 VMs are optimized for high-performance computing, like financial calculations and weather simulation. That's pretty specific and pretty expensive. There's a new tool in Azure that can make finding the right VM size much easier than reading through all these descriptions.

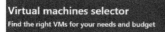
Virtual machines selector
Find the right VMs for your needs and budget

Ready when you are—let's find your VMs

Find VMs by workload type
Select your workload and requirements.

Find VMs by OS and software
Select the operating system and software that you'd like to run on the VM.

Find VMs by deployment region
Select the region where you'd like to deploy the VM.

Start here

Start here

Start here

Help us make this tool better. Did this tool help you find what you're looking for?
If no, tell us what you were looking for.

Yes   No

The virtual machine selector lets you find VM sizes by workload type, OS and software or by deployment region. I won't go through all the screens, but you can select things like the type of operating system and the minimum and maximum number of CPUs and RAM, and it'll produce a list for you. You select a VM size when you create the VM, but it is possible to resize the VM later. That's called scaling up if you're choosing a VM size with more CPU or RAM, or scaling down if you change to a smaller VM size. That's part of the elasticity in the cloud that we talked about previously. You don't have to create a new VM if you need extra processing power, and you can release those resources when you're done with them. Let's talk about the related resources that a VM needs. A virtual machine needs a disk to store the operating system. That's created when you create the VM, and it gets managed by Azure in Azure Storage. It's basically your copy of the VM image. You can also add data disks if you need to store a lot of data as part of your VM. Maybe you need database storage or some other file storage attached to your VM. A VM also needs to exist on a virtual network in Azure, generally referred to as a VNet. That's how it can communicate with other VMs and out to the internet. So even if you only have a single VM, it needs an Azure

Virtual Network. You can either create one while creating the VM or you can attach a VM to an existing virtual network. The VM needs a network interface in order to communicate on the network, and you can have a public IP address for the VM so it can be remotely accessed. That could allow you to use the VM as a web server. You can also set up security rules to filter network traffic between resources on the virtual network using network security groups. We'll talk more about networking in the next module. So each of these is considered a resource in Azure with their own configuration screens, and when you add managed data disks, those have associated costs. Accessing those managed disks also have costs as storage transactions, and any data that comes out of Azure is also charged. That's actually true of Azure in general. It's free to put data into Azure, but there are egress charges when data comes out, like if you're using your VM as a web server, the data in the responses incurs charges. But these are very, very small charges, just something to be aware of when you're pricing out a solution that involves virtual machines. You can estimate your costs in Azure using the Azure pricing calculator. When you add a VM, it will add the related resources that can incur charges. Some related resources, like virtual networks, are actually free. Next, let's talk about the availability options with virtual machines in Azure.

Chapter 17 Azure VM Scale & Availability Sets

By now, you understand that Azure Virtual Machines are hosted on physical machines in an Azure datacenter. Sometimes those physical machines need maintenance or something fails or they need to be restarted. That's just reality. So if you design your solution with a single VM, you're introducing a single point of failure into your application. For that reason, a datacenter is organized into update domains and fault domains, and you can take advantage of these to create a highly available solution using multiple virtual machines. Update domains are groups of virtual machines and the underlying physical hardware that can be rebooted at the same time. Fault domains define a group of virtual machines that share a common power source in the datacenter and a common network switch. When you're creating a virtual machine in Azure, you can choose to create it in an availability set with other VMs. When you do that, Azure places your VMs in separate update domains and fault domains. So you're essentially telling Azure that these VMs are part of an application so Azure can help with the resiliency and availability. This doesn't protect you from things like operating system or application-specific failures, but it does limit the impact of potential hardware failures, network outages, and power interruptions. And you actually need to create at least two VMs within an availability set if you want the 99.95% uptime guarantee in the Azure service-level agreement. To use these VMs for redundancy in a solution, you'd need to put them behind a load balancer. Users access a web server from a single IP address and URL, but the load balancer routes the traffic to one of the VMs in the solution based on availability and load. To make that easier, though, Azure offers something called virtual machine scale sets. These let you create and manage a group of identical virtual machines, and Azure will put them behind a load balancer for you. You can configure virtual machine scale sets to scale with demand so Azure can add and remove VMs from the scale set as needed, and of course you configure the parameters around that. Those VMs are spread across fault domains, so you have that protection as well. Virtual machine scale sets let you maintain a consistent configuration across your VMs. You get resiliency if one of the VMs has a problem, and the autoscaling feature helps with application performance. If you plan to set up a large-scale solution that requires a lot of VMs working together, up to 1000 VMs are supported in a virtual machine scale set.

Chapter 18 How to Create a Virtual Machine in Azure

We could start from the shortcut on the left menu, but let's go to All services and search for virtual machines. I'll click that in the search results, and let's create a VM from the Create button at the top. There's a few options here.

Azure virtual machine with preset configuration just narrows down the VM sizes based on whether you intend this VM for development or production. Azure Arc lets you manage VMs in environments outside Azure, including your on-premises environment. And Azure VMware Solution virtual machine lets you move VMware-based workloads from your datacenter to Azure. Let's just create a VM in Azure. That brings us to the create screen with all the tabs across the top. We'll go in order here.

Create a virtual machine

Basics   Disks   Networking   Management   Advanced   Tags   Review + create

Create a virtual machine that runs Linux or Windows. Select an image from Azure marketplace or use your own customized image. Complete the Basics tab then Review + create to provision a virtual machine with default parameters or review each tab for full customization. Learn more

ⓘ This subscription may not be eligible to deploy VMs of certain sizes in certain regions.

Project details

Select the subscription to manage deployed resources and costs. Use resource groups like folders to organize and manage all your resources.

Subscription * ⓘ	Azure subscription 1
Resource group * ⓘ	(New) Resource group
	Create new

Instance details

Virtual machine name * ⓘ	
Region * ⓘ	(Europe) Norway East
Availability options ⓘ	Availability zone
Availability zone * ⓘ	Zones 1

ⓘ You can now select multiple zones. Selecting multiple zones will create one VM per zone. Learn more

Security type ⓘ	Standard
Image * ⓘ	Ubuntu Server 20.04 LTS - Gen2 (free services eligible)
	See all images	Configure VM generation
Run with Azure Spot discount ⓘ	☐

Review + create   < Previous   Next : Disks >

I won't go through every option on these screens, just some key ones. We need to put this VM in a resource group, and all the related resources will get created there too. We could use the existing resource group, but let's just create a new one. That'll make it easier to delete these resources later. I'll give this new resource group a name. Now I have to give the VM a name. This can be pretty much anything, but you'll probably develop a naming convention for your organization. Next we choose a region. There are only a few regions available because this is a free Azure trial subscription. In a pay-as-you-go subscription, the list is much bigger. Next we choose the availability option. We can choose to use availability zones. This relates back to the discussion on Azure regions.

82

Create a virtual machine

Basics   Disks   Networking   Management   Advanced   Tags   Review + create

Create a virtual machine that runs Linux or Windows. Select an image from Azure marketplace or use your own customized image. Complete the Basics tab then Review + create to provision a virtual machine with default parameters or review each tab for full customization. Learn more ☐

ℹ This subscription may not be eligible to deploy VMs of certain sizes in certain regions.

Project details

Select the subscription to manage deployed resources and costs. Use resource groups like folders to organize and manage all your resources.

Subscription * ⓘ   Azure subscription 1   ⌄

         Resource group * ⓘ   (New) vm_rg   ⌄
                                     Create new

Instance details

Virtual machine name * ⓘ   vm1

Region * ⓘ   (US) West US 3   ⌄

Availability options ⓘ   Availability zone   ⬚

Availability zone * ⓘ   No infrastructure redundancy required

                                    Availability zone
                                    Physically separate your resources within an Azure region.

                                    Virtual machine scale set
Security type ⓘ   Distribute VMs across zones and fault domains at scale

Image * ⓘ   Availability set
                                    Automatically distribute your VMs across multiple fault domains.

Run with Azure Spot discount ⓘ   ☐

Review + create   Previous   Next : Disks >

Most regions have availability zones where there are separate datacenters in the region. If you're planning on creating multiple VMs for your solution, you can choose which zone to put the VM in. There are also virtual machine scale sets available and availability sets. Let's choose Availability set. And since there isn't an existing one to add this VM to, I'll create a new one. We can configure the number of fault domains and update domains. Let's just leave the defaults and click OK. Next we choose the image we want to use to create this VM. We can choose from various flavors of Linux or versions of Windows.

I'll just choose a Windows Server image. Next we choose the size. There are a few popular sizes listed here, and we can browse all the sizes and their specs if we want to.

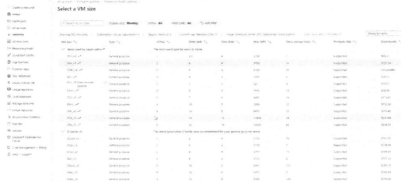

But let's choose the smallest D-series VM listed here. Next we need an administrator name. This will be a local account on this VM. We can add other accounts for access later.

84

After that, we can open some inbound ports. You'll want at least RDP enabled on a Windows VM so we can remote into it. So I'll leave port 3389, the default RDP port.

Next let's go to Disks.

We can choose the type of disk to use for the operating system, and we can add data disks here, but we can also do that after the VM is created. So let's move on to Networking.

Create a virtual machine

Basics Disks **Networking** Management Advanced Tags Review + create

Define network connectivity for your virtual machine by configuring network interface card (NIC) settings. You can control ports, inbound and outbound connectivity with security group rules, or place behind an existing load balancing solution.
Learn more ⬚

Network interface

When creating a virtual machine, a network interface will be created for you.

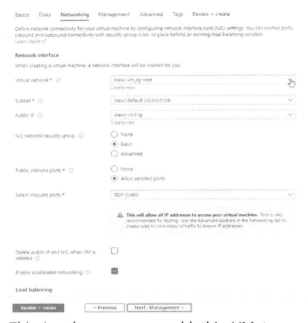

This is where we can add this VM to an existing virtual network or create a new one. Since we don't have an existing VNet, we'll create one. And you can break that VNet into subnets, and then you can place VMs in different subnets and control communication between them. Let's leave the defaults. And the public IP address will get created too. The security on this VNet will be configured to allow access from port 3389 the internet so we can remote in.

86

We could configure load balancing here if we intend to have multiple VMs as part of this solution.

Let's go to Management. Here we can configure options like boot diagnostics, which lets you debug problems booting up your virtual machine.

You can also create a system-managed identity, which is an Azure AD-managed service account for this VM. So you can do things like grant this VM's service account access to a database or to a storage account in Azure. You can enable auto shutdown. Shutting down a VM in Azure will save you money on compute charges, but you still pay for the storage of the underlying VM. So if this is a VM for development, let's say, you might only need it running during business hours. You can also shut down a VM yourself anytime you want. Let's go to Advanced, and this is where we can configure applications to install after deployment and run custom scripts while the VM is being provisioned.

And we talked about tags earlier, which help with managing large numbers of VMs. Let's review this configuration and create this VM.

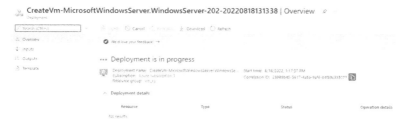

Next, we'll explore the management options once the VM is created.

Chapter 19 How to Explore Azure Virtual Machines

It took about 2 minutes for everything to get created.

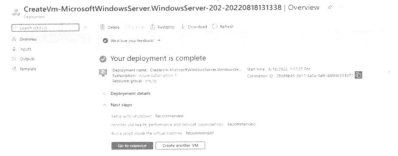

We could go to the VM configuration screen from here, but let's go to All resource groups and let's see the resource group that was created.

You can see all the related resources that were created with the VM itself, like the virtual network, the operating system disk, the network interface, public IP address, and even the availability set is created as a separate resource with its own configuration. Let's drill into the VM. On the Overview tab, you can see the public IP address for this VM. So this is how you would access it from the internet. There's also the private IP address, which is the IP address of the VM on the VNet that was created. And on the Overview tab, you can also stop the VM, and this is how you can save on compute charges when not using the virtual machine.

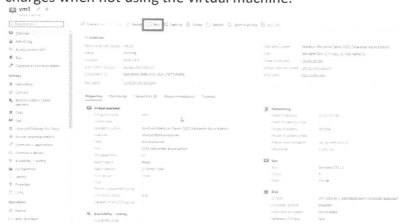

This releases the server resources associated with the VM, like the underlying CPU and RAM. The Networking tab allows us to manage the ports that are open. We could open up port 80 for HTTP traffic here, for example.

Disks are where you can attach data disks if you need more storage later.

On the Size tab, you can resize the VM. So we could scale it up if we found that the workloads that we're putting on here are more than the VM can handle.

You just choose the new size and click Resize. If the VM is running, this will cause it to restart. On the Configuration tab, you can manage settings like the licensing for the Windows operating system. You might have existing Windows Server licenses you'd like to use in order to save on Azure costs.

Identity is where you enable the managed identity we discussed during the VM creation screens, and that allows you to provide access to other Azure resources using the Azure Active Directory identity of this VM. Backup is where you can configure options for backing up this VM. Azure has a service called Azure Backup where you can store backups of VM disks, file shares, and blobs in Azure storage. And even databases running on Azure VMs can be backed up. Of course, there are additional costs associated with storing backups. Azure Site Recovery provides disaster recovery by replicating a VM to a different Azure region.

You can use this service to fail over your Azure VMs to another region and also to replicate VMs from other environments for failover to Azure, like on-premises VMs and even Windows virtual machines in Amazon Web Services. The Updates tab lets you use other services in Azure to help you provide updates to this VM.

With Infrastructure as a Service VMs, you're responsible for updating them. Azure does help with this, though, by allowing you to leverage a service called Azure Automation to push out updates to VMs that are enrolled with the service. You need to configure that and schedule the updates, though. This works for Windows and Linux VMs. Now let's see how to connect to this VM remotely.

On the connect page, you can connect using Remote Desktop Protocol, SSH or using a service called Azure Bastion, which lets you connect using your browser and the Azure portal. RDP is the traditional way to log into a Windows VM, so let's choose this. Azure is going to create a file for us to download. I'll go to my Downloads folder and let's edit this file. If you've used Remote Desktop Connection before, you see this is just a standard file with the IP address of the VM and the RDP port 3389 already configured. The only account that has access to this VM right now is the local administrator account we created on the VM, so I'll use a different account, and the name is the VM name, backslash, the account name, and the password I used during the VM creation. Once it connects, we're brought into the remote session. Server Manager opens on the VM, and here we can manage the VM and even add it to a domain.

I've used Azure VMs many times to create test environments in the cloud by creating a VM and installing Active Directory and then joining VMs to the network, just like you would on-premises. That's a standalone environment. If you want to give Azure AD users access to this VM and the applications on it, there's a way to do that using Azure AD Domain Services.

Chapter 20 Azure AD Domain Services

First of all, Azure Active Directory is not the same thing as Active Directory on-premises. They both store user identities and allow you to create groups of users for security purposes, but Azure AD was built for the cloud and it uses web authentication protocols for authenticating users like OAuth 2.0 and OpenID Connect. Cloud native services like Azure App Service use these protocols by default. The authentication technologies used most often in on-premises Active Directory is Windows Integrated Authentication, which uses Kerberos and NTLM protocols. With Windows Integrated Authentication, a user logs into the local network and a security token gets passed around so they can get authenticated by any computer that's joined to the network, including web servers. That functionality is provided by domain services, which is just a part of Active Directory. Many legacy applications use Windows Integrated Authentication, so if you're moving them to VMs in Azure, that can be a showstopper. You may not want to modify those applications to use another authentication method, or in the case of commercial off-the-shelf software, you probably can't change the authentication methods that they use. One possible solution if you have an on-premises Active Directory infrastructure is to extend your on-premises network to the cloud and use your Active Directory Domain Services, at least for users in your on-premises Active Directory. You would join the VMs in Azure to the same network as on-premises, so really there's no connection to Azure AD for those servers. For on-premises users accessing applications on the VMs, though, they could still authenticate with Windows Integrated Authentication. But user identities stored only in the cloud have no connection, and you may be looking to minimize your dependency to on-premises AD or you don't plan on having a hybrid cloud at all. So there is a solution in Azure AD, and it's called Azure Active Directory Domain Services. It's not enabled by default, you need to turn it on, and it provides the ability to join virtual machines to managed domain where the user identities are stored in Azure AD, but the VMs can use legacy authentication methods like Kerberos and NTLM. When you set up Azure Active Directory Domain Services, Azure deploys two domain controllers into your selected Azure region, and you don't need to manage or update them. It's handled for you. Information from Azure AD is synchronized into Azure AD Domain Services. Then, applications, services, and virtual machines connected to the managed domain can use common AD features like Domain Join, Group Policy, LDAP, Kerberos, and NTLM authentication. If you have on-premises Active Directory, you learned that you can synchronize users and groups from your on-premises Active Directory to Azure Active Directory. That's not the same thing as joining the two networks. They're still separate, there's just an agent installed in your environment that synchronizes the user accounts into Azure Active Directory on a continuous basis. Then those users can be granted access to applications in Azure. Even though they're accessing the application from on-premises, it's their Azure AD identities that are used. They can still access applications hosted on those virtual machines that use legacy authentication protocols. Before we leave the discussion of virtual machines, let's talk about Azure Virtual Desktop, next.

Chapter 21 Azure Virtual Desktop Basics

Azure Virtual Desktop is a desktop and app virtualization service in Azure. It was previously called Windows Virtual Desktop. Azure Virtual Desktop is used to provide Windows desktops to users with computers actually running in Azure. The user logs into a computer in Azure where all their applications are installed and all their data is accessible, but none of it is stored on their local computer and all the processing by the applications is being done in the cloud. Users can access their remote desktop and applications from any device. There are native apps provided for Windows, Mac, iOS, Android, and an HTML5 interface is also provided, so the remote desktop can be accessed using a web browser too. What's the purpose of Azure Virtual Desktop? What problems does it solve? It separates operating systems, data, and apps from local hardware. That enables central management and security of user desktops with less IT management required. You don't need desk-side support because all the apps are running remotely in the cloud. Azure Virtual Desktop provides a separate compute environment for users outside of their local device, so the chance of confidential information being left on the user device is greatly reduced. It also lets you provide standard images to users with all the tools they need already configured without having to procure hardware, set it up, and ship individual computers to users. They just access the virtual computers from their existing devices. You can choose images for Windows 11, 10, and Windows 7 with extended support until 2023, and also Server operating systems like Windows Server 2022, 2019, 2016, and 2012 R2. You can also create or upload your own image with all the software and configuration needed for users. At sign in, the user profile is dynamically attached to the computing environment and appears just like a native user profile on a local machine. Users have access to their own data, and users with privileges can even add and remove programs without impacting other users on the same remote desktops. Azure Virtual Desktop is similar to Remote Desktop Services and Windows Server, but if you've ever set up that environment in an enterprise, you know there are multiple roles and multiple servers required for scalability. You can avoid all that configuration by using Azure Virtual Desktop. So, it's really a Platform as a Service offering to provide remote virtual machines. In the past, if you wanted to provide client operating system VMs to users in Remote Desktop Services, you had to have a single VM for each user. To have multiple users use the same VM and conserve resources, you needed to use a server operating system, but Azure Virtual Desktop supports Windows 10 or 11 multi-session, which means you don't have to overprovision VMs. You can let users share the resources of a single VM. Users on a multi-session environment still have a unique secure experience, and they can use all their apps, like Office 365. The user's data and files are persisted on a separate disk that gets attached when the user logs in, so they get their desktop settings and application settings as if it's their own computer. But the user profile is separated from the operating system, so you can update the operating system and not lose the user's profile. Azure Virtual Desktop works with a couple of features that you've already learned about. You can domain join Azure Virtual Desktop VMs to Azure Active Directory Domain Services or to an existing domain in Active Directory if you've created a hybrid cloud. Azure AD provides a secure, consistent sign-on experience that allows users to roam from device to device. And it also lets you use Azure multi-factor authentication for another layer of security. Now let's move on from virtual machines and talk about hosting containers in Azure

Chapter 22 Azure Container Options

Containers are a way to wrap up an application into its own isolated package. It's for server-based applications and services, so web apps are a typical example. When an app is deployed using a container, everything the application needs to run successfully is included in the container, like runtimes and library dependencies. This makes it easy to move the container around from your local workstation to VMs in your on-premises environment that have the container runtime installed or to a managed container hosting service in Azure, like Azure Container Instances or the Azure Kubernetes Service. The main characteristic of a container is that it makes the environment the same across different deployments, so containers reduce problems with deploying applications. Let's talk about how containers are different from virtual machines. Virtual machines run on some sort of infrastructure, whether it's your laptop or it's a physical server in a datacenter in Azure. There's a host operating system that might be Windows, Linux or macOS. Then we have a hypervisor layer, and this is what runs the virtual machine and provides resources to it from the host operating system. Hyper-V is Microsoft's hypervisor technology, but there are others like VMware and KVM. Then there's the virtual machine. The virtual machine contains a full copy of an operating system, and it virtualizes the underlying hardware, meaning the CPU, memory, and storage. It also contains the application that you want to run. If you want true isolation of your applications, you'll have a copy of a VM for each application that you deploy, and that VM will need to have all the runtimes and libraries installed that the application needs. If you want to run three applications in isolation, then you'd be running three virtual machines on this hardware, each with a guest operating system that might be 800 MB in size, and each VM would require a certain amount of CPU and memory allocated to it because, again, virtual machines virtualize the hardware. Containers, on the other hand, virtualize the operating system. The host could be a physical or a virtual server, and on top of the operating system there's a runtime. This is kind of like the hypervisor for virtual machines, but it's for containers. On top of the runtime are the containers, which just contain the application along with any dependencies for that application, like frameworks and libraries for connecting storage, for example. These are the same types of things you would normally install on a VM to run your application. The containers emulate the underlying operating system rather than emulating the underlying hardware. This makes containers smaller in size than a virtual machine and quicker to spin up because you're only waiting for the app to launch, not the operating system. Because containers are so lightweight, you can host more containers on the host VM or physical server than using traditional virtual machines for each application, so there's obvious cost savings associated with that. A container is an instance of a container image. An image is a read-only template with instructions on how to create the container, and the container is the runnable instance of the image. You can create your own container images by leveraging existing images and adding the frameworks, any dependencies, and finally the code for your application. Then you can deploy the container in a repeatable way across environments. Container images get stored in a container registry. A container registry is a service that stores and distributes container images. Docker Hub is a public container registry on the web that serves as a general catalog of images. Azure offers a similar service called Azure Container Registry, which provides users with direct control of their images, integrated authentication with Azure AD, and many other features that come along with its Azure integration. I just mentioned Docker Hub. A Docker container is a standard that describes the format of containers and provides a runtime for Docker containers. Docker is an open source project that automates the deployment of containers that can run in the cloud or on-premises. Docker is also a company that promotes and evolves the technology, and they work in collaboration with cloud vendors like Microsoft. Docker has a runtime process that you can install on any workstation or VM, and there are services in Azure that provide that runtime for you. Remember that containers are portable, so they can be moved around to different hosts. Now let's talk about the different ways you can host containers. You can set up a local environment by installing the Docker runtime. Then you can develop your app locally and package up all its dependencies into the container image that you want to deploy. You could also host a container on-premises on your own hardware or virtual servers by installing the Docker runtime there. You can deploy containers on your own VMs in Azure. If you just need a small dev environment or you're not ready yet to move into container-specific services, you can still package your application into containers and deploy those onto VMs that you control. Of course, you'll need to maintain and patch those VMs, but it can at least get you started with some of the benefits that containers offer in terms of deployment and agility. With each of these approaches, you need to install the container runtime, but Azure has several Platform as a Service offerings for hosting containers. Azure Container Instances, or ACI, is a service that provides a way to host containers without having to maintain or patch the environment. It hosts a single container instance per image, so it's intended for smaller applications like simple web apps or DevTest scenarios, but it still has obvious advantages to deploying containers to your own virtual machines because you get a managed environment where you only pay for the containers. Azure Kubernetes is a fully managed container management system that can scale your application to meet demands by adding and removing container instances, as well as monitoring the deployed containers and fixing any issues that might occur. Kubernetes is an open source project, and it's one tool in a class of tools called container orchestrators. Azure Red Hat OpenShift is a service in Azure that's a partnership between Red Hat and Microsoft, and it allows for running Kubernetes powered OpenShift. If your organization is already using OpenShift, this is a way to move to a managed hosting environment in the cloud. Azure Spring Apps is for hosting containers that run Java Spring apps, so it's tailored to that specific platform. You can actually deploy containers to Azure App Service also. So in addition to deploying code onto Azure App Service, you can package web apps as containers and host them in App Service. You can also deploy containers to Azure Functions for event-driven applications. And a relatively new service in Azure for hosting containers is Azure Container Apps. This is a managed serverless container platform for running microservices. This service is also powered by Kubernetes, but it doesn't provide direct access to the underlying Kubernetes configuration, which makes management a lot easier. So the choice of how to host your containers comes down to the development platform your team uses, what orchestration platform they might be accustomed to, and how much control you want over the management of the service. Let's take a look at the simplest of the container hosting options. Azure container instances

Chapter 23 How to Create an Azure Container Instance

From All services, I'll search for container instances. There are a few other services here, like Container Registry for storing your custom containers, and Container Apps, which is another service for hosting the running of your containers. But we'll choose Azure Container Instances, a simple service for running single containers. And let's create one from the menu.

As always, we need to choose a resource group to store the metadata about the container. I'll choose the one we created earlier. Let's give this container a name, and this name only needs to be unique within the resource group. There's a lot of regions we can choose from to deploy this container instance, but I'll just leave the default. Next we can choose to deploy our container from a container registry. Azure has its own container registry service, or you could choose another service like Docker Hub, and that can be a public or a private registry with a login. But let's choose a quickstart image just to get up and running. I'll select the helloworld Linux image. And you can change the resource requirements for the container if you'd like, so the number of virtual CPUs and RAM that the container uses. Let's close this and move to the Networking tab.

Here you can create a public IP address and DNS name. So this will get prepended on the Azure service URL. You can configure environment variables here and the restart policy for the container.

This is where an orchestration service like Azure Kubernetes offers a lot more functionality. We won't add any tags. And let's create this container instance. It'll take almost a minute to create this in Azure.

And once it's created, we can navigate into the container instance. We have some monitoring happening on the Overview page.

On the Containers page, there's the container we created. It says the state is Running. Let's go back to the Overview page, and the fully qualified domain name is here on the right. This is the DNS name we added with the rest of the URL provided by Azure. Let's paste this into another browser tab.

Welcome to Azure Container Instances!

We get a basic web page that was served by the container, so we know the container is running in Azure Container Instances. Let's go back into the container on the Containers tab. And there are logs available here, so you have some visibility into the output from the container, and you can even remote into the container and get a command prompt so you can run shell commands here.

I can list out all the files and folders that are on this quickstart container.

So it's serving the default page using Node.js. That's a quick look at containers and one of the Azure services that can host them for you. Next, let's talk about Azure app service

Chapter 24 Azure App Service Fundamentals

I mentioned that you can use App Service to host containers, but it's also the Platform as a Service offering for hosting code directly, meaning the App Service is more like traditional web hosting where the frameworks are already installed on the servers, like .NET, PHP or Java, and you can deploy your code onto those servers. The difference with traditional web hosting is that Azure handles the management and patching of the underlying servers for you, but you do have lots of configuration options. Azure App Service can host web applications, API apps, which are web services that use the REST protocol, and it can host the back-end code for mobile applications, which are really just web services. You can deploy containers to Azure App Service too, but you don't have to. And there's also a feature of App Service called WebJobs that let you run services on the underlying VMs of the App Service. WebJobs can run continuously or on a schedule. They can run as executable files or they can run scripts like PowerShell or Bash scripts. So if you're running Windows services on your on-premises web servers now and wonder how you can do that in Azure, WebJobs offer that kind of functionality. There are other services in Azure to accomplish those types of tasks, and we'll look at some of them in the serverless computing section. App Service started out as a service called Azure Websites, and when you create a new App Service, the default URL is still suffixed with azurewebsites.net. And yes, you can use your own custom domain name with Azure App Service. This is just the default URL that first gets created. So an App Service is basically an individual website or API web service or mobile back end that you host. They're all really the same thing, just code that's hosted on a web server.

Before you can create an App Service, though, you need an App Service plan. The App Service plan defines the size of the underlying infrastructure, which are actually just virtual machines in Azure. But remember, you don't patch or maintain those VMs and you have limited access to them. You can run more than one App Service on a single App Service plan. When you create an App Service plan, you choose the size of the VMs, meaning the CPU, RAM, and storage by selecting the plan type, also known as the pricing tier. Depending on the pricing tier, you also have access to different features of an App Service plan. Let's create an App Service plan next and explore the features of Azure App Service in the process.

Chapter 25 How to Create an Azure App Service

We won't create an App Service plan first. We'll just do it during the creation of the App Service. I'll do that by using the shortcut on the left menu for all App Services in this subscription. Let's create a new one. And the first thing is the resource group to put this App Service in.

Let's create a new resource group for this. I'll just give it a name. And now let's give this App Service a name. This name needs to be unique across all of Azure because it's suffixed with azurewebsites.net. So this part here can't be the same as any other website on all of Azure. But remember, you can add your own domain name later. This is just the default one for creating the App Service. Next, we can choose whether to publish code or a Docker container or a static web app. For code, you choose a runtime stack, and this will be available on all the underlying web servers that the code is deployed to. The runtime you choose here will dictate which operating systems are available below. You can deploy your own Docker container from a container registry. And the Static Web App option is when you're just deploying front-end code. There's no code running on the server, so there's no runtime framework option.

This actually brings you to another service in Azure for hosting these types of static web apps, and that service uses Azure Functions for back-end logic. Static web apps integrate directly with GitHub or Azure Pipelines to pull your code, so it's a serverless environment where you don't need an underlying App Service plan. You can create one of these apps from the All services menu. It's just here is an easier way to get to that service, but it does seem a bit confusing. Let's choose a traditional code deployment, and I'll choose .NET 6, which is available on Windows and Linux VMs. Then we need to select a region where this will get deployed. If my subscription had an existing App Service plan in this region, I could choose to deploy the App Service onto that plan. But since it doesn't, a new App Service plan will get created. Because I'm using the free trial, I don't have the option to change from the free pricing tier. They're all using the free pricing tier right now because I've scaled them down to that plan to save money. Let's create a new App Service plan, and I'll give it a name.

Spec Picker   ×

Dev / Test	Production	Isolated
For less demanding workloads	For most production workloads	Advanced networking and scale

Recommended pricing tiers

| F1 | Shared infrastructure
1 GB memory
60 minutes/day compute
Free | D1 | Shared infrastructure
1 GB memory
240 minutes/day compute
15.23 CAD/Month (Estimated) | B1 | 100 total ACU
1.75 GB memory
A series compute equivalent
44.55 CAD/Month (Estimated) |

See additional options

Included features

Every app hosted on this App Service plan will have access to these features.

Custom domains / SSL
Configure and purchase custom domains with SNI SSL bindings

Manual scale
Up to 3 instances. Subject to availability.

Included hardware

Every instance of your App Service plan will include the following hardware configuration

Azure Compute Units (ACU)
Dedicated compute resources used to run applications deployed in the App Service Plan. Learn more

Memory
Memory per instance available to run applications deployed and running in the App Service plan.

Storage
10 GB disk storage shared by all apps deployed in the App Service plan.

And now we can change the size, which is really changing the pricing tier. It defaults to the S1 pricing tier under the Production grouping of tiers, but we can switch to the Dev group. Below the pricing tiers are the options that are available for each one. As I change pricing tiers, features are added. With the D1 pricing tier, we can use custom domains. At B1, we can add VM instances manually when we want to scale out the resources to handle increased load. And at the S1 tier, we get autoscale and staging slots and all the features we need.

Included features

Every app hosted on this App Service plan will have access to these features:

Custom domains / SSL
Configure and purchase custom domains with SNI and IP SSL bindings

Auto scale
Up to 10 instances. Subject to availability.

Staging slots
Up to 5 staging slots to use for testing and deployments before swapping them into production.

Daily backups
Backup your app 10 times daily

Included hardware

Every instance of your App Service plan will include the following hardware configuration:

Azure Compute Units (ACU)
Dedicated compute resources used to run applications deployed in the App Service Plan. Learn more

Memory
Memory per instance available to run applications deployed and running in the App Service plan.

Storage
50 GB disk storage shared by all apps deployed in the App Service plan.

Going up from there just increases the amount of CPU, RAM, and storage on the underlying servers. So let's choose this S1 tier, and let's move to the Deployment tab. Here we can set up continuous deployment so our code gets pulled from a GitHub repository automatically.

Let's move on to Networking. We could make it so this App Service is able to call into resources in a virtual network.

Let's leave the default, though. And on the Monitoring tab, we could create an instance of Application Insights, which would collect all sorts of metrics from the App Service, like user behavior and performance of the app. But let's turn this off for now.

We can enable it after the App Service gets created. We won't create any tags, so let's create this App Service. Once it's ready, let's actually go to the tab with all the App Service plans. This is the plan that was created with the App Service. In the App Service plan, there's a tab for apps. There's only one App Service here, the one we just created. Further down the menu, you can change the pricing tier if there's features you need to use or you just need more powerful VMs.

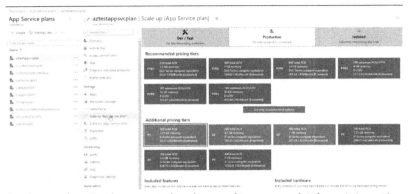

And on the Scale out tab, depending on which pricing tier you're on, you can add VMs to the plan. And, of course, there are costs associated with that.

And you can also configure autoscaling. So when a certain metric is reached, more VMs will be added. In the list here, there are lots of metrics you can have the App Service plan watch, like the amount of CPU being used, the disk queue length, and the percentage of RAM being used. Then you can configure some logic to add or remove VMs under certain conditions.

Let's close this, and let's go back to the Apps tab and drill into the App Service we created. So this is a web app that can use .NET for its server-side logic. We haven't deployed any code here, but there is a default page created for you that you can access from this Browse button. That opens up a tab with the URL that we chose during creation, so we know that the servers are running and serving content.

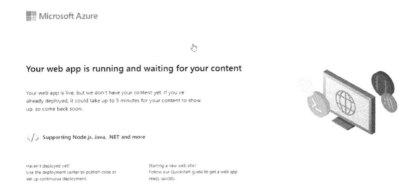

Back in the App Service, let's explore some of the things we can configure. You can add a custom domain.

You can either purchase that through a third party and just verify it here in which case you'd need to point your DNS provider to this IP address or to the URL that you saw on the browse page depending on the type of DNS record that you use, or you can actually buy an App Service domain through

Azure right here in the portal. Let's look at the Configuration tab. This lets you add name value pairs that can be read by your application code. You can also add connection strings to databases here. This lets you keep configuration and secrets out of your code.

If you've written ASP.NET applications before, you know there's a configuration file in your project. Any values here with the same name as what's in that file will override the values in the file, so administrators can manage configuration in the portal. Notice there's a checkbox for deployment slot settings. Deployment slots let you create different environments like dev, user acceptance testing, and production.

So you can have a different version of your web app in each of them, and you can promote your web app through the environments from right here in the portal, and the application settings and database connection strings that we saw can be unique to each deployment slot. So the code gets promoted and the values change for each environment. Now let's take a look at authentication. One of the great things about Azure App Service is that you can let it handle authentication for you. You just choose the provider that your user base uses, and you can use multiple providers.

Add an identity provider

You could use Azure Active Directory, so accounts need to exist there. Or you could use outside authentication providers, like Facebook, Twitter, or pretty much any service that uses this protocol called OpenID Connect. That works with OAuth 2.0, which is a standard on the web. Remember we talked about that when we talked about Azure Active Directory Domain Services. One of the scary things about turning over management of your web servers to a third party, even Microsoft, is how do you troubleshoot that when there's a problem? Same with a deployment. You don't have access to the file system directly, but you can turn on quite a bit of logging, including logs from the web server and from the application.

Those can get stored in Azure Storage as files, or you can have them written onto the local server in the App Service plan, in which case you can actually stream them from here and see the logging in real time. You can stream the logs onto your local computer using Visual Studio or PowerShell also. There's a lot more here that can help you with troubleshooting. Under the advanced tools, there's a link to the Kudu portal. That's an application that gets installed with your App Service that provides all sorts of information about the environment like system information and environment variables on the servers.

Under the Tools menu, there's a way you can deploy your web app by dragging a zip file containing the website right into the browser here. There are a lot of other ways to deploy apps to Azure App Service too, but we'll stop here. Next, we'll look at serverless computing in Azure and Azure Functions in particular.

Chapter 26 Serverless Computing in Azure

There's always servers involved in Azure. The term just really refers to how little you might need to interact with those servers. Serverless computing is about letting developers focus on the code and business logic that they're developing and not on the underlying infrastructure. The environment is set up for you, and it scales automatically to meet demand, but you don't need to do any configuration to make that happen, even the minimal config you need to do with App Service or virtual machine scale sets. Serverless computing also differs from the other compute models you've seen in that you're only charged when the code runs, so you don't need a virtual machine or an App Service running, waiting to do the work. The two main services in Azure that are considered serverless computing are Azure Functions and Azure Logic Apps. Logic Apps don't really fall under the Azure compute category. They are now categorized as part of the integration category of services, but they're used so often with Azure Functions that it's worth mentioning here. Both of these services can be used independently, but are often used together to build solutions. Azure Functions allow you to run small pieces of code that you write yourself. Functions are started by triggers, which could be an HTTP call to the function endpoint, an event that happens in another Azure service, like a blob getting created in Azure Storage, or you can run the code based on a timer event. You can write functions in C#, Java, JavaScript, TypeScript, Python, and even in PowerShell. Azure Functions can run completely serverless, and this is called the consumption-based model. But if you already have an Azure App Service plan that you're paying for, you can also leverage that to host Azure Functions. Azure Logic Apps allow you to design workflows right in the Azure portal, so you don't need to write any code with Logic Apps. You can automate business processes when you need to integrate apps, data, and services. Logic Apps have a huge library of connectors to everything from SharePoint and Azure Storage to Zendesk and SAP. When there isn't a built-in connector that suits your requirements, you can always write code in an Azure Function and call it from a Logic App. So even though Logic Apps are very powerful, it's always good to know that when you hit a wall in terms of functionality, there's a way to write code to accomplish what you need. So for an example of how these can work together, you could create a Logic App that watches an email account for an email with attachments, then cleanses the body of the email using an Azure Function. Then the Logic App could create a blob in an Azure storage account and store the email and the attachment there. In terms of choosing one over the other, if you need a solution that calls well-known APIs, Logic Apps are a good place to start because of all the connectors available. If your solution needs to execute custom algorithms or do special data lookups, Azure Functions would be a starting place because you already know that you need to write code. Let's create an Azure Function next.

Chapter 27 How to Create an Azure Function

This will just be a simple HTTP trigger that returns HTML to the browser. I'll start by going to All services and searching for Function Apps.

A Function App is the container that holds multiple functions. Click Create, and we get brought to the creation screen. Let's create this Function App in the resource group.

We need to give this Function App a name. And similar to Azure App Services, this name needs to be unique across Azure because it's suffixed with azurewebsites.net. So you can start to see the relationship here between Function Apps and Web Apps in the Azure App Service. Next, we select to deploy code or a container. Because I'm using the free trial subscription here, only code is available. I'll select the runtime stack as .NET, but you can see there are other options here, like Node.js and Java. I'll leave the default framework version, .NET 6, and I'll leave the default region too. You can deploy Function Apps onto Linux or Windows. It just depends on the runtime stack you've selected. .NET runs on both, but not all the frameworks do. And the plan is the most important thing here.

The consumption-based plan will take care of all the sizing and scaling of the VMs for us, and we'll only be charged based on when the functions are called. The other options are grayed out because I'm using the free Azure trial. But normally, you can select to create this Function App on an existing App Service plan right alongside your other web apps and API apps. Or you can choose the Function Premium plan, which adds some network and connectivity options and avoids having to warm up the underlying VMs, so the performance can be better.

Create Function App ...

Basics   Networking   Monitoring   Tags   Review + create

Function Apps can be provisioned with the inbound address being public to the internet or isolated to an Azure virtual network. Function Apps can also be provisioned with outbound traffic able to reach endpoints in a virtual network, be governed by network security groups or affected by virtual network routes. By default, your app is open to the internet and cannot reach into a virtual network. These aspects can also be changed after the app is provisioned. Learn more ⬈

⚠ Network injection is only available in Functions Premium and Basic, Standard, Premium, Premium V2, Premium V3 Dedicated App Service plans.

Enable network injection   ○ Off ⦿ On ○

And this is where the Function Premium plan provides networking options to restrict access to only virtual networks, not the public internet. On the Monitoring tab, we have the option to enable Application Insights for deep monitoring, just like with App Services.

Create Function App ...

Basics   Networking   Monitoring   Tags   Review + create

Azure Monitor application insights is an Application Performance Management (APM) service for developers and DevOps professionals. Enable it below to automatically monitor your application. It will detect performance anomalies and includes powerful analytics tools to help you diagnose issues and to understand what users actually do with your app. Learn more ⬈

Application Insights

Enable Application Insights *   ⦿ No ○ Yes

Once it's created, let's navigate into the Function App. So this looks a lot like an App Service already. There are deployment slots, configuration, authentication, and custom domains. But under the Function grouping, there's this Functions tab, and there aren't any functions yet. So again, the Function App is the container, and you can have multiple functions here. Okay, now let's create the function.

The first thing is the development environment. You can develop functions using VS Code or another editor with core tools installed like Visual Studio. Or you can develop right here in the portal in the editor. So let's just stick with that. Next, we choose the type of trigger, so what's going to cause this function to run? It could be an HTTP call to the endpoint, it could run on a timer, or this Function App could watch for events in Azure, like when a blob is added to a specific container in Azure Storage or a document changes in a Cosmos DB database. Let's go with the HTTP trigger.

This is how you would call the function from another program, like a Logic App for example. We can change the function's name, and we can choose the authorization level. This has to do with whether or not the caller needs to supply a key, which is just a shared secret.

So you can prevent unauthorized callers from causing this function to run and costing you money. Let's just leave it wide open for the example though, and let's create this function. Once it's created, we're brought into the function. We've got some options along the left here.

Let's click Code + Test. That opens up the editor where you can modify the default code. This just gives you a starting place to see how the function is structured. The default code will write to the log, and it will look for a string in the query string value and send back a response over HTTP. You can write some really complex functions to interact with other services and perform whatever logic you want to code. But this is an easy-to-understand example, so let's just stick with this. Next on the menu is the Integration tab where you can see how the function is laid out and make modifications here. This is just an overview, so we won't go into this. But let's go back to the code and test, and let's run this function.

Let's copy the function URL. So this is the endpoint that the caller would use. They could do that programmatically to get the results back, but let's open up a new browser tab and paste this in. I'll increase the font size.

This HTTP triggered function executed successfully. Pass a name in the query string or in the request body for a personalized response.

It says the function ran successfully and that we can pass a name in the query string. So functions are an easy way to deploy small packages of business logic onto a managed environment and can provide cost savings over hosting a full-blown app service. In summary, you learned about computer options in Azure, starting with the service delivery models, then looking at virtual machines, containers, Azure App Service, and Azure Functions. Next, we'll look at networking in Azure.

Chapter 28 Azure Networking

Azure has a number of products for networking that allow you to create secure networks for your virtual machines and other Azure resources so those resources can communicate with each other and with the internet. The underlying physical network and components are managed by Microsoft, and you configure virtual versions of everything that you need. An Azure virtual network is a fundamental building block for your private network. A VNet enables many types of Azure resources to communicate. A virtual network has an address space that you define in Azure, which is a group of IP addresses that can be assigned to resources like virtual machines. A VNet is segmented into one or more subnetworks called subnets, which are allocated a portion of the VNet's IP address space. Then you deploy Azure resources to a specific subnet. A VM is assigned to a subnet, and VMs can communicate with other VMs on the same network. But you can apply security rules to that traffic using network security groups, or NSGs. These allow you to filter network traffic by allowing or denying traffic into and out of the subnet. Virtual machines are deployed into virtual networks, but you can also deploy other Azure resources into a VNet, networking components, like Azure Firewall, Application Gateway, and VPN Gateway. You can deploy data-related resources like Redis Cache and Azure SQL Managed Instances, and analytics resources, like Azure HDInsight and Azure Databricks. And Azure Kubernetes Service gets deployed into a VNet also. You can also configure App Services to have a private IP on your VNet, which enables private connections to App Services, which have traditionally only been available over the internet. By default, resources assigned to one virtual network can't communicate with resources in another virtual network. So there's some inherent security controls built in, but you can enable that communication between virtual networks using a feature called VNet peering. You can enable VNet peering between virtual networks in the same region, as well as VNets in different Azure regions, and the traffic flows privately over Microsoft's backbone network. You can connect an on-premises network to an Azure virtual network also using a VPN gateway or using a service called ExpressRoute. Virtual machines on a VNet can communicate out to the internet by default. But in order for inbound communications to take place from the internet, the virtual machine needs to be assigned to public IP address. Technically, the public IP address gets attached to the network interface of the virtual machine. So each of these is a separate resource in Azure with their own configuration. I mentioned network security groups, or NSGs. You also use these to control the inbound and outbound traffic to the internet. You can assign a network security group to the subnet or directly to the network interface of a VM. Then you can filter traffic with rules based on the source and destination IP addresses, the ports being accessed, and the protocol being used, like TCP or UDP. Now let's talk about load balancing in Azure. In order to distribute traffic between virtual machines for high availability, you can create a load balancer. There are public load balancers in Azure, which load balance internet traffic to your VMs. You can actually use a public load balancer to allow traffic to your VM without needing to attach a public IP address to the VM. And there are also internal or private load balancers where traffic is coming from inside the network. A public load balancer can provide inbound connections to VMs for traffic coming from the internet. It can translate the public IP address to the private IP addresses of the VMs inside a VNet.

It's a high-performance solution that can handle a lot of traffic, but it's just a load balancing and port forwarding engine. It doesn't interact with the traffic coming in. It just checks the health of the back-end resources. When you're exposing resources to the internet, particularly servers on your internal virtual network, you usually want more control over the traffic. That's where Azure Application Gateway can offer more features and security for publishing applications to the internet. Application Gateway is a web traffic load balancer that exposes a public IP to the internet, and it can do things like SSL termination. So traffic between the client and the App Gateway is encrypted, but then the traffic between App Gateway and the back-end virtual machines can flow unencrypted, which unburdens the VMs from costly encryption and decryption overhead. App Gateway supports autoscaling, so it can scale up and down depending on traffic load patterns. It supports session affinity for applications that require a user to return to the same web server after they've started a session. It can do rewriting of HTTP headers and can make routing decisions based on more than just the IP address and the port that was requested. And App Gateway also uses a service called Web Application Firewall, which protects your web applications from common exploits and vulnerabilities like SQL injection attacks and cross-site scripting. So again, Application Gateway is more than just a load balancer. If you search for load balancing in the Azure portal, you'll see descriptions of all the options. Besides Load Balancer and Application Gateway, there are two other options that relate to load balancing across different regions.

Traffic Manager allows you to distribute traffic to services across global Azure regions. Front Door has more capabilities for application delivery. We'll look a little closer at some of the major components of virtual networking in Azure. We'll create a virtual network and subnets. Then we'll create a virtual machine and attach it to the existing VNet. Next, you'll see how to use network security groups to allow traffic to the VM from the internet. After that, we'll peer two virtual networks so the VMs on the VNets can communicate. Then we'll discuss the options for connecting on-premises networks to Azure using VPN Gateway and then ExpressRoute. Next, we'll discuss Azure DNS for managing DNS services alongside your other Azure resources. And finally, we'll talk about private endpoints in Azure, which bring platform services like App Services and storage accounts into your private virtual network. So next, let's create a virtual network.

I'll start by going to All services and searching for virtual network.

Click this, and there aren't any created yet, so I'll click Create. As always, we need a resource group. I'm going to create a new one, so I'll just give it a name, and let's call this vnet1, and I'll place it in the closest region to me. Next, let's configure the IP address space for this VNet.

This is called CIDR notation. The number after the slash tells how many addresses are in the range, starting at the number before the slash. So a /16 means there are about 64,000 IPs available in the address space. We can assign these IP addresses to virtual machines and other services that can be addressed within a VNet. When you configure your IP address space, the IP addresses are private to your VNet. The only time it matters is when you want to connect this VNet with another network, like another VNet in Azure using peering or with your local network on-premises using VPN Gateway or ExpressRoute. In that case, those IP addresses can't overlap with this address space. We can break this up into smaller blocks of IP addresses using subnets, and then we can apply security to a subnet. I'll call this WebSubnet because I want to put web servers in this subnet. I'll give it an address range that starts within the range of the VNet and has a smaller block of IP addresses. In CIDR notation, a larger number means a smaller group of IPs. So a /27 is only 32 IP addresses. We can attach service endpoints to the subnet.

Service endpoints allow traffic to specific services in Azure over the Microsoft backbone. So VMs on the subnet could connect to Azure SQL or Azure Storage without having to connect to the public endpoints on the internet. Let's create this subnet, and let's create another subnet. Let's call this AppSubnet. So I might put application servers on this subnet and have them only accessible from VMs on the web subnet. Then you can use network security groups to enforce that. I'll give this subnet a range that starts higher than the highest IP available in the WebSubnet. And let's make this a /24, so there are 256 IP addresses available on this subnet.

Create virtual network

Let's add this, and let's move on to the Security tab. Here, you can enable a bastion host, which is a VM that lets you remote into the virtual machines in this VNet without having to connect to them directly, so that's for security. We can enable DDOS standard protection.

Create virtual network

Every VNet comes with basic protection against distributed denial of service attacks. By enabling standard protection, you get additional metrics and access to experts within

Microsoft if an attack is launched against one of your applications. That comes for an additional charge, which is why you have to enable this. Azure Firewall is an intelligent firewall security service. It can watch for patterns and alert you to traffic coming from known malicious IP addresses and domains and deny that traffic. But let's leave these off, and let's move ahead and create this VNet.

Once the VNet is created, I'll go to the shortcut to all VNets. On the menu here, you can see the IP address space we configured, and you can modify it from here.

You can create and remove subnets. And down here, you can specify the DNS servers to use. You can let Azure handle DNS resolution for you, or you can add the IP address of your own DNS servers.

DNS resolves domain names to the IP addresses of servers, so you might create your own network in a VNet with a VM for Active Directory, VMs for applications, and a VM for hosting DNS services. You might do that if you're setting up a lab environment in Azure here, for example. Setting that VM as the DNS server here will allow all the VMs on the network to resolve your internal domain names to the IPs of the servers, but you can actually use a service called Azure DNS for that also. And on the tab for peerings, you can peer this VNet with other VNets in Azure, so the VMs and resources can communicate. If you have any resources that have been assigned IP addresses on the VNet, their network interfaces will show up here. We don't have any, so let's create a virtual machine next and add it to this VNet.

Chapter 30 How to Add Virtual Machine to VNET

So we have a VNet, but it doesn't have anything on it. So let's create a virtual machine just like we did earlier, but this time, we won't create a new virtual network at the same time. We'll add the VM to the existing VNet. We went through all this earlier, so I'll move quickly through this. Let's put this VM in the same resource group as the VNet. We don't have to, but that'll make it easier to delete everything at once later. But this VM does need to be in the same region as the VNet. Let's turn off the availability options and change the VM image from Linux to Windows Server.

I need to enter a username and password for the local administrator account. Now let's move to the Disks tab, and I'll leave the defaults.

Create a virtual machine

Basics   **Disks**   Networking   Management   Advanced   Tags   Review + create

Azure VMs have one operating system disk and a temporary disk for short-term storage. You can attach additional data disks. The size of the VM determines the type of storage you can use and the number of data disks allowed. Learn more

Disk options

OS disk type * ⓘ	Premium SSD (locally-redundant storage)
Delete with VM ⓘ	☑
Enable encryption at host ⓘ	☐

ⓘ Encryption at host is not registered for the selected subscription. Learn more about enabling this feature

| Encryption type * | (Default) Encryption at-rest with a platform-managed key | ∨ |
| Enable Ultra Disk compatibility ⓘ | ☐ Ultra disk is not supported for the selected VM size Standard_DS1_v2 in Canada Central |

Data disks for web1

You can add and configure additional data disks for your virtual machine or attach existing disks. This VM also comes with a temporary disk.

LUN	Name	Size (GiB)	Disk type	Host caching	Delete with VM ⓘ

Create and attach a new disk   Attach an existing disk

And Networking is where I want to assign this VM to the existing VNet. Remember the VM is being created in the same Azure region as the VNet is in so that VNet is available in the drop-down list here.

Create a virtual machine

Network interface

When creating a virtual machine, a network interface will be created for you.

Virtual network * ⓘ	vnet1 / Create new	∨
Subnet * ⓘ	Websubnet (10.20.0.0/27) / Manage subnet configuration	∨
Public IP ⓘ	(new) web1-ip / Create new	∨
NIC network security group ⓘ	⦿ None ◯ Basic ◯ Advanced

⚠ All ports on this virtual machine may be exposed to the public internet. This is a security risk. Use a network security group to limit public access to specific ports. You can also select a subnet that already has network security groups defined or remove the public IP address.

| Delete public IP and NIC when VM is deleted ⓘ | ☐ |
| Enable accelerated networking ⓘ | ☑ |

Load balancing

You can place this virtual machine in the backend pool of an existing Azure load balancing solution. Learn more

Load balancing options ⓘ	⦿ None
	◯ Azure load balancer Supports all TCP/UDP network traffic, port forwarding and outbound flows
	◯ Application gateway Web traffic load balancer for HTTP/HTTPS with URL based routing, SSL termination, session persistence, and web application firewall.

You also need to select which subnet to put this virtual machine on. Technically, it's the network interface attached to this VM that will get the IP address from the subnet. The

140

default for security is that a network security group will get created and assigned to the network interface of this VM. But we're going to create a separate network security group and assign it to the subnet, not to the VM. So I'll turn this off for now. That's all I want to change in the defaults, so let's skip ahead through these tabs and create this VM. It'll take a minute or so to create this, and once the VM is created, let's navigate into it from here. I'll go to the Connect screen.

This is where we downloaded the RDP file to connect into the VM. It says here that the port prerequisite is not met. That's because there's no network security group that will allow traffic to this VM from the internet. Let's download the RDP file and try to connect anyway just to be sure. I'll open the file and click Connect, and I don't even get to the login screen because Azure won't allow the connection to the VM over port 3389.

So let's fix that in the next chapter.

Chapter 31 How to Create a Network Security Group (NSG)

We can't connect into this VM from outside the Azure VNet. Let's fix that by creating a network security group, or NSG, and opening up port 3389 to the internet. I'll go to All services again and search for network security. Click on Network security groups, and there aren't any yet in the subscription. This is a different subscription from the free trial that I used earlier in the course when I created that VM. Otherwise, the network security group attached to the network interface of that VM would show up here. I'll create a new network security group. We need to put this in a resource group, so I'll use the same one as the VNet and the VM, and that updates the region for me. And I'll give this a descriptive name.

Create network security group

Basics   Tags   Review + create

Project details

Subscription * | Visual Studio Professional   ∨ |

    Resource group * | networking1_rg   ∨ |
                           Create new

Instance details

Name * | vnet1websubnetnsg |

Region * | Canada Central   ∨ |

That's all the configuration you can do when you create the NSG, so let's skip tags and create this. Once the NSG is created, let's navigate into the resource. On the Overview tab, it shows the default inbound and outbound security rules.

Network security groups allow you to permit or deny traffic between sources and destinations and to be specific about which ports and which protocol are permitted or denied. Before we add an inbound rule to allow port 3389 from the internet, let's just verify that this NSG isn't attached to a network interface for a virtual machine. If it was, that would show here. And this isn't associated with any subnets either, so let's do that first.

I'll select the VNet that's in the same region as this NSG, which is the one we want and then associate this with the subnet that the VM is on, which is the WebSubnet. Now the security rules of this network security group are being applied to the subnet that the VM is on. So let's go to Inbound security rules, and let's add a new rule. I won't go through each of these options. But if you wanted to allow HTTP traffic from the internet to a web server in the subnet associated with this NSG, you would allow ports 80 to the IP address of the VM or to any VM on the subnet, which is the default here, Let's do something similar, but allowing RDP traffic, which changes the port to 3389.

And that's all we need to do. So let's just change the name of the security rule and add it to the NSG. Now it shows at the top of the list because it has higher priority than the other rules.

These rules are processed based on priority, the lower number taking precedence. So this RDP rule overrides the rule at the bottom to deny all inbound traffic. Now let's go back to the list of virtual machines and drill into this VM and go to the Connect tab.

Now it shows that the inbound access port check past, so we should be able to connect using RDP. Let's download the RDP file, although we could use the one we downloaded before. Nothing's really changed. And I'm getting brought to the login screen, so that's progress. I'll enter the credentials of the local administrator on this VM. Okay, I can accept the certificate errors, and I'm brought into the remote desktop of the virtual machine in Azure. So the network security group enabled access from the internet from my local computer. Let's just wait until the connection is completed. Now I'll open up the command prompt, and let's run the ipconfig command. This shows us the IP address of this VM. It's been assigned an IP address on the subnet of vnet1.

```
Windows IP Configuration

Ethernet adapter Ethernet:

   Connection-specific DNS Suffix  . : v2tz0ozeg5ue3cjrd53al0l55h.ux.internal.cloudapp.net
   Link-local IPv6 Address . . . . . : fe80::c5b1:4bca:c158:d42d%6
   IPv4 Address. . . . . . . . . . . : 10.20.0.4
   Subnet Mask . . . . . . . . . . . : 255.255.255.224
   Default Gateway . . . . . . . . . : 10.20.0.1
```

Next, let's see how to set up VNet peering, so this VM can access a VM on another VNet.

Chapter 32 How to Peer Virtual Networks

Now let's see how to allow resources in different virtual networks to communicate with each other by peering the virtual networks. I've created another VNet for this demo. The type is kind of small here, but the VNets have different address spaces, and the IP addresses in each address space don't overlap.

I've also created another virtual machine. And if I drill into it, it shows here that the VM network interface is attached to a different VNet and subnet. The private IP address of this VM on the VNet is 10.0.0.4. Let's remember that.

I've still got the Remote Desktop window open to the VM on the other network, the one that we created earlier. Let's open up the command prompt. It still shows the results of ipconfig, which shows that this VM is on the first VNet, vnet1. Let's try and ping the VM on the other VNet. I've turned off the firewall on that VM by the way, so it will allow ICMP traffic, which is what ping uses. The request is timing out as expected.

146

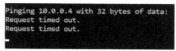

Pinging 10.0.0.4 with 32 bytes of data:
Request timed out.
Request timed out.

Let's go to all virtual networks, and let's go into vent1. You can actually do this from either direction, vnet1 or vnet2. Let's go to Peerings on the menu and add a peering.

I'll give this link a descriptive name to show what it's meant to do, and the default is to allow traffic between the VNets. It's going to create a peering in the other VNet, so we need to give that one a name too. And now let's select the VNet to peer with. I'll select vnet2 and accept the defaults, and let's add this peering. That's all there is to it.

147

It says the status is connected. Let's navigate to vnet2 from the link here, and let's go to Peerings, and there's the other side of the peering.

Now let's see if we can ping the virtual machine in vnet2 from the virtual machine in vnet1. I'll open up the Remote Desktop session again, and I'll just press the up arrow key to show the last command and hit Enter. Now the ping is working, so we successfully peered the two VNets.

```
Pinging 10.0.0.4 with 32 bytes of data:
Reply from 10.0.0.4: bytes=32 time=2ms TTL=128
Reply from 10.0.0.4: bytes=32 time<1ms TTL=128
Reply from 10.0.0.4: bytes=32 time<1ms TTL=128
Reply from 10.0.0.4: bytes=32 time<1ms TTL=128

Ping statistics for 10.0.0.4:
    Packets: Sent = 4, Received = 4, Lost = 0 (0% loss),
Approximate round trip times in milli-seconds:
    Minimum = 0ms, Maximum = 2ms, Average = 0ms
```

So that's how you can allow VNets in Azure to communicate with each other. Next, let's see how to allow on-premises networks to communicate with resources in Azure VNets.

Chapter 33 Azure VPN Gateway Basics

When you want to connect your on-premises network to an Azure VNet, there are a couple of ways to do it. In this chapter, we'll talk about VPN gateways, and in the next, we'll talk about Azure ExpressRoute. What does it mean to connect your networks? It means that from the computers and servers joined to your on-premises network, you can access the virtual machines and other Azure resources that have private IP addresses on that VNet in Azure. To the users on your local network, there's no difference accessing an application on a web server in Azure than there is accessing one on the local network, and that web server in Azure doesn't need to be exposed to the internet. The connection from on-premises is taking place over a private secure connection. To make that connection between networks, you can use a VPN gateway in Azure. VPN Gateway creates a private encrypted tunnel over the public internet. If you connect to your local office now using a VPN, it's basically the same thing. Azure VPN Gateway is made up of one or more VMs that get deployed into a subnet in your Azure VNet. That subnet needs to have a specific name, and you can't configure the VMs for the gateway subnet. You connect to the VPN gateway through its public IP address. If you're connecting your entire on-premises network to Azure, then the VPN gateway needs to connect to a VPN device on your network that has a public IP address to the internet. The traffic between the on-premises network and the Azure VNet flows through the gateway. There are a few different types of connections. Let's take a look at the documentation to see some diagrams.

Site-to-Site VPN

A Site-to-Site (S2S) VPN gateway connection is a connection over IPsec/IKE (IKEv1 or IKEv2) VPN tunnel. S2S connections can be used for cross-premises and hybrid configurations. A S2S connection requires a VPN device located on-premises that has a public IP address assigned to it. For information about selecting a VPN device, see the VPN Gateway FAQ - VPN devices.

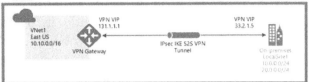

You can create a VPN gateway that connects to your on-premises network. One major stipulation is that you have to make sure that the IP address ranges of the VNet in Azure don't overlap with your on-premises IP addresses. A virtual network in Azure can only have one VPN gateway, but you can make multiple connections to it.

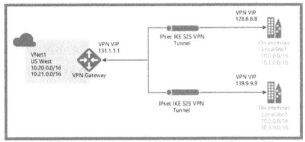

So if you have different regional offices with different networks, you can connect them to the same VPN gateway and the same VNet in Azure. There's a second type of connection possible, which is called a point-to-site VPN. This is where a single computer connects to the VPN gateway.

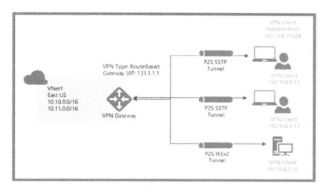

You might use this if you're working from home. It doesn't require the local computer to have a public IP address or a VPN server, like with the site-to-site VPN, but you need to authenticate using certificates uploaded to Azure and on your local computer. It's also possible to use VPN Gateway to set up a connection between two VNets in Azure.

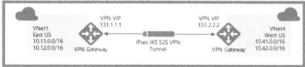

That's an alternate to VNet peering. You might do this if you have older VNets in Azure that were created with the classic deployment model, and you want to join them with newer VNets that use the resource manager model. You can't have more than one VPN gateway in an Azure VNet, but you can connect to a VNet using both VPN Gateway and ExpressRoute. The difference is that VPN Gateway uses the public internet, and ExpressRoute uses a private connection that's not over the public internet.

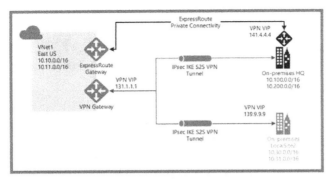

You might do this in order to use VPN Gateway as a failover if, for some reason, the ExpressRoute connection isn't available. That's a lot cheaper than maintaining a backup ExpressRoute connection.

Chapter 34 Azure ExpressRoute Basics

The other type of connection you can make from your on-premises network to Azure is an ExpressRoute connection. The connection is made through a third-party service provider that's partnered with Microsoft. You connect to the service provider, and they connect directly to the Microsoft edge servers. So the traffic doesn't get routed over the public internet. There are actually two ExpressRoute circuits created, so there's built-in redundancy. ExpressRoute can connect your network to multiple VNets in Azure, which is called private peering. You can also connect to Azure public services, like App Service endpoints and storage accounts, as well as Microsoft 365, which used to be called Office 365, and Dynamics 365, which is a Software as a Service customer relationship management system. This type of connection used to be called public peering, but it's now called Microsoft peering. ExpressRoute requires you to work with a third-party provider, and they're partnered with Microsoft to connect to Azure. These providers have infrastructure at data centers where they're collocated with Microsoft edge servers. Examples of these providers are companies like AT&T or Verizon, but there are many regional providers, and they're listed on docs.microsoft.com by location. Each ExpressRoute circuit has a fixed bandwidth, and you choose a plan between 50 Mbps and 10 Gbps. The speeds available depend on the service provider that you work with. There's also something called ExpressRoute Direct where you can establish a direct connection to Microsoft's global network at peering locations around the world. This gives you increased speed and encryption options and, of course, increased cost. So ExpressRoute direct is for big corporate clients with major security requirements like banks and government. You can choose to be charged based on how much data you transfer out of Azure, which is metered billing. Inbound data is always free, or you can pay a monthly fee for unlimited data. The standard ExpressRoute plan gives you access to all the regions in a geopolitical area, but there are two other plans available. The local plan gives you access to only one or two Azure regions near the location where you're peering. You don't pay additional charges for egress for the data coming out of Azure, so this can be economical for large data transfers. And the ExpressRoute Premium add-on gives you global connectivity to any region in the world. So if there's a lot of data moving between your on-premises network and Azure, ExpressRoute can give you the best performance. Let's talk about Azure DNS next.

Chapter 35 Azure DNS Basics

Azure DNS is a way to manage your DNS records right in Azure alongside all your other Azure resources. First, let's review what DNS is. When you create a service in Azure, like an App Service or an Azure Function, they get a name that's suffixed with azurewebsites.net. And when you create a VM, there's a public IP address. You can also add a DNS name label to the public IP address of the VM right in the Azure portal, so you don't have to use the IP address to access it. But again, it ends in an address that you don't control. It's the region name, then cloudapp.azure.com. But when you're publishing your applications for clients, you'll want a custom domain name. Usually, your application name .com or .net or ending in a region-specific suffix, like .ca for Canada. You purchase the custom domain name from a domain registrar, and they're responsible to make sure that no one else owns the domain name. If it's available, you pay an annual fee to reserve the use of the domain name. There are a lot of domain registrars, and the biggest one is GoDaddy. Once you own the domain name, it needs to be hosted by a DNS provider. DNS stands for domain name system, and it's the network of DNS servers all over the world that resolve domain names to the IP addresses of the servers that host the corresponding applications. Your DNS provider makes sure that all those servers can find your domain name and resolve it. Often, when you purchase a domain name, that same company, like GoDaddy, will often let you host the DNS entries with them, but you don't have to. You can host them with any DNS service, and that's what Azure DNS is. Azure DNS is a hosting service for DNS domains that provides name resolution by using Microsoft Azure infrastructure. That's the definition right from the Microsoft docs. Azure isn't a domain registrar. Azure doesn't register your domain name, but they can manage the DNS for it. You can actually purchase domains in Azure using a service called App Service Domains. But App Service Domains actually use GoDaddy for the domain registration and Azure DNS to host the domain name resolution. So you can purchase app service domains for Azure App Services, and everything gets configured for you to point the domain name to the app service. But because they're managed by Azure DNS, you can actually modify the DNS records to point the domain to another Azure service, like a virtual machine or an Azure storage account. If you host your domain name with another DNS provider, you can transfer it to Azure DNS. Then you can manage the DNS records alongside all your other Azure resources, which means you can enable role-based access control to control who in your organization has access, and you can get activity logs to monitor when records are modified, which can help with troubleshooting. DNS domains are hosted on Azure's global network of DNS name servers so that helps with reliability and performance. Besides managing DNS for public domains so they can be resolved from the internet, Azure DNS can also support private DNS domains. That means you can use your own custom DNS domains in your private virtual networks rather than have to set up your own DNS servers on your VM on your VNet. It's great to be able to manage public and private domains in one place. Azure DNS also supports alias record sets. That means you can use an alias record to refer to an Azure resource, like the public IP address of a VM or a content delivery endpoint. Then, if the IP address changes, Azure automatically updates the records. If you manage your DNS records outside of Azure, you might not update those records right away if there's a change in Azure, and then users won't be able to access your service. So having that be automatic with Azure DNS can be really helpful. Next, let's talk about private endpoints.

Chapter 36 Azure Private Endpoints

Private endpoints allow you to essentially bring a public Azure service into your own VNet, so the service can get referenced with a private IP address. When you create a service in Azure, like an App Service, it has public endpoints. That means there's an address on the internet where that resource can be reached. For App Service, that's a URL, the name of your App Service, then azurewebsites.net. That resolves to an IP address. But in certain situations, that IP address can actually change, like during the renewal of an SSL certificate. So really it's the URL that's the endpoint. Azure takes care of the resolution to the underlying IP address for other services, like Azure Storage. You can go to the Endpoints tab and see the public endpoints for your instance of the service. In this case, the endpoint is the name of your storage account, then the individual service in Azure Storage, like the Blob Service, File Service, or Queue Service, and then it's always core.windows.net. These endpoints allow people to reach the blobs and files in the particular service from the internet, but you'll see that you can apply security to the endpoint But, what about if you don't want your App Service or storage account to be accessible from the internet? You only want resources on your own Azure VNet to be able to access the service, so virtual machines on your VNet. Or if you've connected your on-premises network to an Azure VNet, you want your users to be able to access the App Service or storage account only through that secure connection and then disable access from the public internet. You can do that by creating a private endpoint for the Azure service. A private endpoint is a network interface that uses a private IP address on your virtual network. So the App Service or storage account gets a private IP address on your

VNet, and you can access it privately and securely using that IP address. For some services, like Azure App Service, creating a private endpoint will automatically prevent access to the public endpoint, so from the internet. For other services like Azure storage, the public internet access isn't automatically disabled, but you can configure that yourself. Private endpoints use a service called Azure Private Link. With Azure Private Link, you can create connections to Azure Platform as a Service offering, and your connection between your VNet and the service travels over the Microsoft backbone network. In order to create a private link to an Azure service, the service has to support it. On docs.microsoft.com, you can see a list of all the resources in Azure that support private link.

Private-link resource

A private-link resource is the destination target of a specified private endpoint. The following table lists the available resources that support a private endpoint:

Private-link resource name	Resource type	Subresources
Azure App Configuration	Microsoft.Appconfiguration/configurationStores	configurationStores
Azure Automation	Microsoft.Automation/automationAccounts	Webhook, DSCAndHybridWorker
Azure Cosmos DB	Microsoft.AzureCosmosDB/databaseAccounts	SQL, MongoDB, Cassandra, Gremlin, Table
Azure Batch	Microsoft.Batch/batchAccounts	batchAccount, nodeManagement
Azure Cache for Redis	Microsoft.Cache/Redis	redisCache
Azure Cache for Redis Enterprise	Microsoft.Cache/redisEnterprise	redisEnterprise
Azure Cognitive Services	Microsoft.CognitiveServices/accounts	account
Azure Managed Disks	Microsoft.Compute/diskAccesses	managed disk
Azure Container Registry	Microsoft.ContainerRegistry/registries	registry
Azure Kubernetes Service - Kubernetes API	Microsoft.ContainerService/managedClusters	management
Azure Data Factory	Microsoft.DataFactory/factories	dataFactory
Azure Data Explorer	Microsoft.Kusto/clusters	cluster
Azure Database for MariaDB	Microsoft.DBforMariaDB/servers	mariadbServer
Azure Database for MySQL	Microsoft.DBforMySQL/servers	mysqlServer
Azure Database for PostgreSQL - Single server	Microsoft.DBforPostgreSQL/servers	postgresqlServer
Azure Device Provisioning Service	Microsoft.Devices/provisioningServices	iotDps

So besides App Services and storage accounts, Azure Cosmos DB supports private endpoints, Azure Container Registry, Azure Service Bus, Azure SQL Database. So chances are if you want to create a private endpoint to a platform as a service offering in Azure, it's probably possible to do it. Let's quickly see how to set up a private endpoint for an App Service. I'll open up the App Service we created earlier. If you go to the Networking menu item, you can configure some options here, including private endpoints.

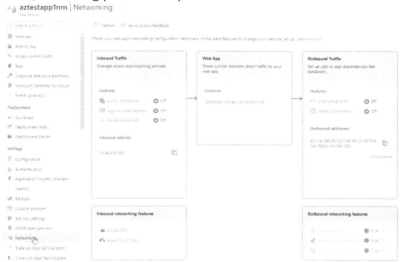

This is available because this App Service was created on the standard pricing tier. If you created yours on the free tier, private endpoints will be grayed out. Let's click this, and here we can create the private endpoint. I'll click Add and select the VNet where I want the private endpoint created and the subnet.

Then I just need to give this a name because it will get created as a separate resource. It'll take a minute or so to create this, and you can watch the status from the

Notifications tab at the top. Once it's created, we could navigate to the resource from here, but let's go to the VNet where it was created. That was vnet1. Under Connected devices, you can see there's the network interface for the virtual machine that was added earlier, and here's the network interface for the App Service.

And you can see they both have private IP addresses from the VNet, and they're part of the web subnet. So that's how you can create a private endpoint for an App Service. In summary, you learned about networking in Azure, starting with an overview. Then you saw how to configure some of the main services, first virtual networks and subnets, then network security groups. After that, you saw how to peer virtual networks in Azure, and then you learned about the ways to connect your on-premises network to Azure using VPN Gateway and ExpressRoute. Then we talked about Azure DNS and how to configure private endpoints to services in Azure. Next, we're going to look at data storage options in Azure.

Chapter 37 Azure Data Storage Options

Modern applications require data to be available quickly and securely from all over the world, and users expect to be able to access, share, and update their data from different devices at any time. Organizations are creating more data than ever, so storing data in the cloud requires addressing new problems in a flexible way, as well as solving old problems in new ways. Azure provides a variety of cloud storage services for different types of data that allows you to choose the storage service that's best optimized for your data and to include several strategies in the same solution, if needed. But common to all the storage solutions in Azure are important benefits like automated backup and recovery, replication across the world to protect your data against unplanned events and failures, encryption capabilities, and built-in security through things like integration with Azure Active Directory for authentication, and developer packages, libraries, and well-documented APIs that can make data accessible to a variety of application types and platforms. Data generally falls into one of three general categories. Structured data is data that adheres to a schema, usually data stored in a database with rows and columns. It's generally referred to as relational data. Azure lets you host databases on virtual machines just like you would on-premises where you're responsible for managing and patching the database product, but Azure also has managed offerings which provide convenience and scalability. For SQL Server, there is Azure SQL Database, and there is also Azure Database for MySQL and Azure Database for PostgreSQL, which are all managed Platform as a Service offerings. Unstructured data is data that doesn't adhere to a schema and is usually data stored in different file formats, so PDF documents, JPEG images, video files and JSON files. For that data, Azure Storage provides highly scalable solutions with Azure Blob storage and Azure File storage. File storage can be attached to virtual machines using the SMB protocol, similar to on-premises file shares, but both types of storage also offer REST APIs, so data can be securely accessed over the internet. Azure Storage also stores large files like disk images and SQL databases. Semi-structured data doesn't fit neatly into tables, rows, and columns. It's often called NoSQL or non-relational data, and it usually uses tags or keys that organize the data and provide a hierarchy. For this type of data, Azure offers Cosmos DB, which is a globally distributed service to store data that's constantly being updated by users around the world. Being able to provision these different types of storage solutions quickly and in a cost effective way helps you respond to business change without the need to procure and manage the costly storage media and networking components required to connect it all together. This makes data storage a very strong value proposition for moving to Azure. We'll be looking at Azure Storage accounts. This is the focus of the data storage portion of the AZ-900 exam. We'll look at redundancy options for storage accounts, so making copies of your data in different locations. We'll create a storage account and explore the features of blobs and files in Azure Storage. Then you'll learn about some of the options for transferring data into Azure using online methods with tools like Azure Storage Explorer and a command-line utility called AzCopy. And for transferring larger amounts of data, there is a service called Azure Data Box where Microsoft will send you hard drives for you to copy your data onto and send back to be copied into Azure. We'll discuss migrating other types of workloads to Azure also, like servers and applications using a service called Azure Migrate. Let's get started by looking at Azure Storage.

Chapter 38 Azure Storage Accounts

Azure Storage is a set of services in Azure that provides storage for a variety of data types using a few different services. Those services are managed under an Azure Storage account. The Blob storage service is for unstructured data like files and documents. Then there is File storage that's similar to Blob storage, except that it supports the SMB protocol, so it can be attached to virtual machines like a network drive, and this makes migrating traditional on-premises applications to the cloud much easier. There is Disk storage which stores the virtual machine disks used by Infrastructure as a Service VMs. There is the Table storage service that lets you store structured data in the form of NoSQL non-relational data, similar to the data you can store using Cosmos DB. And finally, there is the Queue service that's used to store and retrieve messages to help you build asynchronous reliable applications that pass messages. Let's talk about some of the general features of Azure Storage. Azure Storage is durable and highly available. Your data is stored three times in the primary data center by default, and you can choose other replication options that copy the data automatically to other regions in Azure. Your data in Azure Storage can be reached over HTTPS from the internet and each of the storage services in an Azure Storage account has its own REST endpoint, but of course, you can apply security controls to those endpoints to prevent unauthorized access. Security is a big topic for storage accounts. At a high level, when you want to control access to the data plane of a storage account to allow access to the data, you can provide access using role-based access control for users with identities stored in Azure Active Directory and that works for the blob, file, and table services in your storage account. Or you can provide a storage account key that gives access to the entire storage account. You can also provide a user with something called a shared access signature. A shared access signature is a security token string, and it can scope access to a particular service like only the Blob service, as well as to a particular container or even an individual blob, and it can also scope access to a range of time and a particular set of permissions like only allowing reads or updates or deletes. A shared access signature gets appended to the end of the URL to a blob or file in Azure Storage so you're able to have pretty fine-grained access control to data in Azure Storage using shared access signatures, and data in your storage account is encrypted. You can even use your own encryption keys. Besides accessing your data using the REST endpoints, there are SDKs for a variety of languages like .NET, Java, PHP, and others, as well as support for scripting in PowerShell and the Azure CLI. Microsoft also offers free tools like Azure Storage Explorer, which provides a graphical user interface and a command-line utility called AzCopy to make it easy to move data into and out of your storage account. There are four types of storage accounts, standard general purpose v2 storage accounts support blobs, file shares, queues, and tables. This is the recommended storage account type for most situations. It offers the most redundancy options, meaning you can have copies of your data in other regions. Premium Block Blob storage is for storing blobs only and it's for scenarios when you need high transaction rates and low latency. You're limited to only storing your data within a single Azure region though. Premium file shares are for high performance file storage, but you could only store files with this type of account, and again, you're limited to storage within a single Azure region. Premium page blobs are for storing larger blobs like databases and VMs for disks. You can store these types of files in general purpose v2 storage accounts too, but the premium page blob account type gives you better performance when it's needed. Again, your redundancy options are limited. All of the premium account types use solid-state drives for low latency and high throughput. You can't change the storage account type after it's been created. You would need to create a storage account of a different type and move your data over. Next, let's talk about redundancy options for Azure Storage accounts.

Chapter 39 Azure Storage Account Redundancy Options

Redundancy with Azure Storage is about protecting your data from unplanned events like hardware failures, network outages, and even natural disasters. You do that by making copies of your data, which is called replication. Your data is always replicated in the primary data center, you can just expand that with other options. There are three categories that group the redundancy options: redundancy in the primary region, redundancy in a secondary region, and read access to data in the secondary region. Let's start with the primary region. Locally redundant storage is the lowest cost replication option. Your data is copied three times within a single physical data center. It protects you from failures of a server rack or a disk drive within the data center, but because all the data is within a single data center, there is still the risk of a data center level disaster like a fire or a flood. To help mitigate that risk, the next storage type is zone-redundant storage. This storage replicates your data across three availability zones in a single region. Availability zones are data centers within a region that have their own separate power, cooling, and networking. Zone-redundant storage isn't available in every Azure region. Locally redundant storage and zone-redundant storage provide redundancy in the primary Azure region that your storage account is located in, but in the event of a regional disaster where multiple availability zones are affected, there are other options that allow you to copy your data to another Azure region. Geo-redundant storage copies your data three times in the primary region within a single data center and also copies the data asynchronously to a single location in a secondary region. The data is copied three times in the secondary data center, it's basically locally redundant storage in two regions. The secondary region is decided by Microsoft and you can't change that, but it's selected to be hundreds of miles away from the primary region to prevent data loss in the event of a natural disaster. Microsoft lists the paired regions on their website. The second option for redundancy in a secondary region is geo-zone-redundant storage. This replication option uses zone-redundant storage in the primary data center and locally redundant storage in the secondary data center. With geo-redundant and geo-zone-redundant storage, the data in the secondary region is only available to be read if you or Microsoft initiates a failover from the primary region to the secondary. You might want to always have the ability for your applications to read the data in the secondary region. To enable this, there are two other account types, read-access-geo-redundant storage and read-access-geo-zone-redundant storage. The two options are similar to the previous ones we discussed, geo-redundant and geo-zone-redundant storage. They just add the ability to always be able to read the data from the secondary region. The replication options available depend on which storage account type you select. Let's create a storage account in the Azure portal.

Chapter 40 How to Create a Storage Account

Let's create an Azure Storage account so we can explore some of the features and configuration options. As usual, I'll go to All services and search for storage. Clicking on Storage Accounts brings us to the list of storage accounts in this subscription. We could have also gotten there from the shortcut on the left menu. From here, let's create a new storage account. The first thing we need to do is choose a resource group for the storage account, I have one created already. Then we need to give the storage account a name and this name needs to be unique across all of Azure because it will become part of the URL to each of the storage endpoints for the blob, file, table, and queue services. Now we choose the region. Before I change the default, I just want to show you how the choice of region affects the redundancy options available.

Create a storage account

Basics Advanced Networking Data protection Encryption Tags Review

Azure Storage is a Microsoft-managed service providing cloud storage that is highly available, secure, durable, scalable, and redundant. Azure Storage includes Azure Blobs (objects), Azure Data Lake Storage Gen2, Azure Files, Azure Queues, and Azure Tables. The cost of your storage account depends on the usage and the options you choose below. Learn more about Azure storage accounts

Project details

Select the subscription in which to create the new storage account. Choose a new or existing resource group to organize and manage your storage account together with other resources.

Subscription *   Visual Studio Professional

    Resource group *   storage_rg
                                  Create new

Instance details

If you need to create a legacy storage accou...   Locally-redundant storage (LRS):
                                                   Lowest-cost option with basic protection against server rack and drive
Storage account name   failures. Recommended for non-critical scenarios.

Region   Geo-redundant storage (GRS):
                                                   Intermediate option with failover capabilities in a secondary region.
Performance   Recommended for backup scenarios.

                                                   Zone-redundant storage (ZRS):
                                                   Intermediate option with protection against datacenter-level failures.
                                                   Recommended for high availability scenarios.
Redundancy   Geo-redundant storage (GRS)

                                                   ☑ Make read access to data available in the event of regional unavailability.

Review   ← Previous   Next : Advanced →

For the East US region, the options are Locally-redundant, so just in a single region, Geo-redundant, so with failover to a secondary region, and Zone-redundant storage. If I change the region to Canada Central, we have all the same choices plus Geo-zone-redundant storage, so that's not available for all Azure regions, but let's go with Locally-redundant storage, the cheapest option. Next, we choose the storage account type which is labeled as performance. The standard selection is for a general-purpose v2 storage account type, but we can change this to Premium and choose from Block blobs, File shares, or Page blobs.

Instance details

If you need to create a legacy storage account type please click here.

Storage account name ⓘ *   stgacctnmtest1

Region ⓘ *   (Canada) Canada Central

Performance ⓘ *
  ◯ Standard: Recommended for most scenarios (general-purpose v2 account)
  ● Premium: Recommended for scenarios that require low latency.

Premium account type ⓘ *   Page blobs

Redundancy ⓘ *
  Block blobs:
  Best for high transaction rates or low storage latency

  File shares:
  Best for enterprise or high-performance applications that need to scale

  Page blobs:
  Best for random read and write operations

Review   < Prev

These account types store data on solid-state drives, but they're limited to just the type of data in the description, so file storage won't let you store blobs, tables, or queues. Each of these options offers better performance and might be suitable depending on your business requirements, but you'll notice that choosing any of these limits the redundancy options to just Locally-redundant storage. Let's change this back to Standard and move to the Advanced tab.

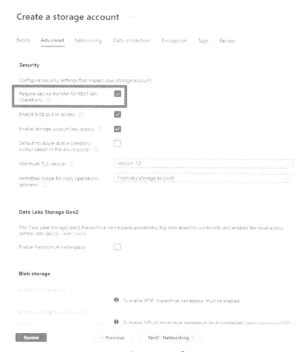

Here, you can choose from some security options like requiring HTTPS on the REST API to the storage account allowing anonymous access to Blob storage, then there is options to Enable hierarchical namespace for the Blob service, which will allow it to be used for Data Lake Storage Gen 2. That adds some security options, and the hierarchical namespace makes it easier to do the type of bulk operations required by big data analysis tools. You can choose the default Access tier when uploading blobs.

Access tiers can have a significant impact on the cost of storing your data, and you can enable large files for Azure File storage.

Normally, file shares are limited to 5 TB in size, but by choosing this option, you can create file shares up to 100 TB. Let's move on to networking.

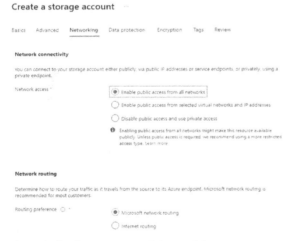

The default is to Enable public access, so this includes the internet and this is for the REST endpoints to all the storage services, which of course, you can secure by requiring the caller to authenticate or you can specify virtual networks within Azure and public IP addresses on the internet that you want to restrict access to. And you can also select to only have the storage account available over a private endpoint. Let's use the default and move on to data protection. You have the ability to Enable soft delete for blobs, containers, which hold blobs, and for file shares.

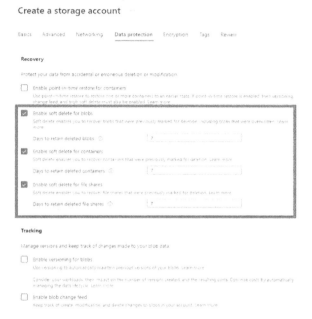

This essentially gives you a recycle bin where you can recover deleted files and folders. Then there are some options for versioning of blobs and enabling the change feed to record when blobs are created, modified, and deleted. Let's move on to encryption. The data in your storage account is encrypted by default, but you might have a need to manage your own encryption keys, maybe for regulatory compliance. You can do that using an encryption key that you   store   in   Azure   Key   Vault.

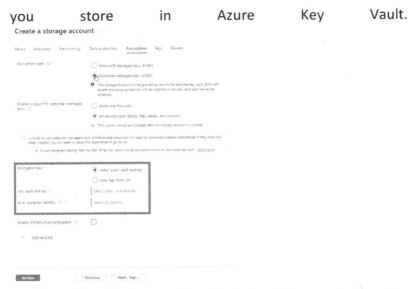

We haven't talked about Key Vault, but it's a central service in Azure to securely store secrets like encryption keys, SSL certificates for web apps, and strings, like database connection strings. They can all be managed in one place and accessed by applications that have permissions. Let's leave the default and let's go to Tags. We won't create any tags. So let's review the configuration and create this storage account.

Once the storage account is created, we can navigate to it by going to all storage accounts and there is the new storage account we created. Before we explore the storage account, let's talk about blob access tiers next.

174

Chapter 41 Azure Blobs and Access Tiers

Now let's talk about blobs and how you can save on storage costs by using a feature called blob access tiers. BLOB is an acronym for binary large object. A blob can be any type of file, including documents, video files, text files, even virtual machine disks. The Blob service is optimized for storing massive amounts of unstructured data, and by unstructured data, I mean data that doesn't adhere to a particular data model or definition. There are three types of blobs you can store: block blobs, stored text, and binary data. They're called block blobs because a single blob is made up of multiple blocks and that helps you optimize uploading. Append blobs are made up of blocks also, but they're optimized for appending only, so they're a good choice for logs where you only add to the file. And page blobs store random access files up to 8 TB in size, so they're used to store disks for virtual machines and databases. Page blobs are made up of 512-byte pages and are designed for frequent random read/write applications, so they're the foundation of Azure Disks. Block Blob storage is the most cost effective way to store a large number of files, and one of the features that helps you save is blob access tiers The cost of Azure storage comes from the amount of storage, as well as transaction costs related to accessing the data. So there are three blob access tiers that you can choose from to tailor these costs to the way that you use your data. The hot access tier is for data that's accessed frequently so it has the highest storage cost, but the lowest transaction costs. Cool storage is for storing data that you don't access frequently, so the storage cost is lower, but the transaction cost is higher when compared to the hot access tier. And the archive access tier is for storing data that you rarely access.

It's very inexpensive to store a large amount of data, but you have to be willing to wait hours to rehydrate the data if you do need to access it, but for organizations that have requirements to archive large amounts of data, there can be big cost savings by using the archive tier. With some data, the need to access it drops as the data ages, so Blob storage also has a feature called lifecycle management, which lets you set policies to move blobs between access tiers so you can design policies that provide the least expensive storage for your needs without having to manually move the data around. Blob storage has a lot of other features too, like creating snapshots of blobs, leasing blobs to prevent other people from modifying them. You can enable soft delete to essentially provide a recycle bin for your blobs, and you can even host static websites directly in Blob storage so you don't have to host simple HTML and JavaScript sites in Azure App service or on a virtual machine. Blob storage also integrates with other Azure services like the content delivery network, so you can optimize the delivery of blobs to clients all over the world. Azure Search integrates with Blob storage too so you can index the contents of blobs, which enables searching inside the contents of the documents like Word docs, PDFs, Excel spreadsheets, PowerPoint files, and lots of other types. So the Blob service and Azure Storage accounts can be an integral part of applications that use unstructured data. Let's talk about File storage next.

Chapter 42 Azure File Attachments

You can attach File storage to virtual machines to act like network drives. The file share will show up as a drive letter in the virtual machine, just like on-premises storage. When you're moving applications from on-premises to the cloud, there is inevitably going to be some applications that rely on data or configuration being stored on a file share. With the SMB support that Azure Files brings, you can migrate those apps much easier. Something that distinguishes Azure file storage from traditional file shares is that you can make the files accessible from anywhere in the world using a URL to the file with a shared access signature appended on the end. Azure file shares can be mounted concurrently by cloud or on-premises deployments of Windows, Linux, and macOS. In order to map an Azure file share to on-premises using the SMB protocol, you need to open port 445, which is used by SMB. If your organization requires that port 445 be blocked, you can use Azure VPN Gateway or ExpressRoute to tunnel traffic. You'll need to set up a private endpoint for your storage account to do that though. Moreover, Azure File shares can be cached on Windows Servers with Azure File Sync. That provides you fast access near where the data is being used. It actually allows you to tier files based on how they're used. You can keep recently accessed files on your on-premises servers while seamlessly moving old and files that aren't used as frequently to Azure. This helps you manage unpredictable storage growth, and essentially turns your on-premises file server into a quick cache of your Azure file share. You do that by installing a sync agent on the local server. Azure Files has different storage tiers. There are premium file shares, which are part of the File Storage storage account type. We talked about storage account types in the overview on Azure Storage accounts. Premium file shares run on solid-state drives so you get high performance and low latency, so single-digit milliseconds for most input/output operations. Transaction optimized file shares are backed by hard disk drives, and therefore, transaction heavy workloads that don't require the low latency of the premium tier. These are good for applications that require File storage as a back-end store. Hot file shares are for general-purpose file sharing, like team shares, and it works well as the storage for Azure File Sync also. Cool file shares offer the most cost-efficient storage for offline archive storage. Hot and cool file shares are similar to the access tiers that you learned about for Blob storage. You choose the storage tier when you create the file share, but with the tiers on the general-purpose v2 storage account type, you can change the storage tier after the file share has been created. So next, let's explore the storage account that we created earlier and upload some data.

Chapter 43 How to Explore Azure Storage Accounts

Let's explore some of the features of the Blob and File services in the Azure Storage account that we created earlier. From the list of all storage accounts, I'll open that one. From the menu on the left, you can access each of the services in this general purpose v2 storage account.

Containers are the Blob service, File shares are the File service, and the Queue and Table services. Below those are general settings for the storage account. Let's look at blob containers. Containers are the logical groupings of blobs. You can think of them like folders, but they're really just a path in the URL to the file. Let's create a new container. I'll just give it a name and you can specify an access level.

This means that you can require everyone accessing blobs in this container to authenticate, which is the private option, or you can allow anonymous read access to just the blobs and not to be able to list the container contents or the container option allows anonymous access to both the blobs and the container. Let's leave this as private and create the container. I'll navigate into the container and it's empty, so let's upload some data. I'll go to my desktop and there are some files in this folder. I'll select them all and click Open. Under Advanced, we can specify the blob type, and we can also specify the access tier.

So if this data is meant to be archived, we can send it right to the archive tier during the upload. We can also specify a folder, which is similar to the container in that it's just part of the path in the URL. Once the upload is complete, I'll close this window and let's click on one of these files. So this just opens the metadata about the file, not the file itself. From here, we can change the access tier of this blob. On the right side, there is a pop-up menu for each blob.

Blob type	Size	Lease state
Block blob	34.51 KiB	
Block blob	2.42 MiB	
Block blob	7.4 MiB	

- View/edit
- Download
- Properties
- Generate SAS
- View versions
- View snapshots
- Create snapshot
- Change tier
- Acquire lease
- Delete

This is where you can download the file or create a snapshot so a version of the file. You can acquire a lease to prevent other users from modifying the file and you can generate a shared access signature. Let's click that. This lets us choose the parameters for the token, like the permissions we want to give, how long it's valid for, and the IP addresses the user must be coming from in order to access this blob.

Let's generate this with the defaults. That gives us a URL to the blob with the shared access signature token appended on the end, but let's close out of the container and go back to the Storage Account menu. Now let's go to File shares and let's create a file share.

You need to give the file share a name and then you can choose the storage tier. Premium isn't available because the storage account was created with a general purpose v2 storage account type, but you can choose between Transaction optimized, Hot, and Cool storage tiers. Let's create this file share. And once it's created, I'll click to open it. From here, we can upload files and change the storage tier. We can also generate a script to run on a virtual machine in Azure, then it will show up on the VM with a drive letter. We can do that for Windows, Linux, and macOS because remember, it's also possible to connect to this file share from on-premises. Let's close out of this and let's go back to the root of the storage account. I want to show you some of the configuration options here. Under configuration, you can change some of the settings we chose when setting up the storage account like the default Blob access tier and the Replication option.

We could change this to Geo-redundant storage. Farther up the menu, there are a number of options under Security and networking. You can create a shared access signature to allow access to the services within the storage account, so this provides more access than the token we generated to the individual blob, and you could also provide the access key to the entire storage account.

This isn't recommended though because it provides full control of the storage account. You can rotate the primary and backup keys here which would remove that access, and the shared access signatures are actually generated using these keys too, so if you wanted to revoke the shared access signatures before they expire, you could just rotate the keys here. On the Networking tab, you can disable access from the internet and you might do this if you set up a private endpoint or you can enable access from your virtual networks.

On the Azure CDN tab, you can integrate the storage account with the Azure Content Delivery Network, which would cache the data in locations around the world for faster access times. We won't go into the Azure CDN here, but it can really increase speed and availability of files to users in locations outside the region where the storage account is located.

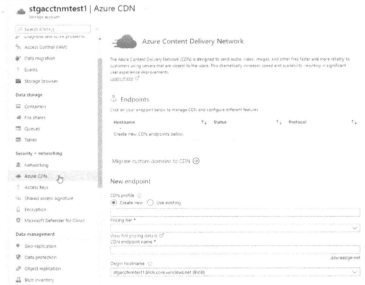

Farther down the menu, there is an option for Static website. This allows you to host static HTML pages and client-side scripts.

This is less expensive than hosting a full app service when all you need is a website without any server-side processing or frameworks installed. Azure Search lets you integrate your storage account with the Azure Search service so your blobs can be indexed and searchable, that includes being able to search the contents of a variety of file types like Word documents and PDFs.

You need to create a search service in order to do that though. We won't go into Azure Search in this book. When you want to access a blob in the Blob service, it would be at this endpoint, followed by the container name and the blob name. Uploading files manually using the Azure portal can be quite time-consuming, so in the next chapter, let's look at other ways to manage files in Azure.

Chapter 44 Azure Data Transfer Options

Let's talk about some of the options for moving data into Azure Storage. The approach you choose depends on a few factors, the amount of data you need to transfer, the frequency, meaning is this a one-time transfer or will you be periodically pushing data into the Azure Storage account, and the last factor is network bandwidth. If you've got a slow connection, transferring large amounts of data can take quite a while. Even if you have a larger connection, you might not want to use up all the network bandwidth for data transfer. For smaller amounts of data, so I'm talking about gigabytes or terabytes of data, if you've got a decent network connection, there are a few tools available. Of course, you can use the Azure portal to upload data to Azure Storage like you saw it earlier, but there is also Azure Storage Explorer, which offers a graphical user interface and makes moving data as easy as using File Explorer, so it's a good choice if you need to delegate some tasks to business users, but it also offers management capabilities for a storage account so it can be used by administrators too. Behind the scenes, Azure Storage Explorer uses a tool called AzCopy. It's actually a command line tool that you can use directly. AzCopy provides features for uploading in a very performant way by leveraging multiple connections at once, and you can integrate AzCopy commands into your scripting activities to copy data to and from Azure. PowerShell and the Azure command line interface also have commands for managing data in Azure. For developers, there are also the client SDKs available in a variety of languages, so you can integrate data ingestion to Azure Storage as part of application development. Earlier, I mentioned Azure File Sync as a way to extend your on-premises file shares to Azure. This way, data that you access frequently is kept on-premises, and data that you use less often is automatically stored in Azure. Azure File Sync is always online, and you don't need to manually move the data to Azure. These are some of the ways that you can get data into Azure using a connection over the internet. Sometimes that's not convenient or even possible due to the amount of data or the throughput of your internet connection. So we'll talk about some options for offline data transfer later, but first, let's take a look at Azure Storage Explorer and AzCopy.

Chapter 45 Azure Storage Explorer

Now let's talk about a tool for managing the data in your Azure Storage account. Azure Storage Explorer is a tool that you can download for Windows, Mac, and Linux and it runs on your local desktop. I've already installed it on my local computer, so let's search for it and open it up.

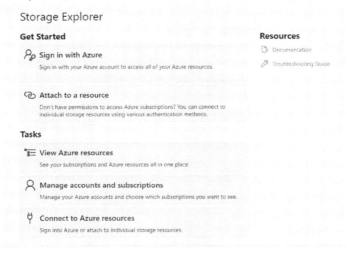

We need to log into Azure, so let's add an account. There are a number of ways to authenticate. You can log into the whole Azure subscription so the administrator would likely do this, or you can scope the login to just the resource the user needs access to like a blob container or a file share. This is great if you want to give access to an end user to upload files to Azure Storage. You don't want them to have any more access than they need so you set the permissions in Azure Storage and have them log into the resource that they need access to.

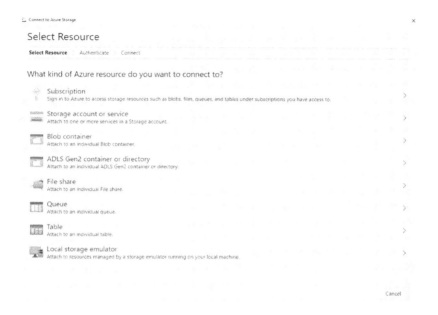

Let's use the subscription option and hit Next. That opens a browser and I'll select my administrator account, enter my password, and I have multifactor authentication enabled so I need to send a code to my phone and then enter that. Now I'm logged in and my account shows here along with the subscriptions that I have access to.

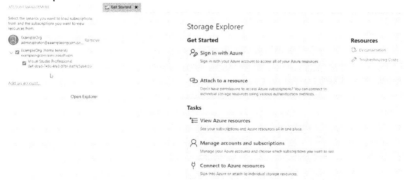

I'll go to the Explorer tab and expand the subscription. All the storage accounts are listed and below that are disks. This is a big advantage to using Storage Explorer. You can manage the disks used by virtual machines in your subscription, and I'll show you that shortly. First, let's expand the storage account we created earlier. If I right-click on that storage account, I have some options to manage it like copying the access keys and setting the default blob access tier. Let's expand the Blob service and click on this container.

The blobs show on the left, and by right-clicking on the container, I can do things like copy the container, get a shared access signature to provide someone else access to the container, and set the public access level.

You can manage the blobs in the container from here also. Right-clicking, you can change the blob access tier for the individual blob. You can acquire a lease, create a snapshot, and edit tags.

Of course, you can upload blobs from here also with the same options you saw in the portal like setting the access tier. Let's cancel out and look at file shares. From here, you can create file shares and upload and download data, and you can get the script to attach this file share to a Windows VM, but let's close this and look at the Tables service. There are some tables here because classic metrics are enabled on this storage account. In the second table here, there is some data, and you can run queries against this data from here if you like.

With the Queues service, you can create a new queue, so this might be for applications or components that need to pass messages. And you can create queue messages from here also, which you might want to do for testing during development.

191

Let's close this storage account and now let's look at disks. I have this resource group that's storing the operating system disk for the VM that I created earlier. From here, you can download the disk image and also create a snapshot, and you can also upload disk images from on-premises to Azure.

You select the operating system type, you can select whether it should be stored on a solid-state drive or a hard drive, and the generation of the Hyper-V image.

Azure Storage Explorer gives you a graphical user interface that lets you do some management of your Azure Storage account, and it's great for transferring data to and from Azure. It also lets you delegate access to other people with an easy-to-use interface. Azure Storage Explorer actually uses a utility called AzCopy to transfer the files, and you can use AzCopy directly too, so let's look at that next.

Chapter 46 How to Use AzCopy to Upload & Manage Blobs

Let's take a look at the AzCopy command line utility. You can download it from docs.microsoft.com, and it's available for Windows, Mac, and Linux. I've already downloaded it, and you just need to unzip it and navigate to the folder where it's stored, it doesn't get installed. I've copied it to the root of my C drive. So I'll open up the Windows command prompt and I'll change directories to the root of the C drive where the AzCopy file is stored. We need to authenticate to Azure, so I'll type azcopy login.

```
c:\>azcopy login
To sign in, use a web browser to open the page https://microsoft.com/devicelogin and enter the code RVKY9e5VE to authenticate.

INFO: Logging in under the "Common" tenant. This will log the account in under its home tenant.
INFO: If you plan to use AzCopy with a B2B account (where the account's home tenant is separate from the tenant of the target storage account),
ease sign in under the target tenant with --tenant-id
```

It says I need to open up a browser and go to microsoft.com/devicelogin and paste in this code, so let's do that. And I'll paste in the code I copied and select my administrator account and just click Continue to log in. Now we can run some commands, but before we do that, I need to show you something in the Azure portal. I'll navigate into the storage account that we're going to be working against with AzCopy. Let's go to Access Control and view my access. I had to give my administrator account this permission called Storage Blob Data Contributor.

That will give the account access to create and modify blobs in the storage account. You don't actually have to log in using Azure AD. You can just attach a shared access signature on all of your calls with AzCopy, but using the Azure AD login is just more convenient. Let's open up the Containers tab and now go back to the command prompt and run some commands. Azcopy make will create the container name at the end of the URL to the Blob service in my storage account.

```
C:\>azcopy make "https://stgacctnmtest1.blob.core.windows.net/azcopycontainer"
```

It says it's being created, so let's go to the portal and refresh the list, and there is the new container. Let's open it up. And now let's upload some files back in the command prompt. I have these files on my local computer. Let's copy the DOCX file. You do that with the azcopy command specifying the source and destination.

```
C:\>azcopy copy "C:\Users\neilm\Desktop\files\documentation.docx" "https://stgacctnmtest1.blob.core.windows.net/azcopycontainer/newname.docx"
```

The source can be a local file or folder or even a container in another storage account, and you can change the name of the file in the destination, so it's the same file just with a different name. It shows that it was successful, so let's go to the portal and refresh the container, and there is the file with the new name. The last thing I want to do is to use AzCopy to change the access tier of one of these files. I want to change it from hot to cool because I know I won't need to access this file, and I'd like to save on storage costs. So back at the command prompt, I'll use azcopy set-properties with a path to the file and the parameter block-blob-tier set to cool.

```
C:\>azcopy set-properties "https://stgacctnmtest1.blob.core.windows.net/azcopycontainer/newname.docx" --block-blob-tier=cool
INFO: Authenticating to source using Azure AD
INFO: Any empty folders will not be processed, because source and/or destination doesn't have full folder support

Job f7840443-f2cd-944a-6101-c266b6bbe81a has started
Log file is located at: C:\Users\neilm\.azcopy\f7840443-f2cd-944a-6101-c266b6bbe81a.log

INFO: Transfers are likely to fail because destination does not support tiers.
0.0 %, 1 Done, 0 Failed, 0 Pending, 0 Skipped, 1 Total,


Job f7840443-f2cd-944a-6101-c266b6bbe81a summary
Elapsed Time (Minutes): 0.0335
Number of File Transfers: 1
Number of Folder Property Transfers: 0
Total Number of Transfers: 1
Number of Transfers Completed: 1
Number of Transfers Failed: 0
Number of Transfers Skipped: 0
TotalBytesTransferred: 0
Final Job Status: Completed
```

No failures, so let's take a look in the portal. And the blob access tier has been changed.

Modified	Access tier	Archive status	Blob type	Size	Lease state
9/7/2022 8:26:29 PM	Cool		Block blob	34.51 KiB	Available
9/7/2022 8:37:17 PM	Hot (Inferred)		Block blob	2.42 MiB	Available

AzCopy is a powerful tool that you can use for managing files in Azure and you can use when creating scripts for batch jobs. Next, let's talk about managed database products in Azure.

Chapter 47 Managed Database Products in Azure

Azure offers managed database solutions for storing structured data in relational databases. Let's start by talking about Microsoft's own relational database management system, SQL Server. There are three offerings for SQL Server in Azure that make up the SQL Server family of products. You can host SQL Server on virtual machines, which gives you full control over the product and all the features you're accustomed to hosting SQL Server in your own on-premises data center, but you can also provision a virtual machine with SQL Server already installed by using the Azure Marketplace, and you can take advantage of pay-as-you-go pricing so you don't have the costly upfront licensing fees. You even have the ability to configure a maintenance window for some automated patching, and you can configure backups using a managed backup service in Azure. Then there is a fully-managed platform-as-a-service version of SQL Server called Azure SQL Database. Most database management functions are handled for you like upgrading, patching, backups, and monitoring. Azure SQL Database is always running the latest stable version of SQL Server with high availability guarantees. There is also flexible pricing models based on either the number of virtual cores or using a unit of measurement called DTUs, which stands for database transaction units, and makes up a combination of CPU, memory, and data throughput. Azure SQL database also has flexible deployment options. You can provision a single isolated database or what's called an elastic pool, which is a collection of databases with a shared set of resources. With single databases, you can still harness the elasticity of the cloud by scaling database resources up and down when needed. There are different service tiers available too like the standard tier for common workloads, the business critical premium tier for applications with high transaction rates, and the hyperscale tier for very large transactional databases. Running SQL Server on a virtual machine, you get access to all the features of the product so there are some limitations to using Azure SQL Database. The majority of core features are available in the managed version, but if you have some specific requirements, you can verify compatibility with Azure SQL Database in the Microsoft documentation. If you have compatibility concerns, there is also a third offering called Azure SQL Managed Instance. It combines the broadest set of SQL Server capabilities with the benefits of a fully-managed platform. It allows you to deploy a managed VM with SQL Server onto your own virtual network. Some organizations have security concerns about deploying databases onto a managed public cloud platform, so SQL Server Managed Instance lets you lift and shift your on-premises databases to the cloud with minimal changes and into an isolated environment with the networking controls while also getting the advantages of automatic patching and version updates, automated backups, and high availability. Those are some of the options for using SQL Server in Azure, but there are other database options available in Azure. Using the Azure Marketplace, you can provision a variety of virtual machines with various relational database systems preinstalled, but of course, you'll be managing those servers and databases yourself. In terms of fully-managed platform-as-a-service offerings, Azure offers Azure Database for my SQL and Azure Database for PostgreSQL. These are hosted versions with pay-as-you-go pricing, and you get high availability and automated patching of the underlying database engine. Next, let's talk about how you can migrate different types of workloads, including SQL Server from your on-premises environment into Azure.

Chapter 48 Azure Migrate Fundamentals

Azure Migrate is a unified migration platform that allows you to start, run, and track your migrations to Azure. It lets you assess your on-premises infrastructure, data, and platforms to determine how to migrate them to Azure. Azure Migrate can assess your on-premises physical and virtual servers for migrating them to Azure virtual machines. It can assess on-premises SQL Server instances to migrate them to SQL running on a VM, an Azure SQL Database, or an Azure SQL Managed Instance. It can assess web applications running on-premises and migrate them to run on Azure App service or the Azure Kubernetes service. For migrating large amounts of unstructured data offline, Databox is a service that's part of Azure Migrate. You can track your data migrations in the Azure Migrate portal, and you can also assess your on-premises virtual desktop infrastructure and migrate it to Azure Virtual Desktop. Azure Migrate is made up of several tools, let's look at some of them. Let's start with migrating servers. The Azure Migrate: Discovery and Assessment tool looks at physical servers hosted on-premises and virtual machines running on Hyper-V and VMware. It assesses whether the VMs are ready for migration to Azure, including the web apps and SQL servers running on the VMs. The tool estimates the size of the virtual machine that will be needed in Azure and estimates the costs for running the servers that you need. The tool also identifies cross-server dependencies and makes recommendations for optimization. You download a virtual appliance to your environment to do the assessment, and it can run on a physical or virtual server. It discovers on-premises servers and sends metadata and performance data to Azure Migrate. Then you can use the Azure Migrate

Server Migration tool to actually replicate your on-premises servers into Azure. You can also migrate servers hosted in other cloud environments. You download and install a replication appliance in your environment and install the mobility service agent on the servers you want to replicate to Azure, Then you can replicate up to 10 servers at once and track the progress in the Azure Migrate portal. The server migration tool also attracts incremental changes to the on-premises disks after the initial replication and makes updates to the disks in Azure. For migrating on-premises SQL Server databases, there is the Data Migration Assistant and Azure Data Migration service. The migration assistant detects compatibility issues that can impact functionality when migrating to newer versions of SQL Server in the cloud or to Azure SQL Database. It can also recommend performance and reliability improvements. For smaller databases, the migration assistant can move the schema data and objects from your source server to your target database in Azure. The Azure Database Migration service is for large migrations in terms of the number of databases and the size of those databases. Both of the tools can move your SQL Server databases to SQL Server hosted on virtual machines, Azure SQL Database, or Azure SQL Managed Instances. Azure Migrate also has tools to assess and migrate.NET and Java web applications hosted on-premises. They can be moved to Azure App Service as containers or as code. You can also use the Azure Migrate App Containerization tool to containerize existing ASP.NET and Java applications and move them to the Azure Kubernetes service. A Docker file gets created and the container is pushed to the Azure Container Registry for deployment to Kubernetes. The process doesn't even require access to your code base. So next, let's take a look at Azure Migrate in the Azure portal.

Chapter 49 How to Use Azure Migrate to Move Apps to Azure

I'll go to All services and search for migrate. This isn't a service that you create, it's a portal inside the Azure portal to organize all your migration projects.

The different migration options are listed on the left menu. Let's go to Servers. I've already created a project, so the instructions for assessment and migration are listed here. Let's click on Discover.

It asks if the servers we want to migrate are virtual or physical, and notice that physical includes servers hosted on other cloud platforms like Amazon or Google. Let's select

Hyper-V. The next screen is where you can download the appliance to your environment that will do the discovery and assessment.

We won't do this. Let's close out of this and let's see what's involved in creating a new project. There is only a few things you need to enter here, the resource group, give the project a name, and you need to select a geography.

Notice this isn't an Azure region. You learned earlier that geography is organized groups of Azure regions. Under Advanced, you can select whether the migration will be over the public internet or a private endpoint. That's all you need to create a project. Let's close out of this though and let's look at another type of project for migrating web apps. I'll create a new project here, and this looks exactly like the servers project, but let's go ahead and create this. I'll use an existing resource group and enter a project name. Now I'll select my Azure geography, and I'll leave the public endpoint.

The project gets created and the steps here are different than for the server project. It says to download the App Service Migration Assistant.

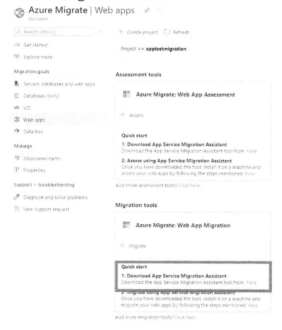

Let's click this link. That brings us to the overview page for the tool. Scroll down and the tool is available here.

App Service migration assistant

Migrate .NET web apps from Windows OS to App Service.

Documentation ›

Download now ›

App Service migration assistant for Java on Apache Tomcat (Linux—preview)

Download prerelease software to migrate Java web apps running on Apache Tomcat web servers to App Service. Or, migrate on-premises Docker containers running on Linux to App Service using Docker Hub or Azure Container Registry.

Documentation ›

Download now ›

App Service migration assistant for Java on Apache Tomcat (Windows—preview)

Download prerelease software for migrating Java web applications on Tomcat web server running on Windows servers.

Documentation ›

Download now ›

App Service migration assistant for PowerShell scripts (preview)

Download prerelease PowerShell scripts for discovering and assessing all Microsoft Internet Information Services (IIS) web apps on a single server in bulk and migrating .NET web apps from Windows OS to App Service.

Documentation ›

Download now ›

Let's download this. I just have to accept the license terms and an MSI gets downloaded to my local computer. Clicking on the file actually runs the installer, although there is no wizard here to step through. So when this is done, I'll minimize this window and there has been a shortcut installed on my desktop. I'll click this to open up the tool. So I have a web server installed on this Windows 10 computer, Internet Information Services, or IIS, is running the same web server that you would install on a production server in your environment. So the tool detects that and scans the web server. There is only the default site running which is just a web page actually, but it did discover the site so let's proceed with this.

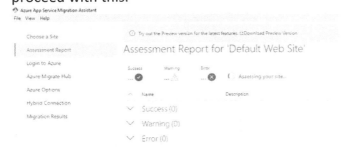

Once the assessment report is complete, it shows all the things that were scanned and it passed all the checks. Next, I'm told to log into Azure. I'll click this and paste in the code that was copied to the clipboard. I need to choose an account, and I'll skip filming all the login stuff because I have multifactor authentication enabled. And once I'm logged in, it asks if I'm trying to sign into the App Service Migration Assistant.

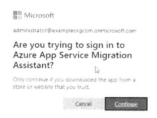

So let's continue and go back to the assistant. Now we can select a project in Azure Migrate. I have several. Let's choose the one I just created. Next, we enter the target in Azure. I'll choose an existing resource group and give this app service a name, which remember, needs to be unique across Azure.

I'll choose an existing app service plan and that's it, let's hit Migrate. And while this is creating the app service in Azure and migrating the code, you can export the Azure Resource Manager template for this app service configuration.

Once the migration is complete, you can navigate to the website deployed in Azure.

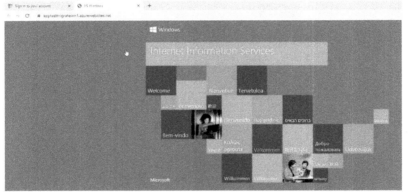

This is just a default web page that gets installed locally with IIS, but it shows that the files were successfully copied into Azure App service. So Azure Migrate makes it pretty easy to move resources from on-premises and other cloud providers into Azure. Next, let's talk about Azure Data Box for moving large amounts of data into Azure.

Chapter 50 How to Migrate Data with Azure Data Box

Azure Data Box is a service where Microsoft will ship you a secure device that you copy data onto and send back to Microsoft to load into at Azure. Data Box is actually part of Azure Migrate. So let's go to the Azure Migrate portal and go down to Data Box on the menu.

You select a resource group for the order, then a source country or region, and a destination. Click Apply and the options are here.

There are three tiers to the service depending on how much data you need to transfer. The standard Data Box service is a secure device that can move up to 80 TB of data. It gets transported to you and you copy your data onto the device and ship it back to Microsoft. Or you can use it to export your data from Azure and copy onto your local network. You might use this to move some virtual machines or databases to Azure in a one-time migration. Keep in mind, this isn't just a hard drive that Microsoft is shipping you. These are pictures of the device from the documentation.

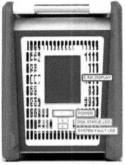 

Data Box front view (left) and back view (right)

It's a rugged device with fast transfer speeds and multiple layers of security and encryption. You can track the status of the transfer right in the Azure portal. For smaller transfers, Azure Data Box Disk can be used. Microsoft can ship you 1 to 5 solid-state disk drives that can hold up to 35 TB of data. The process is the same, and one of the advantages is that it can use USB 3.0 to copy the data locally, so you don't need a network interface like you do with the standard Data Box. You might use this to send backups to Azure Backup without having to transfer them over the network or to seed files in Azure File Sync. On the other end of the spectrum, if you need to transfer more data than the standard Data Box service, you can go with Azure Data Box Heavy. This is a device with 800 TB storage capacity, and it uses a high-performance 40 Gbps network interface. You might use this to move your virtual machine farm or SQL Servers to Azure in a lift and shift type scenario. There is another service available for Microsoft for drive shipping also called the Import/Export service. This allows you to ship your own disk drives to Microsoft to load the data into Azure Blob or File storage. You can also ship disks to Microsoft and have them load your blob data onto the disks to be shipped back to you. There is another product with Azure Data Box and it moves data online so it's not storage that you ship back and forth to Azure. Azure Data Box Gateway is a virtual device hosted in your on-premises environment. You write data to the device like using a file share and then as the data is written to the gateway device, the device uploads the data to Azure Storage. You might still use Data Box for the initial offline transfer and then use Data Box Gateway for incremental ongoing transfers over the network. In summary, you learned about storage options in Azure. We went into depth on storage accounts and their configuration options. We created a storage account and explored blobs and files. You learned about data migration options like using Azure Storage Explorer to upload small amounts of data and Azure Data Box for transferring large amounts of data offline. You also learned about using Azure Migrate to move different types of workloads to Azure. Next, we'll look at ways to manage Azure other than using the Azure portal, as well as monitoring tools in Azure to ensure the health and performance of your resources.

Chapter 51 Azure Resource Manager Basics

So far, we've been creating resources in Azure using the Azure portal. That's a pretty intuitive way to do it, but there are also several tools for managing Azure from the command line and using infrastructure as code. Central to all of Azure Management is Azure Resource Manager, which goes by the acronym ARM. ARM is the deployment and management service for Azure and it's central to all the creation, deletion, and modification of resources that you do in Azure. When you're using the Azure portal, you're really just using a website that sends requests to the ARM endpoint. ARM handles authentication using Azure Active Directory and authorizes that you can perform the action that you're attempting to perform. ARM then sends the request to the Azure Service that you're attempting to create or manipulate. That could be an app service, a virtual machine, an Azure SQL Database, a machine learning workspace, anything in Azure that's a resource, which is basically everything in Azure. ARM is used by all the tools that you use to manage Azure. The Azure portal is an obvious tool, but you can also use PowerShell to create and manage resources in Azure. It's actually done through a set of cmdlets that you install as the Azure PowerShell module. PowerShell works from a Windows, macOS, or Linux computer, and with PowerShell, you can write scripts to automate a series of tasks, so it's really powerful. There is also the Azure command-line interface, or Azure CLI. The Azure CLI is a set of commands used to create and manage Azure resources and it's also available for Windows, macOS, and Linux. It runs in the Windows command prompt on Windows or the Bash Shell on Linux. You can download and install PowerShell or the Azure CLI onto your local workstation, but there is also something called the Cloud Shell in the Azure portal that lets you use these scripting tools right from within the portal in your browser, so you don't need anything installed locally. There is a mobile app for managing Azure that lets you use a graphical user interface on your phone to create and manage Azure resources and receive alerts. There are also SDKs for different programming languages that allow you to call the Azure Resource Manager endpoints so you can build Azure management into a custom solution. Azure Resource Manager was introduced in 2014. Before that, there was the classic deployment model where every resource existed independently. You couldn't group resources together. The concept of resource groups was a major addition that came with ARM. Azure Resource Manager also brought the ability to use Resource Manager templates, which allow you to define your infrastructure using JavaScript Object Notation, or JSON. That lets you deploy infrastructure as code to create the resources for your solutions. And the Azure Resource Manager model also brought the concept of tags which allows you to logically group the resources in your subscription. We're going to look at different ways to manage Azure using the Azure CLI, Azure PowerShell, and we'll see those in the Azure Cloud Shell also. Then you'll learn about Resource Manager templates for deploying infrastructure in a repeatable way. Then I want to show you some of the services in Azure that can help with monitoring and troubleshooting your deployed solutions. Azure Service Health gives you a view of the health of the overall Azure service, so you'll know if there are problems with the platform that could be impacting your applications. Azure Monitor integrates with all the Azure services to provide monitoring of different metrics with alerts you can set up to know when there is an issue. Azure Monitor also contains log analytics which provides extensive logging capabilities that can help with troubleshooting. You'll learn about Microsoft Defender for Cloud which assesses the security of your cloud workloads, provides recommendations, and alerts you to security events. After that, we'll discuss Azure Advisor which provides recommendations for configuration of your deployed resources. Next, you'll see the Azure mobile app, which is a native app for your phone to manage your Azure subscription and receive alerts. Finally, we'll talk about Azure Arc, which lets you monitor resources that are deployed outside of Azure. We've got a lot to get through, so let's start by looking at the Azure CLI next.

Chapter 52 Azure Command Line Interface

The Azure CLI lets you manage Azure resources from the command line. You can download it to your local workstation, and it's available for Windows, Mac, and Linux, and I'll show you later that it's also available right in the Azure portal using the Cloud Shell. All Azure CLI commands start with az, then the command. Before you can use the CLI with your Azure subscription, you need to log in. That's done with the az login command. The first command I'll run is to get the list of resource groups in this subscription. Azure CLI commands are organized into groups and subgroups. Az is actually the parent group, and group is the name of the set of commands for resource groups, then list is the actual command. I'll hit Enter to run this.

```
{
  "id": "/subscriptions/0ef1dba3-743c-4fe2-97bf-8d81c3e64c20/resourceGroups/websitesRG",
  "location": "centralus",
  "managedBy": null,
  "name": "websitesRG",
  "properties": {
    "provisioningState": "Succeeded"
  },
  "tags": null,
  "type": "Microsoft.Resources/resourceGroups"
},
{
  "id": "/subscriptions/0ef1dba3-743c-4fe2-97bf-8d81c3e64c20/resourceGroups/pieshoprg",
  "location": "canadacentral",
  "managedBy": null,
  "name": "pieshoprg",
  "properties": {
    "provisioningState": "Succeeded"
  },
  "tags": null,
  "type": "Microsoft.Resources/resourceGroups"
},
{
  "id": "/subscriptions/0ef1dba3-743c-4fe2-97bf-8d81c3e64c20/resourceGroups/pssamples",
  "location": "eastus2",
  "managedBy": null,
  "name": "pssamples",
  "properties": {
    "provisioningState": "Succeeded"
  },
  "tags": null,
  "type": "Microsoft.Resources/resourceGroups"
}
```

That gives us back a list of the resource groups and their properties, and this is showing a JavaScript Object Notation format, or JSON. Let's run this again, but this time, we'll use a global argument called output, and this lets you format the output of any query. You can modify this to include whatever properties you want, but let's move on. Another useful global argument is help, this will give you information at whatever level you use it. So by typing help after the subgroup name called group, we get a list of all the commands that are available in that subgroup.

```
Group
    az group : Manage resource groups and template deployments.

Subgroups:
    lock    : Manage Azure resource group locks.

Commands:
    create : Create a new resource group.
    delete : Delete a resource group.
    exists : Check if a resource group exists.
    export : Captures a resource group as a template.
    list   : List resource groups.
    show   : Gets a resource group.
    update : Update a resource group.
    wait   : Place the CLI in a waiting state until a condition of the resource group is met.

To search AI knowledge base for examples, use: az find "az group"

Please let us know how we are doing: https://aka.ms/azureclihats
```

There is the list command we used. Let's try using the help argument at the root, the az group. That gives us a list of all the subgroups which have commands for the different services in Azure.

```
ppg                             : Manage Proximity Placement Groups.
private-link                    : Private-link association CLI command group.
provider                        : Manage resource providers.
redis                           : Manage dedicated Redis caches for your Azure applications.
relay                           : Manage Azure Relay Service namespaces, WCF relays, hybrid
                                  connections, and rules.
reservations        [Preview]   : Manage Azure Reservations.
resource                        : Manage Azure resources.
resourcemanagement              : Resourcemanagement CLI command group.
restore-point                   : Manage restore point with res.
role                            : Manage user roles for access control with Azure Active Directory
                                  and service principals.
search                          : Manage Azure Search services, admin keys and query keys.
security                        : Manage your security posture with Microsoft Defender for Cloud.
servicebus                      : Manage Azure Service Bus namespaces, queues, topics,
                                  subscriptions, rules and geo-disaster recovery configuration
                                  alias.
sf                              : Manage and administer Azure Service Fabric clusters.
sig                             : Manage shared image gallery.
signalr                         : Manage Azure SignalR Service.
snapshot                        : Manage point-in-time copies of managed disks, native blobs, or
                                  other snapshots.
sql                             : Manage Azure SQL Databases and Data Warehouses.
sshkey                          : Manage ssh public key with vm.
staticwebapp                    : Manage static apps.
storage                         : Manage Azure Cloud Storage resources.
synapse             [Preview] : Manage and operate Synapse Workspace, Spark Pool, SQL
                                  Pool.
tag                             : Tag Management on a resource.
term            [Experimental] : Manage marketplace agreement with marketplaceordering.
ts                              : Manage template specs at subscription or resource group scope.
vm                              : Manage Linux or Windows virtual machines.
vmss                            : Manage groupings of virtual machines in an Azure Virtual Machine
                                  Scale Set (VMSS).
webapp                          : Manage web apps.
```

There is the appservice subgroup, the Cosmos DB subgroup, the group subgroup that we've been using for resource groups, and there is a subgroup called resource for managing resources. Let's use that one. And we'll list out the resources in a resource group. Let's use the second resource group here. I'll use az resource list, then we need to use some parameters. Resource-group is the name of the group we want it to list the contents of, and let's format the output as a table again. So there is just two resources in this resource group, an app service plan, which is actually called a serverFarm type behind the scenes in Azure, and a site, which is an appservice.

Name	ResourceGroup	Location	Type	Status
pieshopsvcplan	pieshoprg	canadacentral	Microsoft.Web/serverFarms	
pieshoptesting	pieshoprg	canadacentral	Microsoft.Web/sites	

Now let's create some resources. First, I'll create a resource group using az group create, then the location parameter, and I'll use canadacentral, and the name of this resource group will be cli_rg. The JSON that's returned indicates that it was created successfully.

```
{
  "id": "/subscriptions/0ef1dba3-743c-4fe2-97bf-8d81c3e64c20/resourceGroups/cli_rg",
  "location": "canadacentral",
  "managedBy": null,
  "name": "cli_rg",
  "properties": {
    "provisioningState": "Succeeded"
  },
  "tags": null,
  "type": "Microsoft.Resources/resourceGroups"
}
```

Otherwise, there would be an error showing. Now let's create an appservice, but first we need an app service plan, so I'll use az appservice plan create then the resource group I want it created in, the name I want to call the appservice plan, and we need to provide a sku, which is the code for the pricing tier. I'll use the standard S1 pricing tier, the same one we used when we created an appservice plan earlier in the portal. It'll take a second to provision this, but then the JSON returns to indicate that it worked.

```
"isSpot": false,
"isXenon": false,
"kind": "app",
"kubeEnvironmentProfile": null,
"location": "canadacentral",
"maximumElasticWorkerCount": 1,
"maximumNumberOfWorkers": 0,
"name": "asp-fromcli",
"numberOfSites": 0,
"numberOfWorkers": 1,
"perSiteScaling": false,
"provisioningState": "Succeeded",
"reserved": false,
"resourceGroup": "cli_rg",
"sku": {
  "capabilities": null,
  "capacity": 1,
  "family": "S",
  "locations": null,
  "name": "S1",
  "size": "S1",
  "skuCapacity": null,
  "tier": "Standard"
},
"spotExpirationTime": null,
"status": "Ready",
"subscription": "0ef1dba3-743c-4fe2-97bf-8d81c3e64c20",
"tags": null,
"targetWorkerCount": 0,
"targetWorkerSizeId": 0,
"type": "Microsoft.Web/serverfarms",
"workerTierName": null,
"zoneRedundant": false
```

Now let's create an appservice for the plan. This is actually a different subgroup. We use the create command in the webapp subgroup passing the resource group name, the appservice plan name, and the name of this app service.

```
"scmIpSecurityRestrictionsDefaultAction": null,
"scmIpSecurityRestrictionsUseMain": null,
"scmMinTlsVersion": null,
"scmType": null,
"sitePort": null,
"storageType": null,
"supportedTlsCipherSuites": null,
"tracingOptions": null,
"use32BitWorkerProcess": null,
"virtualApplications": null,
"vnetName": null,
"vnetPrivatePortsCount": null,
"vnetRouteAllEnabled": null,
"webSocketsEnabled": null,
"websiteTimeZone": null,
"winAuthAdminState": null,
"winAuthTenantState": null,
"windowsFxVersion": null,
"xManagedServiceIdentityId": null
},
"slotSwapStatus": null,
"state": "Running",
"storageAccountRequired": false,
"suspendedTill": null,
"tags": null,
"targetSwapSlot": null,
"trafficManagerHostNames": null,
"type": "Microsoft.Web/sites",
"usageState": "Normal",
"virtualNetworkSubnetId": null,
"vnetContentShareEnabled": false,
"vnetImagePullEnabled": false,
"vnetRouteAllEnabled": false
```

It looks like it was created, so let's go to the Azure portal and check. I'll go to Resource groups, and there is the resource group we created using the CLI. It only shows the appservice plan, but sometimes there is just a delay in it showing up in the portal, so I'll hit Refresh, and there is the app service.

Let's click the Browse button and make sure it's working with the default page.

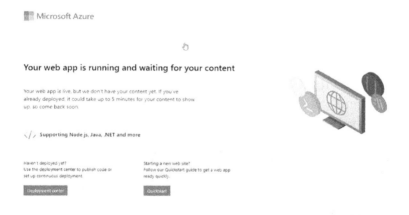

That's how to use the Azure CLI to query and manage resources in Azure. Next, let's look at Azure PowerShell.

Chapter 53 Azure PowerShell

Another way to manage Azure resources is using Azure PowerShell, which is a module for PowerShell that you can install. PowerShell runs on Windows, Mac, and Linux, and Azure PowerShell requires PowerShell version 7 or higher, so you might have to install that first, which is what I had to do on my Windows 10 computer. Then you can install the Azure PowerShell module from right within PowerShell using the install module command. Let's open up PowerShell 7 which runs alongside previous versions of PowerShell. Just like with the Azure CLI, the first thing you need to do is authenticate to Azure. In PowerShell, that's done with connect az account. A browser opens up just like with the CLI allowing us to enter our credentials. I'll use the administrator account in my Azure Active Directory tenant, and I'm already logged in so I don't have to enter the password. Back in PowerShell, it shows that I'm authenticated. Now let's run some commands against Azure. First, let's list the resource groups in the subscription. That's done with Get-AzResourceGroup with no parameters.

```
ResourceGroupName : websitesRG
Location          : centralus
ProvisioningState : Succeeded
Tags              :
ResourceId        : /subscriptions/0ef1dba3-743c-4fe2-97bf-8d81c3e64c20/resourceGroups/websitesRG

ResourceGroupName : pieshoprg
Location          : canadacentral
ProvisioningState : Succeeded
Tags              :
ResourceId        : /subscriptions/0ef1dba3-743c-4fe2-97bf-8d81c3e64c20/resourceGroups/pieshoprg

ResourceGroupName : pssamples
Location          : eastus2
ProvisioningState : Succeeded
Tags              :
ResourceId        : /subscriptions/0ef1dba3-743c-4fe2-97bf-8d81c3e64c20/resourceGroups/pssamples

ResourceGroupName : cli_rg
Location          : canadacentral
ProvisioningState : Succeeded
Tags              :
ResourceId        : /subscriptions/0ef1dba3-743c-4fe2-97bf-8d81c3e64c20/resourceGroups/cli_rg
```

PowerShell commands always start with the action verb so get, in this case. That returns the list, but we can format this in PowerShell too. To do that, you send the output of the first command into another PowerShell command using the pipe operator. So we'll use the Format-Table command with the AutoSize parameter. That's easier to read.

```
ResourceGroupName Location      ProvisioningState Tags TagsTable ResourceId                                                          ManagedBy
----------------- --------      ----------------- ---- --------- ----------                                                          ---------
websitesRG        centralus     Succeeded                        /subscriptions/0ef1dba3-743c-4fe2-97bf-8d81c3e64c20/resourceGroups/websitesRG
pieshoprg         canadacentral Succeeded                        /subscriptions/0ef1dba3-743c-4fe2-97bf-8d81c3e64c20/resourceGroups/pieshoprg
```

Let's clear this, and now let's list the contents of the resource group we created using the CLI. That's Get-AzResource with the ResourceGroupName parameter, and we'll pipe this to Format-Table. So there is the app service and app service plan we created.

```
Name         ResourceGroupName ResourceType               Location
----         ----------------- ------------               --------
asp-fromcli  cli_rg            Microsoft.Web/serverFarms  canadacentral
web1nmfromcli cli_rg           Microsoft.Web/sites        canadacentral
```

Now let's add a storage account to this resource group. First, I'll create a variable to hold the name of the region where I want the storage account created. You can start to see how PowerShell can be used for scripting. Now let's call New-AzStorageAccount passing in the name of the resource group, the name we want to give the storage account, then for the location, we'll use the variable we created. Next is the sku name. I'll use the locally redundant storage option, and finally, the kind of storage account which will be StorageV2.

```
StorageAccountName ResourceGroupName PrimaryLocation SkuName      Kind      AccessTier CreationTime        ProvisioningState EnableHttpsTrafficOnly LargeFileShares
------------------ ----------------- --------------- -------      ----      ---------- ------------        ----------------- ---------------------- ---------------
stgacctnmclitest01 cli_rg            canadacentral   Standard_LRS StorageV2 Hot        8/31/2022 6:56:09 PM Succeeded         True
```

It shows that the provisioning succeeded, so let's go to the Azure portal and take a look. I'll go to resource groups again and I'll open up the cli_rg, and there are the app service resources.

So using Azure PowerShell or the Azure CLI, you can use commands to manage Azure and also integrate those commands into scripts for more complex operations and deployments, but you do need to install the tools locally. If you're working remotely or don't have permissions to install applications on your local computer, there is an easier way to use the Azure CLI and PowerShell right in the Azure portal using your browser. Let's look at that next.

Chapter 54 How to Use Azure Cloud Shell in Azure Portal

You can run Azure CLI and PowerShell commands right in the Azure portal using the Cloud Shell. Cloud Shell runs on a temporary host container in the background and it requires an Azure file share in an Azure storage account. You only need to create this once, and it will get mounted each time you use the Cloud Shell, so you can persist files that you upload between sessions. You choose either the Bash shell or PowerShell here, but you can change between them any time after this gets created. You can change the options for the storage account creation if you like, the region and resource names, but I'll just leave the defaults.

Let's create the storage account for the Cloud Shell. Once the storage account is created, it'll connect the terminal. You can resize the window, and let's make the text a little bigger from the Settings menu. Let's clear this, and since we're in the Bash shell, it's the clear command. Because I'm already logged into the Azure portal, I don't need to authenticate like I did with the Azure CLI installed on my local computer, so let's run a command against this subscription. I'll just run the az group list command.

Now let's look at the menu across the top. If you have problems starting the Cloud Shell, like if it hangs during connection, you can restart it from here. This can come in handy. You can upload and download files. You might have scripts you want to run here or you might upload a file with variables that you want to use when running commands. Remember, there is a file share attached, so those files are only accessible to you. You can actually see the files and edit them right here too. If I expand this and click on a file, it opens in the editor on the right, and I can modify the contents, but let's hide this and now let's switch over to the PowerShell version of the Cloud Shell.

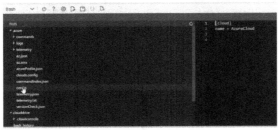

I'll just confirm, and the terminal connects again. I'm already authenticated in the portal, so I can run PowerShell commands here.

Before we leave the Cloud Shell, I just want to show you that besides accessing it here in the Azure portal, you can also go to shell.azure.com, and that opens a full screen version of the Azure Cloud Shell. Depending on your device format, that might be easier to use.

Chapter 55 Azure Resource Manager Templates

Now let's talk about using Azure Resource Manager templates to deploy resources in a repeatable way. Many development teams are adopting agile methods and quick iterations where they want to deploy repeatedly and know that their infrastructure is in a reliable state. That's a big part of DevOps where the traditional division between developers and IT operations roles has disappeared. Teams are now managing infrastructure using code, so those definitions can be stored in code repositories alongside the source code, and they can be deployed in repeatable ways, sometimes using the same continuous integration continuous deployment process that's used to deploy web applications and database code. To implement infrastructure as code, Azure has Resource Manager templates. These are files written using JavaScript Object Notation, or JSON, and the contents define the infrastructure and configuration for all the Azure resources in your solution. It uses a declarative syntax, which means you state what you intend to deploy without having to write a series of programming commands to create it. Once you write the code in the template, you can deploy it in a variety of ways. In the Azure DevOps service, Azure Pipelines allow you to automate code deployments to hosting environments and you can deploy Resource Manager templates as part of an Azure Pipeline too. You can also deploy templates from within GitHub using GitHub Actions, which is a service that's similar to Azure Pipelines. It's also possible to deploy templates using PowerShell or the Azure CLI, and you can also deploy templates using the Azure portal. Let's take a look at how to do that. I'll open up the list of resource groups and drill into the one we created using the Azure CLI. There are three

223

resources in this resource group, an app service, an app service plan, and a storage account.

Every resource in Azure is defined by an ARM template. Let's look at this storage account. If we go down to the export template tab at the bottom, Azure will generate an ARM template based on the current configuration.

Parameters are broken out by default, so it's easy to change the name of the storage account when you deploy a new one using this template, but you can turn off that feature and have the name generated inline in the JSON.

Often, you'll want to deploy groups of resources though, so let's go back to the resource group and there is a tab on the menu here too that will generate an ARM template with all the resources in this resource group, but it's also possible to select just the resources you want and export the template from the menu here at the top. Now we've got just the app service plan, which is called serverFarms in the JSON, and the app service whose resource type is actually called microsoft.web/sites. From this screen, you can download the template and that creates a zip file with the template and a file with the parameters.

If I double-click the template file, it opens in Visual Studio Code, which is the default editor on my local computer. So you could use this as a starting place and modify it to configure or add resources.

```json
template.json  ×

{
    "$schema": "https://schema.management.azure.com/schemas/2019-04-01/deploymentTemplate.json#",
    "contentVersion": "1.0.0.0",
    "parameters": {
        "sites_webinmfromcli_name": {
            "defaultValue": "webinmfromcli",
            "type": "String"
        },
        "serverfarms_asp_fromcli_name": {
            "defaultValue": "asp-fromcli",
            "type": "String"
        }
    },
    "variables": {},
    "resources": [
        {
            "type": "Microsoft.Web/serverfarms",
            "apiVersion": "2022-03-01",
            "name": "[parameters('serverfarms_asp_fromcli_name')]",
            "location": "Canada Central",
            "sku": {
                "name": "S1",
                "tier": "Standard",
                "size": "S1",
                "family": "S",
                "capacity": 1
            },
            "kind": "app",
            "properties": {
                "perSiteScaling": false,
                "elasticScaleEnabled": false,
                "maximumElasticWorkerCount": 1,
                "isSpot": false,
                "reserved": false,
                "isXenon": false,
                "hyperV": false,
                "targetWorkerCount": 0,
                "targetWorkerSizeId": 0,
                "zoneRedundant": false
            }
        }
```

Let's go back to the browser though and let's see how we can deploy the template from here. Now when you're generating a template like this from the existing state of deployed resources, you often need to massage it a bit.

Besides changing the names of resources to deploy new instances, sometimes there are things included that actually can't get deployed. Let's edit this template. I'll scroll down to the bottom, and there are two entries for snapshots.

The documentation says that these are read-only, which means they can't be deployed, so let's remove them and let's save these changes. Okay, now let's create a new resource group to deploy this template to. The parameters from the template are showing here, so let's change the name of the app service and the app service plan.

Custom deployment
Deploy from a custom template

Basics   Review + create

Template

Customized template
6 resources

Edit template   Edit parameters   Visualize

Project details

Select the subscription to manage deployed resources and costs. Use resource groups like folders to organize and manage all your resources.

Subscription *   Visual Studio Professional

Resource group *   (New) arm_rg
Create new

Instance details

Region *   Canada Central

Sites_web1nmfromcli_name   web1nmfromcli

Serverfarms_asp_fromcli_name   asp-fromcli

That's all we need to do. The validation passed, so let's create this.

Custom deployment
Deploy from a custom template

Validation Passed

Basics   Review + create

Summary

Customized template
6 resources

228

It'll take about a minute to deploy the resources in the template.

And it says the deployment is complete. Let's go to the Resource groups tab and there is the new resource group. There is an app service and an app service plan. Let's drill into the app service, and I'll just click browse to make sure it's running.

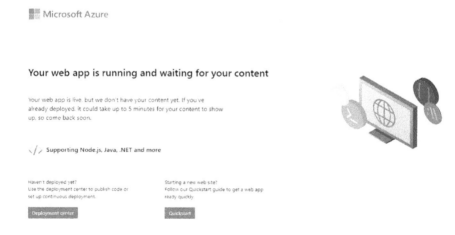

So that's how you can use Azure Resource Manager templates to deploy resources in a repeatable way. Next, let's talk about monitoring the health of the Azure platform.

Chapter 56 Azure Service Health

Azure Service Health keeps you informed about the health of your cloud resources. This includes information about current and upcoming issues that might impact your deployed resources like outages and planned maintenance. There is actually three services that make up service health. Azure status gives you information on service outages across all of Azure, Service Health is a personalized view of the services and regions that you're actually using, and Resource health provides information on your specific resources. Let's look at these. Azure status isn't part of the Azure portal. You go to azure.status.microsoft. It gives you an overview of all the Azure services and their current status. So this is a high-level view of Azure.

The regions are organized into high-level groupings with each region and columns and Azure services and rows, it's quite a long list of services. Let's go to the Azure portal and look at Service Health, which is the recommended way to check the health of your resources. I'll search for it under All services.

So Service Health scopes the affected services to just the ones that you use, so you might not be impacted by an outage in Azure Front Door, for example, if you're not using that service. Azure Service Health will trim those notifications to just what matters to you. You can find out about planned maintenance in Azure that might affect you, so you might want to notify clients of an upcoming event or reschedule an application deployment. There is some planned maintenance here for Azure App Service in regions where I have app services deployed. Notice the impact category says that there is no impact expected.

Health advisories are changes in Azure services that require your attention. For example, if features in a service that you use are being deprecated or you need to upgrade your web applications because the framework version in Azure App Service is being updated.

There is also a link to Health history here which has one of the same links from planned maintenance, but also this historical entry about a DNS failure with Azure Monitor. Security Advisories are notifications or violations that might affect the availability of your Azure services.

The Resource health tab lets you scope to just certain resource types in your subscriptions.

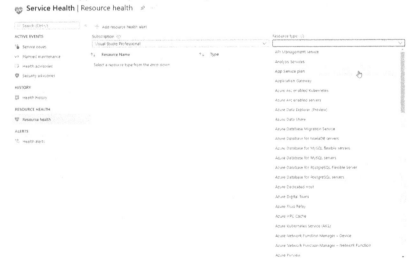

The first two app services are grayed out because they're on a free pricing tier where resource health isn't available, but these other two are on the standard pricing tier, so you can get a quick summary of the overall health and drill in to see more.

If there were issues here, there would also be information on actions that Microsoft is taking to fix the problems and it would identify things that you can do to address them.

You can see a history of the health of the resource if you need to do some historical troubleshooting, and you can add a health alert from here also. Let's back out and let's add a service health alert. You can use this to be notified when there are any changes to a particular service, you can filter the alerts to just service issues or health advisories, security alerts, or planned maintenance, and you can filter the services and regions that you want to be notified about.

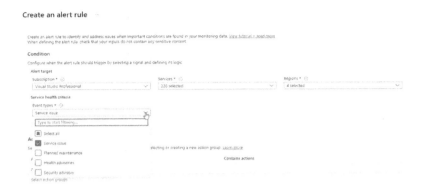

The alerts get sent to an action group. Let's open this up and create a new action group. Let's just move ahead to the Notifications tab.

You can just have an email sent to the people in the Resource Manager role, or you can set up a custom notification for email, text message, and automated voice message, and there is an option here for Azure app push notifications.

You can get notified on your mobile device through the Azure app too. So Azure Service Health can make you aware of when there is an issue with the underlying platform that can prevent you from chasing down a problem with your application when it isn't your application at all. But sometimes the problem isn't with the entire service, it's with your resource. So let's look at how to monitor resources next.

Chapter 57 How to use Azure Monitor

Azure Monitor is a service in Azure that collects metrics and logs from the Azure resources in your subscription. You can use these to check on the performance and availability of your applications and services. Metrics are numerical values that describe some aspect of a system at a particular point in time, and they're constantly being collected. This could be things like the response time of a web application, the amount of CPU being used on a VM, the amount of data coming out of a storage account. Metrics are good for alerting and fast detection of issues. The tool in Azure Monitor that helps you explore the collected metrics is called Metrics Explorer, and it's available inside each Azure resource. Logs, on the other hand, are different kinds of data that are organized into records with different properties for each type of log entry. Logs are good for troubleshooting issues and for analyzing trends. Azure Monitor includes a tool called Log Analytics, which is used to edit and run queries on the log data. It uses a powerful query language called the Kusto Query Language that's kind of like SQL, and it lets you sort, filter, and visualize the data in charts. Another service that's part of Azure Monitor is Application Insights. This monitors the availability, performance, and usage of your web applications. For Azure App Service, you can turn on Application Insights and it will monitor your app from the hosting environment, so things like performance counters on the servers, Docker logs, and you can set up web tests to send requests to your application. You can track API calls and dependencies outside of your application also. For deeper monitoring, you can use the Application Insights SDK to include instrumentation right in your code, and it's available for a number of programming languages. So your application doesn't need to be hosted in Azure to send data to Application Insights from the SDK. Let's take a look at the documentation.

Metrics and logs are collected from different sources inside Azure, and you can collect data from virtual machines outside Azure by installing agents on the machines. Then the data is stored as metrics, logs, and traces, and traces refers to distributed traces. When you have an application with different components deployed to different virtual machines or app services or containers, distributed traces are the data gathered from each of those hosts so it traces a web request through the different tiers of the application and all that data is linked together through some correlation id, which is all possible by using Application Insights. The data that gets collected by Azure Monitor gets used in different ways. Experiences are visualizations and queries that are organized for you already. You'll see shortly in Azure Monitor that these are also called Insights with Application Insights being one of them. You can visualize the data in Azure Monitor using dashboards and a Microsoft service called Power BI. There are tools in the Azure portal to inspect the metrics and log analytics for querying the logs, and you can respond to changes in the metrics by setting up alerts and performing actions like autoscaling an app service to add virtual machines when the load is heavy or calling other services to perform an action like a Logic app.

Chapter 58 How to Explore Azure Monitor

Now let's take a look at Azure Monitor in the Azure portal. Let's look at the central Azure monitor service in this subscription.

On the overview page, there are shortcuts to the same things as on the menu on the left. Metrics are all the metrics collected by the different resources we've deployed. You need to drill into individual resources in order to view the metrics. If I apply this, the metrics are scoped to the ones that are relevant just to this app service, like average response time and the number of requests. Logs are where you can query the logs sent to your Log Analytics workspace.

There are pre-built queries here to get you started and they fall into categories like alerts, audit logs for Azure Active Directory. You can actually send metrics to Log Analytics too so they can be queried like other logs. And there are performance queries here related to Azure functions. Let's just pick a query and run it. This shows you the syntax of the Kusto Query Language so you can start to write your own queries.

You can access Service Health from within Azure Monitor too. Insights are referred to as curated visualizations. It's a customized monitoring experience for a particular service. Application Insights is for web applications, and it can collect information from outside the application from the hosting platform, as well as from inside the code of your web application.

The virtual machine insights allows you to monitor the health and performance of your windows and Linux VMs inside Azure, as well as virtual machines hosted on-premises or even in other cloud environments. To enable that, you need to install an agent on the virtual machines to send data to Azure Monitor. You can monitor the overall health of your storage accounts. There are some metrics here, and the Capacity tab tells you the amount of storage being used by each service in the storage account. Network insights gives you a view of the health and metrics for all your deployed networking resources.

This is good for checking on application gateways and load balancers, but not all networking resources have health checks. You can also set up connectivity tests to monitor things like latency between VMs and storage and applications hosted in Azure and on-premises, which also requires installing agents to run the connectivity tests. Let's take a look at setting up alerts for metrics in Azure Monitor. Up at the top of the menu is the Alerts tab. From here, you can create an alert rule. Let's create an alert for an app service.

Next, we set up conditions for the alert. There is a number of metrics to choose from here. Let's select CPU time.

This is the amount of CPU consumed by the app in seconds. We could scope this metric to a particular virtual machine in the underlying app service plan if there is more than one. And we can set the alert logic so when the total CPU time is greater than 80 seconds, then the alert will get fired. Let's finish this part. And next, you decide what happens when the alert is fired. Just like with the service health alerts, you do that with an action group. We don't have any created, so let's create one.

I'll create it in the same resource group and give this action group a name. And next, we set up the notification type. I'll choose the push notification option, and this can be an email, text message, voice message, or we can push out a notification to the Azure app on the mobile device of this user. Let's give this notification a name.

And besides sending a notification, you can also configure an action when the alert is fired. That could be calling an Azure function or a Logic app, calling a webhook in an outside web service.

There is lots of options for taking actions when an alert gets fired. We'll skip tags and let's create this action group. And now let's create the alert rule. Now let's move forward and create this alert.

You can see all the alerts from the Alert Rules tab at the top. Next, let's look at using Azure Monitor metrics and logs from right inside Azure resources.

Chapter 59 How to Use Azure Monitor Metrics in a Resource

Azure Monitor collects metrics for Azure services by default, it's turned on automatically. So let's navigate into a service that we've created like this app service we deployed earlier using an ARM template.

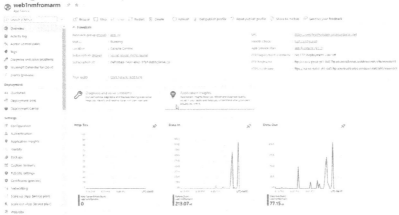

Right on the overview page, there are charts showing things like HTTP server errors, the amount of data moving in and out of the app service, the number of requests, and the average response time. These are coming from Azure Monitor and these are just predefined views of the metrics that are being collected. You can dig deeper by going down the menu to the Monitoring group and clicking Metrics.

Most Azure resources have a Monitoring section on the menu, although the exact tabs might be different depending on the service. We have a blank slate here. Because we're inside a resource already, some of these items are already populated like the scope of the resource and the metric namespace. The same metrics are here that you saw on the charts on the overview page, but there are others too like CPU time for the underlying virtual machines in the app service plan. Let's select that. It shows a slight spike here around 6 PM.

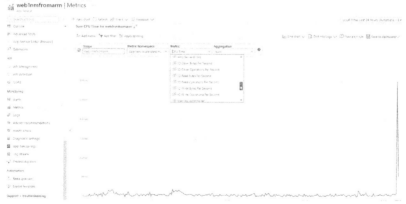

If we scroll further down the list, there are all sorts of metrics around IO, and there is the number of requests. Let's choose that.

It shows 125 total requests. With these charts, you can choose a different aggregation. So instead of summing all the requests, we could show the count at different time periods or the average requests. Let's try a different metric like Private Bytes, which is the working memory set on the server that the app service has allocated.

If this number keeps growing, you might have a memory leak in your application. Depending on the resource, you can apply splitting to the graph. In the case of an app service, I've increased the instance count of the underlying app service plan, so there are two virtual machines, and we can split the graph to show how the metric, Private Bytes in this case, applies to each VM. Let's see what that looks like for a different metric. Let's try Response Time.

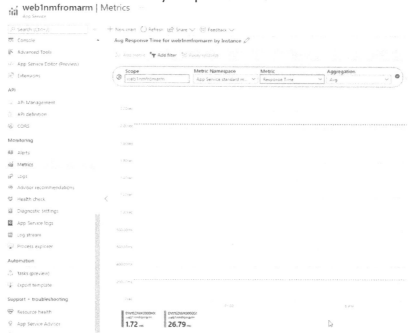

It looks like there is quite a difference here, but that's probably because I just added the second instance a short time ago, so it hasn't serviced many requests. Across the top, you can give the chart a name, and you can pin it to the dashboard so it will show up on the main dashboard page along with any other charts and graphs that you want to see every time you log in. That's a quick look at metrics in this app service. Let's look at logs next.

Chapter 60 Log Analytics in Azure Monitor

Now let's look at Logs. I'm still inside the app service. There are a bunch of predefined queries that you can run against the log data that's been collected, but before we can do that, we have to enable that log collection.

You do that from the Diagnostic settings. Let's add a diagnostic setting. Depending on the resource you're in, there are different types of logs available, and you can choose to send metrics also.

Diagnostic setting

Save X Discard Delete Feedback

A diagnostic setting specifies a list of categories of platform logs and/or metrics that you want to collect from a resource, and one or more destinations that you would stream them to. Normal usage charges for the destination will occur. Learn more about the different log categories and contents of those logs

Diagnostic setting name *

Logs	Destination details
Categories	☐ Send to Log Analytics workspace
☑ HTTP logs	☐ Archive to a storage account
☑ App Service Console Logs	☐ Stream to an event hub
☑ App Service Application Logs	☐ Send to partner solution
☑ Access Audit Logs	
☑ IPSecurity Audit logs	
☑ App Service Platform logs	

Metrics

☑ AllMetrics

We need to give this diagnostic setting a name and then you choose where you want to send the logs. Log Analytics is the obvious choice where you can aggregate all your logs together and run queries. There is a default workspace created automatically, but you can have multiple Log Analytics workspaces. You can send these logs to a storage account and specify how long you want to retain each of the log types for. You can stream the logs to an event hub where they can get ingested by another Azure service or you can send the logs to a third-party tool, maybe you have one in your organization already and you want to keep all the logs together. Let's just send these logs to Log Analytics and save this setting. Now that we have a diagnostic setting, we can go to the Logs tab, which lets us run queries against the data. You can choose a pre-built query from here, and these queries fall into the categories on the left menu.

Let's scroll down and choose the query related to response times. This is actually a metric that's being sent to Log Analytics. You can see the Kusto Query Language syntax here, and this is a good way to learn how to write queries by using these pre-built ones.

We just turned on logging so there won't be any data yet. I'll go to the default page in the app service, which is already open, and keep refreshing it so there is data generated. It won't show up right away in the logs, but it will come back later when the data is available. There is a chart generated from the results of this query, and the individual data is showing on the Results tab.

So even though this is metric data like we saw in the metrics demo, because it was sent to Log Analytics, there is individual records for each web response here, it's not aggregated like in the Metrics Explorer. Let's try a different query, the one for HTTP response codes. It's showing that all the response codes were in the 200s, which indicates successful HTTP responses.

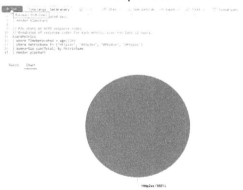

You can do some formatting of the chart from right here, and across the top, you have some options. You can share this query, you can create an alert based on this query, and you can export the query results to a CSV file, Excel, or to Power BI, and you can also pin the query to the dashboard just like on the Metrics tab. Let's navigate out of here and look at another resource group. This one has a storage account. Let's open that up. And down the menu on the storage account, there is a Monitoring section here too.

Some of the items are different from the app service, but we've got logs and metrics here too. You can scope the metrics to each of the services in the storage account and there are different metrics here that apply to Azure storage, so things like the count of blobs in the containers or the ingress of the data that I uploaded.

On the Logs tab, there are custom queries here related to storage, and you still need to turn on logging from the Diagnostic settings, but here you can set up logging on the individual services in the storage account. That's a quick look at logs. Remember, in the central Azure Monitor service, you can access the logs for all the resources you've configured to send logs to Azure Monitor, then you can write custom queries to correlate data across services. Next, let's look at Azure Advisor.

Chapter 61 How to Optimize Resources using Azure Advisor

Microsoft refers to Azure Advisor as a personalized cloud consultant that helps you follow best practices to optimize your Azure deployments. It's actually a great tool to provide recommendations on how to improve performance, availability, and security of your Azure resources, as well as recommending ways that you can save on costs in Azure. Let's go to All services and search for advisor, and click on here to open up Azure Advisor. It refreshes your recommendations when it loads.

These are personalized recommendations, so Azure is looking at the resources that you have deployed, it's not just providing a list of generic recommendations. This dashboard provides a summary of the recommendations broken down by five categories, cost, security, reliability, operational excellence, and performance. You can click on the tiles at the bottom to get links to each of the recommendations or you can use the menu on the left. Let's look at the security recommendations.

The first one says Accounts with owner permissions should be MFA enabled. So it's telling me to enable multifactor authentication on all the administrator accounts. There is a medium impact recommendation that storage accounts should use a private link connection. Some of these might not make sense for the design of your solution, so you can actually turn these off individually so you don't keep seeing them. Let's go to the next page. Here is one that has a quick fix.

It says web application should only be accessible over HTTPS. Let's click this. On the remediation steps, it says I can just select the app service and click the Fix button.

Web Application should only be accessible over HTTPS

It will turn on a setting in the app service that only allows incoming traffic over HTTPS so HTTP is disabled. So in some cases, Azure Advisor can make the required changes for you, otherwise, it will just describe what you need to do. Let's go back to the main screen and let's look at the Reliability tab.

There is just one recommendation and it's for the virtual network being used by the virtual machine that I created. It says add NAT gateway to your subnets to go outbound. If I click on the link, it brings me to a screen to create a NAT gateway.

Create network address translation (NAT) gateway

In this case, it isn't fixing the problem for me, but it's making it easier to fix. We won't complete this though. Let's go back and move on to cost recommendations. There actually aren't any, but there is this link to the list of cost recommendations that Azure Advisor uses.

This is a way to be proactive and configure your resources to best save on costs. The first recommendation is for compute and it says to use standard storage for disk snapshots rather than using premium storage. For another service like Azure storage, it has a recommendation about retention policies for log data so you're not storing old data you'll never use. Operational excellence has to do with deployment best practices and things like creating service health alerts. I don't have any recommendations here and performances to help improve the speed of the applications I have deployed. Again, you can view the standard list of recommendations here to get an idea of what Azure Advisor looks for. The last thing I want to show you is on the Overview page.

At the bottom, you can download the recommendations in PDF and CSV format, so you could share this report with other team members who might not have access to the Azure portal. Next, let's step outside of the Azure portal and look at the Azure app, which allows managing Azure from your mobile device.

Chapter 62 Azure App for Mobile Devices

Let's take a look at the Azure app. This is a tool that lets you monitor the health and status of your Azure resources, quickly diagnose and fix issues, and you can even run commands using the Cloud Shell.

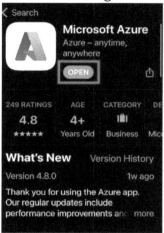

You can download the app from the Apple App Store and from Google Play. I've already installed the app on my iPhone so let's open it up. I'm logged in and I've chosen a subscription. On the home page here, any alerts would show right away. I don't have any so let's scroll down, and I have access to Service Health from here too.

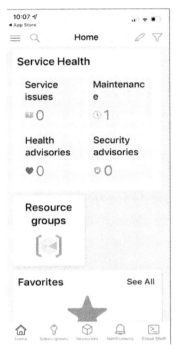

There aren't any service issues, but there is a maintenance notification. It's something about routine maintenance on app services. So I can see the Maintenance window and the impacted regions, and there is more detail further down. It says there is no impact expected.

2022-08-23 1:12:03 AM

Service: App Service
Region(s): Australia Central,
Australia East, South Africa North,
West US 3, East Asia, Canada
Central, UK West, East US 2,
West US, Korea South, South
Central US
Stage: Planned
Impact Category: No impact
expected
*You're receiving this
notification because you
currently use App Service.*
Summary: Azure App Service will
begin upgrading your resources
as part of routine scheduled
maintenance in around 7 days.
Once started in a given region,
upgrades generally take between
24-78 hours to complete. You
may receive more than one
notification per region if a
subscription has resources on

Back on the home screen, you can create shortcuts to resources that you frequently check on. Let's open up all the resource groups. I'm going to open up a resource group where I know there is a storage account. There is cost management information here showing how much this resource group is costing me.

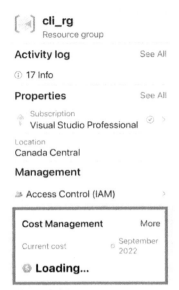

cli_rg
Resource group

Activity log See All

ⓘ 17 Info

Properties See All

Subscription
Visual Studio Professional ⊘ >

Location
Canada Central

Management

Access Control (IAM) >

Cost Management More

Current cost September 2022

⊚ **Loading...**

Resources

At the bottom are the resources, so I'll drill into this storage account. I can see some metrics that show me the health of the storage account, and these are coming from Azure Monitor. The Resource health tells me that the storage account is available.

Activity log See All

ⓘ 1 Info

Metrics See All

Average success E2E latency

— Success E2E Latency

Resource health

⊘ Available >

Properties See All

Subscription
Visual Studio Professional ⊘ >

262

There is some information about the resource, and at the bottom is Access Control. So I can give someone access to the storage account from here, which can be handy if you're out of the office and there is an issue or a new client needs to upload files.

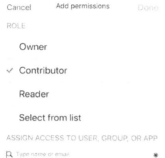

Let's back out of here and go back to the list of resource groups. I'll choose one that has a virtual machine in it. I'll open up this virtual machine. You can see the metrics for the virtual machine and you can restart the VM from here if there is a problem.

I'll actually shut it down so I don't incur compute charges. And you can even connect to this VM. This button will launch another app, Microsoft Remote Desktop. Let's back out of here and go back to the home screen. At the bottom, you can open up the Cloud Shell.

You can choose between the Bash Shell and PowerShell, and from here, you can type in PowerShell and Azure CLI commands to manage your resources. Let's run this az group list command, and we get back information on all the resource groups in the subscription.

```
{
    "id": "/subscriptions/0efldba3-743c
-4fe2-97bf-8d81c3e64c20/resourceGroups/
websitesRG",
    "location": "centralus",
    "managedBy": null,
    "name": "websitesRG",
    "properties": {
        "provisioningState": "Succeeded"
    },
    "tags": null,
    "type": "Microsoft.Resources/resour
ceGroups"
},
{
    "id": "/subscriptions/0efldba3-743c
-4fe2-97bf-8d81c3e64c20/resourceGroups/
pieshoprg",
    "location": "canadacentral",
    "managedBy": null,
    "name": "pieshoprg",
    "properties": {
        "provisioningState": "Succeeded"
    },
    "tags": null,
    "type": "Microsoft.Resources/resour
ceGroups"
},
{
    "id": "/subscriptions/0efldba3-743c
-4fe2-97bf-8d81c3e64c20/resourceGroups/
pssamples",
    "location": "eastus2",
    "managedBy": null,
    "name": "pssamples",
    "properties": {
```

We can switch to PowerShell and it will restart the Cloud Shell. The last thing I want to show you is that from the menu at the top left, you can manage your log in and change directories, and you can even access support requests from here.

So the Azure app provides an easy way to perform some Azure management tasks from your mobile device. Next, let's talk about Azure Arc.

Chapter 63 How to Manage Resources Outside Azure using Azure Arc

Azure Arc is a service in Azure that allows you to manage resources outside of Azure. So resources that you host on-premises or in other cloud platforms like Amazon Web Services or Google Cloud. You can manage a few different types of resources hosted outside of Azure. You can manage Windows and Linux physical servers and virtual machines, that means being able to monitor them, secure them, and update them from within Azure Arc. When you're hosting your virtual machines on private cloud platforms like VMware vSphere or Azure Stack HCI, you get additional integration with Azure Arc like the ability to perform lifecycle operations like provisioning, restarting, resizing, and deleting virtual machines as if they were hosted in Azure. SQL Server instances hosted outside of Azure can be managed using Azure Arc also, and with Azure Arc, you can manage Kubernetes clusters running on-premises and with other cloud providers. Remember, Kubernetes is an orchestration service for containers. You can apply Azure policies to the Kubernetes clusters to enforce configuration and compliance. Once you have Kubernetes clusters being managed, you can run other Azure services on them like data services. SQL managed instances and postgreSQL hyperscale databases are available running on Kubernetes. You can deploy Azure machine learning workloads onto those clusters also. And you can deploy Azure App Services on Azure Arc-enabled Kubernetes clusters, including web apps, function apps, and even Logic apps so your developers can leverage the features of app service while you maintain corporate compliance by hosting the app services on internal infrastructure or leveraging your existing investment with other cloud providers. You get features of Azure Resource Manager when your resources are managed using Azure Arc. That includes organizing resources using management groups and tags, searching and indexing them using Azure Resource Graph, security and access control through role-based access control and subscriptions, automation using templates and extensions, and update management. For physical and virtual machines hosted outside Azure that you want to manage with Azure Arc, you install the Azure connected machine agent on the servers. That lets you proactively monitor the operating system and workloads running on the machine, and you can leverage Azure features like update management to manage operating system updates. You can apply Azure policies to audit settings inside the machine. You can leverage Microsoft Defender for threat detection and Microsoft Sentinel to collect security-related events, and you can collect log data using the Log Analytics agent. The data gets sent to a Log Analytics workspace.

Chapter 64 How to Add Local Server to Azure Arc

Let's look at Azure Arc in the Azure portal. I'll go to All services and search for Arc. When Azure Arc opens, all the infrastructure services that can be hosted are listed on the menu.

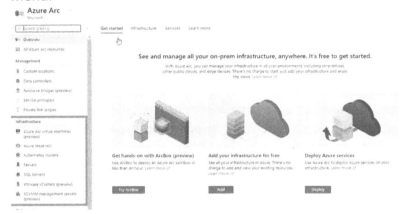

The data services are below and the application services are below that. Let's go to Servers. These are the physical and virtual servers that you host on-premises or in cloud environments other than Azure. There aren't any being hosted, so let's add one. I'll add a single server, and this will be a virtual machine running on my local computer using Hyper-V.

It says the server will need HTTPS access to Azure services for outbound connectivity. It'll need local admin permissions and the server can connect over a public endpoint, so over the internet, or using a private endpoint. We also need an existing resource group to add the server to. I'll click Next, and I've already created a resource group for this which will change the region to Canada Central.

This VM will be using the Windows operating system, but it could use Linux. And connectivity will be over the internet. Next, we can fill out some tags. The default ones define the location of the server. You can add your own custom ones also. On the next page, a script is generated. We need to run this script on the local server in order to download and install the agent and connect the server to Azure Arc, so I'll copy this script. And I have this virtual machine running on my local computer using Hyper-V. I'll search for PowerShell and open it up as an administrator. Now I'll paste in the script I copied from the Azure portal, and let's run this script on the local VM. It'll take a few minutes because it's downloading the agent from Azure.

```
    Invoke-WebRequest -Uri "https://gbl.his.arc.azure.com/log" -Method "PUT" -Body ($logBody | ConvertTo-
    Write-Host  -ForegroundColor red $_.Exception
}

VERBOSE: Installing Azure Connected Machine Agent
VERBOSE: .NET Framework version: 4.7.3190
VERBOSE: Downloading agent package
VERBOSE: Installing agent package
Installation of azcmagent completed successfully
time="2022-09-05T13:43:57-04:00" level=info msg="Connecting Machine. This might take a few minutes."
To sign in, use a web browser to open the page https://microsoft.com/devicelogin and enter the code E
Q6DB2Y62 to authenticate.
```

Next it's asking me to sign into Azure by going to microsoft.com/devicelogin and entering the code here. So let's open up a browser and navigate to the URL and it's asking for the code, so I'll switch back to PowerShell to enter it in. Now I need to authenticate. My administrator account has already logged into the browser so I'll use that and it has MFA enabled, so I get a code sent to my phone. I'll enter that in, and now it says Are you trying to sign in to Azure Connected Machine Agent?

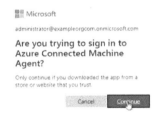

So I'll hit Continue, and now we can go back to PowerShell, and it'll continue with the installation.

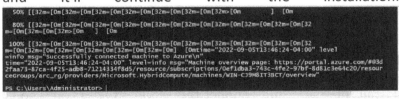

Once that's done, the machine should be getting managed by Azure Arc. Let's go back to the Azure portal. I'll close out of this and out of the Add server screen, and we're already on the Servers tab so I'll just hit Refresh. There is the server that was added and it says it's connected. There is information here about the operating system and tabs along the left with actions we can perform on this VM. Let's look at Security. Microsoft Defender is running on this virtual machine now, so it's scanning for threats, and there are also recommendations being made related to security.

One of them says that Log Analytics agent should be installed on Windows-based Azure Arc-enabled machines. So Log Analytics doesn't get installed by default, that's another agent we can install on the local VM. We can also manage operating system updates on this VM using Azure automation, and there is something called Automanage that will apply a preset configuration to the VM depending on whether it's being used for dev or production, and that includes things like backup and monitoring.

You can also assign policies to the VM so you can assess it for compliance to rules set up in Azure Policy. There is a lot of functionality here that makes it seem like this virtual machine is running right inside Azure, but of course, it's not, it's running on my local computer. So Azure Arc provides a lot of possibilities for simplifying your resource management across other clouds and on-premises. Let's have a quick review of what you've learned. We started with understanding how Azure is implemented physically with regions and data centers and logically with subscriptions and resource groups. You saw how to use the Azure portal and learned a bit about Azure Active Directory for controlling access. Next you learned about Azure compute. We looked at virtual machines, containers, and Azure App Services for hosting web apps, as well as Azure Functions for smaller pieces of code. Then you saw some of the main features of networking in Azure, like virtual networks, network security groups, Azure DNS, and private endpoints. You also learned about connecting your on-premises network to Azure using VPN Gateway and ExpressRoute. Then you learned about data storage in Azure with Azure Storage accounts, including how to copy files in Azure and migrate data into the cloud. Then you learned about managing and monitoring Azure using features like the Azure CLI and Resource Manager templates and services like Azure Monitor and Azure Arc. We've covered a lot in Azure, but there are a lot more features and services that are worth checking out like solutions for big data ingestion and analysis, solutions for the Internet of Things, machine learning services, and artificial intelligence. Those things actually used to be part of the AZ-900 Azure Fundamentals exam, but they were removed probably because they're pretty advanced and aren't relevant to as many people as these topics, but I encourage you to jump in and try Azure, create a free trial account, and take some of the services for a drive.

BOOK 2

MICROSOFT AZURE
SECURITY AND PRIVACY CONCEPTS

CLOUD DEPLOYMENT TOOLS AND TECHNIQUES, SECURITY & COMPLIANCE

RICHIE MILLER

Introduction to Azure Identity Services

In the following chapters, we'll be taking a look at Azure identity services. We will first focus on Azure identity services, so we're going to be taking a look at authentication and authorization, we're going discuss Azure Active Directory, and discuss the benefits of multi-factor authentication. We'll cover Azure AD and discuss why it's important to a secure deployment inside Azure. We'll take a look at role-based access control too. Role-based access control gives you granularity of permissions assignment inside Azure. We'll also take a big look Azure governance and policies. We'll look at practical things we can do to make sure that we stay within certain compliance standards, looking at both Azure governance features and documentation to back them up. We'll take a look at securing network access. Almost all the Azure projects I work on have some sort of virtual networking involved in them, and managing access to those virtual network can be a bit challenging. We'll also take a look at reporting and compliance. We'll detail some of common compliance standards your organization might be interested in and tools we can use to achieve them. You might be asking yourself, why is this important to you? Well, if you're thinking about deploying resources to the cloud, a good understanding how they can be securely deployed is important to you. The hat of that is authentication, you must have a good understanding of how your users, computers, and applications are authenticated and authorized to use Azure. Also, monitoring is so important to us today. Understanding how we monitor the security posture of our organization, how we comply to various security standards is vital for all deployments. So if you're interested in any of these areas of

Azure, then this book is for you. I would recommend this book to anyone that's interested in securing compliance in Azure, anyone that's thinking about migrating or deploying workloads to Azure and anyone that's studying for AZ-900 exam because this book is part of a series of books that should prepare you well for that certification. There are some prerequisites that would be recommended before starting this book. First of all, a familiarity of cloud concepts, a basic understanding of cloud computing. Even if you don't meet these prerequisites, then as long as you have an interest in Microsoft Azure, then you'll benefit from this book. Let's now talk about authentication and authorization and how the two compare. When we think about authentication, we need to think about the act of proving who or what something is. Authentication is something we do on almost a daily basis in our lives. Each time you show your pass to get into a building, each time you provide a copy of your signature that can be compared with a copy on file, or each time you go through a passport control on your holiday, we're going through a process of authentication. Authentication works hand in hand with authorization. Once you can guarantee beyond a reasonable doubt who or what something is, you can then authorize them to do certain things. So think about the passport analogy. When I travel to some countries, my passport is required to prove who I am, but then a visa is required to show that I'm allowed to enter that country and what I can do when I'm there. The passport is authentication. The visa is authorization. Authorization is saying, now that we can prove who this person is, this is what they can then do. In Azure, authentication is provided by Azure AD and authorization is provided by role-based access control. There may be some overlapping areas, but this is the list I came up with. A user logs in with a password is authentication. This is an example of something the user knows being used to authenticate them. A user uses their thumbprint to get access to a laptop. This is an example of using biometrics. The third example is a bit more general A user proves she's a member of your staff. Well, if they prove they're a member your staff, they've authenticated. The next three are authorization. Once you've been authenticated, you can be given the rights to create virtual machines, get access to files, allowed access to a building. Hopefully, you could see the flow here. Authentication has to take place first, and then authorization can occur.

Chapter 1 Azure Active Directory Fundamentals

Fundamental to authentication in Azure is Azure AD. So now, we're going to give you a good grounding in what Azure AD is. Azure Active Directory sits at the heart of authentication for the Microsoft cloud. If you've ever signed up for an Azure subscription, Office 365 or any of the Dynamics products, then you're using Azure AD. When using any of these products, if you've created a user, a group, you've granted permissions, then you've been using Azure Active Directory. Azure Active Directory underpins the security for all these products. When using these products, an Azure Active Directory tenant is created for you. This is dedicated for your company's exclusive use. Usually, an organization will have one Azure Active Directory tenant that manages the security for each of their Microsoft products, so for each Azure subscription or each Office 365 installation that they have. But Azure Active Directory is not just about securing access to Microsoft products, Azure Active Directory can also be used to secure access to your on-premise applications, third-party applications, and applications provided by other cloud providers. When we think Azure Active Directory, think single sign on. A user will have a single user account that can be used to access all these different applications. If your company uses Microsoft products, then you're probably already using Active Directory Domain Services on-premise. Azure AD is not the same product, so let's try and compare the two. Azure AD is all about user and computer registration and providing single sign on capabilities for Users and Computers. Active Directory Domain Services also performs Users and Computers registration. Azure AD does not give access to Group Policies, but Active Directory Domain Services does. Azure AD cannot perform trust relationships, whereas Active Directory Domain Services can. When thinking about Azure AD and single sign on, also think about application management. Applications can register for Azure AD, so your users can be given single sign on access. Active Directory Domain Services offers application and device management, as well as application deployment. Active Directory Domain Services supports both Kerberos and NTLM as authentication protocols. Active Directory Domain Services also gives you access to schema management so that you can add custom objects and attributes into the domain service. Finally, Active Directory Domain Services follows a hierarchical design using domains, trees, forests, and organizational units. It scales almost infinitely, whereas Azure AD is a flat structure, which offers limited scale. For most organizations that already use Microsoft products, when moving to Azure, you'll use a mixture of Active Directory Domain Services on-prem and Azure AD in the cloud. But there is a third option as well. In Azure, we have another domain service called Azure AD Domain Services. The names are very similar here, but we have three distinct products. We have Azure AD. This is for single sign on and application integration. We have Active Directory Domains Services. This is the full Active Directory Domain Service that we've used for years on-premise. And sat between the two, we have Azure AD Domain Services. Azure AD Domain Services was introduced several years ago now. It was initially introduced to make it easier to migrate legacy applications as it supports both NTLM and Kerberos for authentication. But it also supports Group Policies, trust relationships, as well as several over domain service features. Azure AD Domain Services is a Platform as a Service offering provided by Microsoft. Instead of you having to manage the virtual machines, the operating systems, and the directory service, you just deploy Azure AD Domain Services and let Microsoft take care of the rest. The question I get asked most often is can Azure AD Domain Services replace Active Directory Domain Services? The answer right now is still no. It's not as feature-rich as Active Directory Domain Services, and there's a little way for it to go before it can replace on-premise Active Directory. Do we need Azure AD? Well, giving a short answer, yes, it's a requirement. If you're thinking about working with Microsoft Azure, then you will need to work with Azure AD. But that doesn't mean we've wasted all our investment with Active Directory Domain Services. In fact, Azure AD and Active Directory Domain Services work very well together. There's a product called Azure AD Connect that we can deploy on-premise. Think of Azure AD Connect as being like a synchronization tool. As I perform actions on-prem, those actions are replicated into the cloud. For example, as I create a new user account on-premise, that user account is replicated in the cloud. Most of your day-to-day administration of users, of groups, will still be done on-premise. We can then feel the benefit of those actions in Azure AD. When we use Azure AD, there are no domain controllers for us to manage, we just access a list of users and groups applications. Azure AD provides us with user management, application integration, and single sign on, and through the use of products like Azure AD Connect, we can integrate with other directory services. Imagine a typical organization. They have different categories of staff. For example, they have a full-time IT staff, full-time end users, as well as contractors who are brought in to work on various projects. What the company would like from us is an understanding of where the different user accounts will be created and managed for these different sets of users. Take a minute and have a think. Where will these user accounts be created for the company? Well, the full-time IT staff can be created on-premise or in Azure AD. The majority of the IT staff will be created on-premise, and their user accounts will then be replicated into Azure so they can be assigned access to perform Azure tasks. Some IT staffed will be cloud-only. That means that their user accounts will just be created in Azure AD. These tend to be top-level administrators who will only need access to Azure and do not need access to on-premise services. Our full-time users should have their user accounts created on-prem in Microsoft Active Directory Domain Services. Remember, Active Directory Domain Services is almost a limiting scale. It's hierarchical, so the bulk of your user management should be done through there. For the company's full-time users that need access to Azure, well, their user accounts can also then be replicated with Azure AD Connect. Contractors will already have user accounts somewhere, either in an on-premise directory service themselves or in an email product like Outlook or Gmail. Using their existing user accounts, we can grant them access to perform admin tasks in Azure subscriptions. As a company, you might have to go through a project where you categorize your staff and discuss how those user accounts can get access to resources we deployed to Azure. When thinking about authentication, Microsoft strongly recommends that we use multi-factor authentication. Multi-factor authentication involves providing several pieces of information to prove who you are. This information includes something you know, like a password, something you have, like a smart card with digital certificates installed, and some think you are, like biometric information. Microsoft Azure provides several different ways for us to enable multi-factor authentication for users and to enforce it.

Chapter 2 How to Work with Conditional Access

One of the key features of Azure AD is Azure AD single sign-on. Single sign-on means the ability for users to use a single set of credentials to access a whole group of applications and services. This way, your users only have one username and one password to remember no matter which applications they're trying to access. We can integrate Azure AD with Microsoft-provided applications, third-party applications, and custom applications that we and our teams develop The goal is that users should be asked for their credentials once and not prompted to provide their credentials over and over again. Some applications that we integrate in Azure AD even include the ability to provision users and assign levels of access to those applications directly from the Azure AD console. But controlling access to all of these integrated applications can be difficult. For example, do you want all of your Azure AD integrated applications to be accessed from outside your firewall? There might be some applications that give access to sensitive information that you only want to be used if the user is at one of your corporate centers. Are there times when applications should only be accessed if the user has used multi-factor authentication to authenticate? Should access to applications be restricted to certain secure devices? There'll be plenty of scenarios when working with integrated applications in Azure where restricted access based on criteria like this will be a good thing. Azure AD Conditional Access can be used to secure access to Azure AD integrate applications based on the criteria previously discussed and more. Azure AD Conditional Access can be used to control access to applications no matter where our users are. We create Conditional Access policies, which at their heart are if-then statements. If the user is authenticated in this way and is using this type of device, then grant access. If not, then deny access. In conditional access policies, signals are used to make decisions. These include IP location information, risk analysis based on the user's login, information about the device the user is using to try and get access to applications, and the application being accessed. Ultimately, the Conditional Access policy is trying to make one of two decisions, either to block access to an application if various conditions in a policy are met or grant access to an application. And even when we grant access, that access can be qualified by enforcing requirements like MFA required or that the user is accessing the application from an Active Directory joined device. Let's take a look at conditional access. In this demonstration, we're going to be working with Azure Active Directory to enable conditional access. We're going to be working with the Azure console and, as always to follow along, you will need the Azure subscription. But be warned, some of the features that we're enabling can incur costs. I'm in the Azure console. Specifically, I'm looking at my Azure AD tenant and a list of its enterprise applications. These are some of the applications that have been integrated with my Azure AD tenant for single sign-on.

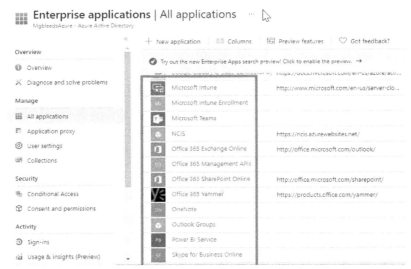

If I select Conditional Access here and then select New policy, we'll start off by giving our new policy a name.

I want this policy to be assigned to a user, so in the Users and group section, I click the blue writing, 0 users and groups selected, and I'm going to choose the Select users and groups radio button and the Users and groups tick box.

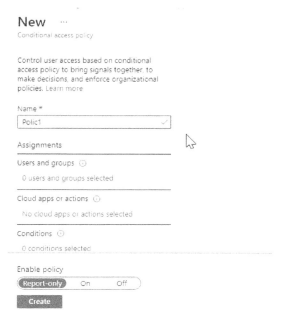

Using search, I'm going to search for the user that I want this policy to be assigned to. But don't forget, you can select groups of users, directory roles or guests and external users. Next, I'm going to choose Cloud apps or actions.

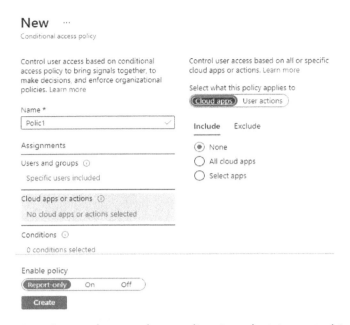

New ⋯
Conditional access policy

Control user access based on conditional access policy to bring signals together, to make decisions, and enforce organizational policies. Learn more

Name *

Polic1

Assignments

Users and groups ⓘ

Specific users included

Cloud apps or actions ⓘ

No cloud apps or actions selected

Conditions ⓘ

0 conditions selected

Enable policy

(Report-only)   On   Off

Create

Control user access based on all or specific cloud apps or actions. Learn more

Select what this policy applies to

(Cloud apps) User actions

Include   Exclude

◉ None

◯ All cloud apps

◯ Select apps

Here I can choose the application that I want this policy to affect. So if I choose the Select apps radio button, and for this demonstration I'll just choose Office 365, but you can select any of the applications that you've integrated with Azure AD.

Select   ✕
Cloud apps

🔍 Search

☐ 🚪 Office 365 ⓘ

☐ aws Amazon Web Services (AWS)
       39271c77-dc15-4bc3-ab83-0d2184b2d9c4

☐ AS Assignment-ournewblueprint
       cc7926f1-68b3-4246-9629-7fc39d7b897d

☐ AK Azure Kubernetes Service AAD Server
       6dae42f8-4368-4678-94ff-3960e28e3630

Selected items

With Office 365 selected, I click Select. We're starting to build up our policy. So far I've identified a user and the Office

365 application. Let's select Conditions. And for this demonstration, we'll choose Device platforms.

Then we'll select Yes to apply this policy to selective device platforms. And we'll say this policy should take effect if the user is using selected device platforms, such as Android, iOS,

and macOS.

I'm happy with my selections, so I select Done. Let's select Locations, and here you'll select Yes to control access based on the physical location.

This time we'll leave the default any location selected, but you can build up a list of trusted locations based on IP addresses. I'm happy with the conditions selected, so if I scroll down a little bit, and on the left-hand side we have Access controls.

In the Grant section, if I select 0 controls selected, here we get to decide whether this policy will block access or grant access based on the conditions that we've input into this policy.

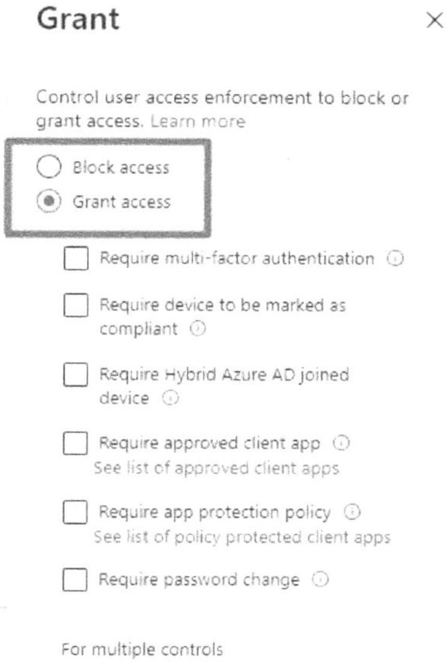

Grant   ×

Control user access enforcement to block or grant access. Learn more

○ Block access

◉ Grant access

☐ Require multi-factor authentication ⓘ

☐ Require device to be marked as compliant ⓘ

☐ Require Hybrid Azure AD joined device ⓘ

☐ Require approved client app ⓘ
    See list of approved client apps

☐ Require app protection policy ⓘ
    See list of policy protected client apps

☐ Require password change ⓘ

For multiple controls

I want this policy to grant the user access to Office 365, but if the user is using one of the device platforms selected, then I require that he is authenticated using multi-factor authentication. So if I select that tick box and then choose Select, notice here this policy can be turned On, Off, but the default is Report-only.

This generates report information that would indicate whether this policy would have taken effect if it was turned on. I want this policy to be enforced, so I'm going to select On. And I'm happy with my policy, so I select Create. It should only take a second, and your policy is created. Now if the user tries to access Office 365 from any of the devices listed, he will be granted access as long as he's logged in with multi-factor authentication. So far, we introduced our customer to a company. You learned the differences between authentication and authorization, and you were introduced to Azure Active Directory. You were shown how to create users and groups using Azure Active Directory, and you were shown how to enable Conditional Access. Next, we're going to look at Azure role-based access control and Azure locks.

Chapter 3 How to Implement Azure Role Based Access Control

In this chapter we'll be looking at implementing Azure role-based access control. We'll begin by discussing shared access to an Azure subscription and how difficult it is to manage multiple user accounts who have different requirements. We'll then move on and introduce you to Azure role-based access control. We'll take a look at the different types of built-in Azure roles and discuss using custom Azure roles. Role-based access control is used daily by your organization. It's central to access control in Azure. Azure provides shared access. By this I mean there are different types of users that require different access to Azure, and we can provide access to them all. Some users will require admin access to Azure while other users will require access to the resources we deploy. Each type of user has to be authenticated and authorized at the correct level, as well as managing each type of user. Each type of user also has to be monitored to make sure they have the correct level of access, but also to make sure they're not trying to breach the access levels they've been assigned. Azure role-based access control is the tool we use to provide shared access. RBAC is made up of several different components, starting off with roles. Roles are groups of permissions that are needed to perform different administrative actions in Azure. We can make users or groups members of different roles that inherit all permissions that are assigned to that role. When using roles, we first choose a built-in role or we create a custom role of our own. We then assign role members before configuring a scope for the role. A scope details where a role can be used. There are many built-in roles, each giving different sets of permissions, but three built-in roles are used more than any other. The Owner role, for example, is used a lot. If you are assigned the Owner role for a resource, you have full control of that resource, including the ability to assign other users and group access. We then have the Contributor role. The Contributor role allows you to do everything except manage permissions, so you would not be able to assign your friend access to the resource with the Contributor role, you would with the Owner role. We then have the Reader role. This role is read-only. It lets you view everything, but you can't make changes. These three roles are used most often in Azure, and these roles can be used to grant access at the subscription level, the resource group level, or to individual resources. Here we've got an example of using roles in Azure. We've got a user, and this user needs full control of the development resource group. The user does not need to assign permissions to the resources, he just needs full access for day-to-day administration. Because the user will be making changes, the Reader role is no good. Because he doesn't want to assign permissions to other users, the Owner role is not required. The Contributor role fits for the user's requirements nicely, so you would assign the user the Contributor role and scope it to the development resource group, giving the user full control of that group. When using roles in Azure, start off by using the built-in roles. There's dozens of these to choose from. Some grant access to Azure resources, some to Azure AD itself, some to applications like Office 365, but if you have a requirement to grant access, start off by looking for a built-in role that meets those requirements. If you can't find the built-in role, then create a custom role. You can use one of the built-in roles as your template. So if you find a built-in role that gives you 90% of what you need, you can copy that role to create your custom role, and then just change the final few percent. Always follow the principle of least privilege. Make users and groups members of roles that allow them to do their job, but no more. A company has different sets of users, like most organizations, and these different sets of users have different requirements. The company will have to go through a process of identifying each of their user's needs and then mapping those needs to the roles that will grant them access to Azure. The company has got three types of users. They have Azure administrators who are quite high-level administrators that need a lot of control in Azure. They have Azure developers who will be working with projects and they will need full control of a subset of resources. And then they have Azure compliance officers. These compliance officers perform audits, making sure the resources that we deploy are compliant with the various standards that the company is trying to certify against. Your organization will go through a similar project to the company, identifying the different types of administrative access required and choosing appropriate roles to make your administration work.

Chapter 4 How to Implement Azure Access & Governance Tools

In this chapter we're going to take a look at Implementing Azure Access and Governance Tools. We'll first discuss the importance of governance tools in Azure. We'll then take a look at Azure policies and initiatives before moving on to take a look at Azure Blueprint. We will demonstrate both sets of governance tools, and we'll discuss the importance of governance generally. We'll discuss how we can use Azure governance tools to restrict the sets of features that can be used in your subscriptions and how we can use Azure governance tools to enforce sets of security standards. Before we get into the Azure governance tools themselves, let's just take a minute to discuss why we need the governance tools in the first place. We will discuss with our security teams the different security requirements we need for our cloud deployments. The actual governance tools gives a way to enforce those requirements. We will have also discussed the technical requirements we need for our various deployments, and again our governance tools gives a way of enforcing those technical requirements. So instead of allowing engineers to make their own decisions that might impact security, scale, and cost of our deployment, the governance tools gives a way of putting guardrails in place that our different users in Azure must follow. One often overlooked component of governance and compliance in Azure it Azure tags. And because they are often overlooked, they're worth a special mention now. Azure tags are key value pairs that we assign to Azure resources. Tags might identify the department or project that particular Azure resource belongs to or identify the cost center that should be paying for the resource. All resources that you deploy to

Azure should be tagged, but we shouldn't leave it up to the individual to apply any old tag. Instead, organizations should have a tagging policy enforced by Azure policies. This way, the tags applied to our resources in Azure will be consistent. Tags can be used to enforce security requirements, so access to resources will be granted only if certain tags are on the resources, tags can also be used to control costs. We can use Azure Cost Analysis to search resources that have a specific tag, let's say a tag for a particular department or a tag for a particular project, and use that information to build cost reports. We can also put in rules that say that if costs for resources associated with a particular tag go above a particular amount, that we'll be informed and even the automation steps can kick in to close those resources down. We can also use tags when we're deploying software. Our DevOps teams can deploy an application, but on its virtual machines they are tagged in a particular way. Two of the most powerful tools available to us are Azure policies and initiatives. What is Azure Policy? Well, at its heart, Azure Policy is a collection of rules. Each policy we create is assigned to a scope, such as an Azure subscription. By creating a set of rules that the user of that subscription has to then abide by, it will mean the resources they deploy will remain compliant with corporate standards. When using Azure Policy, we create a policy definition, a policy assignment, and policy parameters. When we create Azure policies, they can be used by themselves or they can be used with initiatives. Initiatives are a collection of policies. These policies tend to be grouped together to achieve a larger goal. It is the initiatives then that we assign to a scope, such as a management group, a subscription or resource group. To use initiatives, we create an initiative definition, an initiative assignment, and initiative parameters. To get us started, there are a set of built-in Azure policies that we can use. We have a built-in policy that controls the characteristics of storage accounts, a built-in policy that controls resource types that can be used inside resource groups. One really useful policy is a policy that controls the locations that can be used by your subscription. So if you only want resources deployed to the UK, we can use this policy to make sure that's enforced with a built-in policy that enforces tags and a built-in policy that controls the size of virtual machines to get deployed. So these five, and several more policies, are available to give us a head start when using Azure policies. When working with Azure, think about your teams and think about the resources that they all need to deploy. You'll then create Azure policies so that those resources can be deployed, but nothing else. This will save you money, but also lead to a more secure Azure deployment.

Chapter 5 Azure Blueprints & Security Assistance

Let's now take a look at Azure Blueprints. Azure Blueprints give us an advanced way of orchestrating the deployment of resources. You may have used ARM templates in the past to deploy virtual machines, virtual networks, entire resource groups. Think of Azure Blueprints as a big extension of what resource templates can already do. One of the benefits of using Blueprints is that they maintain a relationship between themselves and the resources that they deployed. If you use a resource template to deploy resources, changing the template later on will have no effect on the deployed resources. If you deploy your Blueprints on the other hand, a change to the Blueprints can affect the deployed resources. Imagine a situation where you've got set of deployed resources and you want to change the roles that associated with those resources. By changing the roles in the Blueprint, it will update those resources for you. Blueprints can include Azure policies and initiatives, as well as artifacts like Azure roles. These can be deployed along with ARM templates to set up your subscriptions or to deploy a set of resources to existing subscriptions. To use Blueprints, we require a Blueprint definition, we publish the Blueprint, and then assign it to a scope. When we create a Blueprint definition, we can provide details of resource groups that we wish to deploy. We could include the Azure resource manager templates that we want to use as part of that deployment, Azure policies to enforce compliance. We can also use Blueprint definitions to assign roles to the resources that Blueprints have deployed. So far, we've used governance tools that allow us to enforce our security and compliance standards on our subscriptions. Azure also has tools that will look at our subscriptions and provide recommendations to us. One of those tools is Azure Advisor, and part of Azure Advisor is Azure Advisor Security Assistance. Azure Advisor Security Assistance integrates with Security Center. Security Center has lots of information from lots of sources. The job of Azure Advisor Security Assistance then, is to filter through all the information and provide best practice security recommendations. Azure Advisor Security Assistance helps prevent, detect, and respond to security threats. You or your team should be using this tool every day to get the latest security recommendations. Configuration of this tool, the amount of information it is gathering, the type of information it is gathering, is controlled through Security Center. It's the results that we're seeing in Azure Advisor Security Assistance. In this demonstration, we're going to work with Azure blueprints before taking a look at Azure Advisor security assistance. Back in Azure portal, I'm in a Blueprints dashboard. If I scroll down here, we're going to create a new blueprint by clicking Create. Like most governance and compliance tools that Azure gives us, we have a choice of where we start from.

We can start from a blank blueprint, or with a set of samples. Again, if I scroll down, we can see some of the sample blueprints that we can choose from.

298

Create blueprint

Other samples

In this example, we're not going to use a sample; we are going to start with a blank blueprint. The first part of creating a blueprint is a very familiar wizard. We need to assign a name to the blueprint and provide a location. The location could be a management group or a subscription.

Create blueprint

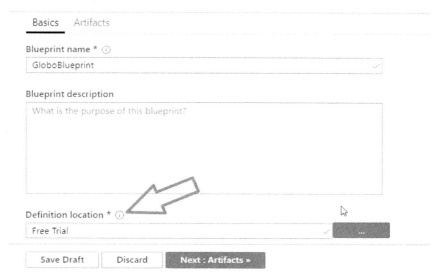

The location you choose dictates where this blueprint can be used. Once we have these basic properties in place, we can click Artifacts. Artifacts control what your blueprint can do.

Let's click Add artifact, and then click the drop-down for Artifact type. Here you can see that we have a choice of four different artifacts that this blueprint can work with; Azure policies, Azure roles, Resource Manager templates, and resource groups.

The first thing I want our blueprint to do is to deploy a resource group, so let's select that. We have to select a name for the artifact, and we can either fill in the properties of this artifact now, or say the properties will be filled in when the blueprint is deployed.

That's the default, and that's what I'll leave it as. So I'll say, add here. Notice how we've got two levels for our blueprint now, subscription and resource group.

So let's add a second artifact, but let's add it to our resource group. Notice the type of artifacts have changed. We can no longer select resource group because you cannot have one resource group inside another. What we can select, though, is role assignment, so let's select that.

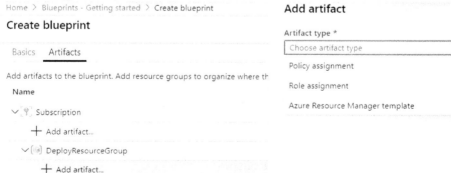

And from the role drop-down, let's choose a role. This time, we will untick the box that says this value should be specified when the blueprint is assigned, and in the Add user, app, or group, we'll select the user. With the role assignment properties filled in, we say Add.

I'm happy with this blueprint, so I want to save the changes. So at the bottom here, we say Save Draft. And it might take a minute, but our blueprint will be saved. We can view our blueprint from the Blueprint definitions section.

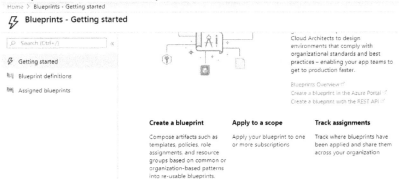

And we can see our blueprint. Draft blueprints cannot be deployed. Blueprints have to be published first. So let's select our blueprint, and at the top left, we can say Publish blueprint. We'll have to provide a version of this blueprint, and then we click Publish.

Publish blueprint

Version * ⓘ

1.0

No previous versions

Change notes ⓘ

Publish   Cancel

It should take no time at all to publish the blueprint. And once we have published it, we can then say Assign blueprint. During the assignment of the blueprint, we can finish off its configuration. So we can choose a location, we can select the version of the blueprint we want to assign, and then as we scroll to the bottom, we can fill in the parameters for the artifacts that we've chosen to deploy.

In our case, a resource group name and location. We don't have the choice of filling the role artifact because we did that when the artifact was added. It'll take a minute to create the blueprint assignment. Once created, we'll see the assignment under Assigned blueprints. Notice the provision section. Right now my blueprint is being deployed. Depending on the size of the blueprint and how much work it's got to do, it could take seconds, minutes, or even hours to deploy your resources. Here we can see my deployment succeeded.

The resource group has been created. If we go inside there and under Access control assignments, we can see that the user has been assigned a contributor role. Back over in Blueprints and Blueprint definitions, we have the option here to edit the blueprint. In artifacts, we'll say add artifacts to the resource group, and for artifact type ,let's choose policy assignment.

Add artifact

And here you can see the Azure policies that we created earlier. So let's choose the require tag Azure policy. Now we've made a change to the blueprint, we say Save Draft, and then we publish the blueprint again, this time with a different version number. Once the draft is published, if we go to Assign blueprint, in the version section we can now see we can assign both version 1.0 and version 1.1.

Location * (i)

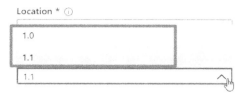

We've seen how we can create blueprints, publish and assign blueprints, and how we can create a new version of blueprints. One more thing to show here, on the right-hand side, you can see the section that says Track assignments.

Let's click Track there. Here we can see our original assignment. If we select that and say Update assignment, through here, we can change the version of the blueprint that's been assigned from version 1.0 to version 1.1. If we scroll down, we can now set a tag for this resource group and say Assign. Here we can see that our change succeeded, and now version 1.1 of our blueprint has been deployed.

↑↓	Version	↑↓	Provisioni...↑↓
	1.1		Succeeded

For the second part of this demonstration, we're going to move away from Azure blueprints and take a look at Azure Advisor security assistance. This is Azure Advisor security assistance.

When you access this tool, it will perform a scan of your subscription, and it's going to make security recommendations. Let's take a look at some of those security recommendations. We can see that I've got 12 recommendations in total. We can see there's 36 security alerts for me to view.

So if we scroll down a bit more, you can see that I've been advised about all sorts of different areas.

High	Vulnerability assessment should be enabled on your SQL servers	1 SQL server
Medium	Management ports should be closed on your virtual machines	1 Virtual machine
Low	Access to storage accounts with firewall and virtual network configurations should be restricted (Preview)	2 Storage Accounts
Low	Diagnostic logs in Logic Apps should be enabled	2 Workflows
Low	Auditing on SQL server should be enabled	1 SQL server auditing setting

The idea here, then, is that we would select one of these recommendations, view the more detailed information about that recommendation, and then decide whether we want to act on the recommendation or not.

MFA should be enabled on accounts with owner permissions on your subscription

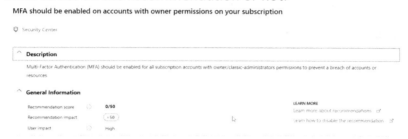

For each recommendation, you should find a description, general information, and then, if you're lucky, remediation steps, which will give you information on how you can remediate this particular issue. We should be using security assistance every day, as our security parts change as resources are deployed and removed from our subscriptions. In summary, you have learned the importance of the Azure governance tools. You learned how to use Azure policies, initiatives and blueprints, and you learned the benefit of regularly using Azure Advisor security assistance. Next, we're going to take a look at securing Azure virtual networks.

Chapter 6 Securing Azure Virtual Networks using NSGs

In this chapter we'll take a look at Securing Azure Virtual Networks. You will learn about network security groups and their use for securing Azure Virtual Networks. We'll demonstrate network security groups before taking a look at a feature called application security group and how we can use application security groups to simplify the management of network security. We'll finish off by demonstrating application security groups. To help us relate network security groups to your corporate network. We will discuss a sample company's security group requirements. We'll also highlight areas where security groups can help secure your deployments, and hopefully by the end you'll have a good understanding of where network security groups and application security groups can help you. One of the key recommendations when planning your network security is to plan your security based around defense in depth. This means planning multiple layers of security so that if one layer is breached, other layers are still there to protect you. In Azure, defense in depth starts with physical security. This is managed by Microsoft. They will protect their physical data centers and the physical infrastructure inside those data centers. Another layer of your defense in depth is Identity and Access Control. This is managed by you by working with products like Azure AD and within a great suite of products like Active Directory Domain Services and Active Directory Federation Services. At the perimeter of your virtual networks in Azure, standard distributed denial-of-service protection is enabled by default. You can choose to enable additional layers of DDoS protection if you feel your organization would benefit from the additional monitoring and security that those additional layers will provide. To protect our Azure Virtual Networks and applications, we can deploy network security groups, firewalls, and gateways to offer protection from layer 4 to layer 7 of the OSI model. To protect your compute and data, we would implement the appropriate operating system security and access controls and encryption. A typical deployment integer would implement all of these layers of protection, defense in depth. So let's start off by looking at network security groups then. Fundamentally, network security groups filter traffic. Each network security group has an inbound list and an outbound list. Inbound traffic is filtered through the inbound list and is either allowed or denied, outbound traffic filtered by the outbound list. Each list contains a series of rules, and each rule has a number, a private number with rule 100 having the highest priority and rule 4096 having the lowest priority. As you create rules in each inbound and outbound list, you must get the order right or you might end up with behavior that you didn't expect. Each network security group we create can be attached to subnets on network cards, and each network security group can be linked to multiple resources so we can reuse network security groups. Network security groups are stateful. That means if I allow traffic inbound, the return traffic will be allowed outbound automatically, and vice versa. If I allow certain traffic outbound, the return traffic will be allowed inbound. This makes network security groups relatively straightforward to administer. There are a lot of network security group properties, but they include a name for the network security group, a priority number, the source and destination of the traffic that we're trying to filter, the protocol we're trying to filter, so TCP, UDP, etc. We include a direction for each rule that we create, so inbound to outbound. We include a port range that rules should monitor for, and this could be an individual port or a set of ports. And finally, an action, either allow or deny. So for each rule that we create, we can either allow traffic or explicitly deny it. Imagine that we've got an Azure Virtual Network, and this network contains two subnets, Subject 1 and Subnet 2, and we can see that Subnet 1 contains two servers and Subnet 2 a single server named Server 3. We will use network security groups to control the flow of traffic inbound and outbound to these subnets and servers. If each subnet requires the same set of rules, then they will use a single network security group. We've got a network security group called NSG1, we created that group and associate it with both subnets. And as traffic flows into those subnets, it will be assessed by the inbound rules of NSG1. Server 2 needs slightly different rules, so I can create another network security group called NSG2, attach that to Server 2's network interface, and NSG2, assess its traffic inbound and outbound for that server. We can have granularity of access using different layers of network security groups.

Chapter 7 Azure Application Security Groups

Now we know about network security groups. Let's have a look at another feature that'll make it easier to work with them, application security groups. Network security groups are a great feature, but they can become complex to manage. Each network security group can contain lots of rules, and the more rules they have, the more complex they are to manage. Network security groups can also be difficult to maintain. The more resources we add to our virtual networks, the more we might have to go back and edit network security groups and sometimes several layers of network security groups at that. Anything we can do to simplify the management of network security groups, then, is a good thing and there are several things we can do. First of all, we can use service tags. Service tags are given to us by Azure. Service tags represent services like Azure load balancer, Azure API management, and locations like the internet. In general, if you want to allow strict default traffic, we can use service tags. We can also make use of default security rules. Default security rules allow common outbound traffic such as internet traffic. They also allow traffic from subnet to subnet and traffic from common services like the Azure load balancer. At the same time, the default security rules restrict the flow of inbound traffic. A third option for simplifying network security groups is to make use of application security groups. Application security groups tend to represent a tier of your application. And if we use them correctly, will mean that network security groups are configured once and do not have to be readjusted every time we add a new subnet or set of servers. So what are application security groups? Well, they allow us to reference a group of resources such as web servers, application servers, or database servers. They can be used as even a source or destination of traffic. They do not replace network security groups. They enhance them. So network security groups are still required. When working with application security groups, we create the application security group, we link the application security group to a resource, we then use the application security group when working with network security groups. Let's say that we have an example of an Azure virtual network with two subnets. If we want to restrict access to these subnets, we can create a network security group and associate it with both subnets. When we create new subnets, we can go back to the network security group and adjust it to include the association with our new subnets. Network security group 1 now is associated with subnets 1, 2, 3, and 4. This generally isn't a problem because we're not adding new subnets every day, but resources are different. We've got two virtual machines, and we want to protect access to these virtual machines by using network security group. As we create the machines, we create a network security group called NSG2, and we associate it with the two virtual machines. These virtual machines are part of our web tier. So as I add more resources in our web tier across a range of subnets, we have to keep constantly going back and adjusting network security group 2. Resources like virtual machines will change much more frequently than subnets will. The more we change the virtual machines across these different subnets, the more we might have to change the network security group. So instead of associating network security group 2 with the constantly changing network interface cards of our resources, we're going to use application security groups. In another example, we've got a fore of nets, and we have an NSG called NSG1. And we create an application security group called web tier that's used by the network security group to allow the appropriate traffic inbound and outbound. With that network security group in place, we just add resources. As we add resources, we just make sure they use the appropriate application security group reference. There's no need to go back to the NSG every time we add a new set of resources. Have a think about your requirements. You might be deploying multi-tier applications. In that case, each tier would get its own application security group. Resources in your DMZ would also have their own application security group, and as we build in automation pipelines to our deployment, the application security group will be part of that pipeline. So as I'm deploying new virtual machines, new containers, we make sure they include a reference to the appropriate application security group.

Chapter 8 Azure Firewall Basics

In this chapter, we will be taking a look at Azure firewalls and user defined routes. We'll first take a look at Azure Firewall and Azure's distributed denial of service protection. We will go on to discuss user defined routes and how user defined routes can help us route traffic through our security appliances. We will learn about the different firewall protection options available to us. Understanding of the different firewall options available to you will lead to a more secure Azure deployment and a more cost effective Azure deployment. Let's begin with Azure Firewall and DDoS. What is Azure Firewall? Well, Azure Firewall is a stateful firewall service provided by Azure. It's a virtual appliance configured at the virtual network level. It protects access to your virtual networks and is a highly available solution. Features of Azure Firewall include advanced threat intelligence, so the firewall service can learn about the traffic going in and out of your network to determine which traffic is good or bad. It supports both outbound and inbound NAT, reducing our reliance on public IP addresses. Azure Firewall integrates with Azure Monitor for all our porting needs. It includes support for network traffic filtering rules so that we can tightly control the traffic flowing through Azure Firewall, and it's almost unlimited in scale. If we want to support a small deployment of just a few services or hundreds or thousands of instances, Azure Firewall will scale. Imagine that we've got an Azure Firewall in place. We've got resource subnets and a separate subnet for Azure Firewall. The Azure Firewall will have a public IP address, and inbound traffic will be directed towards the Azure Firewall service. We'll then have NAT rules and intelligent protection looking at all that traffic that's coming in and then passing the good traffic towards our back-end resources. Azure Firewall works hand in hand with Azure DDoS protection. Azure DDos protection provides DDoS mitigation for networks and applications. It's always on as a service. So right now if you're using Azure, you're using Azure DDoS protection. It provides protection all the way up to the application layer. And like Azure Firewall, integrates Azure Monitor for reporting services. Features offered by Azure DDoS protection include multi-layered support, so protection from layer 4 attacks up to layer 7 attacks, attack analytics, ao we can get reports on attacks in progress, as well as post attack reports. Like the firewall service, we have scale and elasticity, so this service will go ahead and try and absorb the attacks that are in progress. Azure DDoS protection also provides protection against unplanned costs. If our service is of scale because of a DDoS attack, then those costs can be recouped. We do need to be aware that Azure DDoS comes in two different service tiers, basic and standard. It is the basic service that's always on for your account. The basic service offers availability guarantees, and it's backed by an SLA, and crucially, is free. The standards here offers everything the basic tier offers, but that includes features like real-time metrics that will monitor when an attack in progress, post-attack reports so you can see details of attacks that have happened and where they came from and what the results were. The standards here also offer live support so you can have contact with DDoS experts at Azure during the attack to help you fight against it. The standards here also integrates with your SIEM systems, but the standard tier is not free. You are charged a monthly fee and a fee based on the usage of the feature of the standard tier. Not everyone will need Azure Firewall or the standard DDoS tier. So think about your network that you have now and think about the networks you'll deploy in the cloud. If you use network firewalls now, you'll probably need Azure

Firewall in the cloud. If you decide that you need Azure Firewall, you'll have to go through a planning phase. During this planning phase, you will figure out what rules will need to be configured in Azure Firewall. As we said a moment ago, the basic tier is free, but you have to ask yourself, do you need that standard tier? As well as Azure Firewall and Azure DDoS protection, you can also deploy virtual appliances for the marketplace. These virtual appliances can add additional protection or be used in place of features like Azure Firewall.

Chapter 9 Azure User Defined Routes

When working with Azure firewall or third-party virtual appliances, you have to think about how traffic is routed around your virtual networks. There may be a requirement to alter the default routing, so that traffic flows through your firewall or virtual appliance you are deploying. And that's where user defined routes come in. When traffic flows around your Azure Virtual networks, it is governed by a set of system routes. These system routes were enabled by default. System routes make sure that resources deployed to different subnets can communicate with each other and the resources deployed to your subnets can connect out to the internet. User defined routes allow us to override Azure's default system routes. They're most often used when we want to fill our outbound traffic through a virtual appliance. Imagine that we got three subnets, and I've got virtual machines deployed to Subnet 1 and Subnet 2. Using the system routes, if traffic wants to leave the internet, traffic rerouted directly from Subnet 1 to the internet and direct them to Subnet 2 to the internet. But let's say I want to deploy a virtual appliance to Subnet 3. I want all traffic going out to the internet to be filtered through that virtual appliance. This is where user defined routes come in. Or we've got the same three subnets, but now I've introduced user defined routes. Can we see how they user defined routes are now filtering the outbound traffic towards our virtual clients first? This virtual appliance can inspect the traffic. It may even alter the traffic before allowing that traffic outbound to the internet. Subnet 3 itself is governed by the system routes for internet access. So using user defined routes, we have a lot of control over the flow of traffic between our subnets and towards the internet. We've got a lot of Azure security options available to us. Let's see if we can try and differentiate between a few of them. So far, we've discussed Azure Firewall and Azure DDoS protection. So hopefully we've got an idea of where those two fit. We also have a feature called Azure Web Application Firewall. Azure Web Application Firewall is designed to publish your applications to the outside world, whether they're in Azure or on-premises, and lures bound traffic towards them. We've discussed network security groups previously, so hopefully we have a good idea of where network security groups fit into our security. We also have a feature called forced tunneling. Forced tunneling allows the control of flow of internet-bound traffic. So instead of traffic being routed directly into that, internet-bound traffic is sent on-premises first where your on-premises security monitoring tools can assess that traffic and decide what is allowed or not. Finally, you can deploy any marketplace devices available. So if you already have an existing skill set on-premises and you want to take advantage of licenses that you already own, you might find a marketplace device that better suits your needs. To help determine when we need to use these six different types of security options, think about these three scenarios. In scenario one, you want to control the flow of internet traffic. You wish to control the flow of traffic heading to the internet so that it can be inspected at layer 7. In scenario two, you've got an Azure-hosted SQL Server. Only traffic from your Azure subnets should be allowed to access the Azure SQL Server. In the final scenario, all internet-bound traffic that's generated by your application servers must be routed through HQ. So take a minute, think about these three scenarios, and decide which of the previous six security solutions would you implement to satisfy the needs of each scenario. There can be a variety of answers here. If I was asked this question, for scenario one, I would say we deploy user defined routes. The user defined routes will allow us to control the flow of traffic, and then would even deploy Azure Firewall or a marketplace device to filter that traffic. For scenario two, well, it's network security groups. Network security groups will allow us to control which traffic is allowed to communicate with those SQL Servers by restricting the source of traffic that those SQL Servers will accept. And for scenario three, forced tunneling. If we want to force internet-bound traffic to HQ, forced tunneling is what we need.

Chapter 10 Azure Information Protection & Security Monitoring Tools

In this chapter we're going to be working with Azure Security and Reporting Tools. We're first going to introduce you to Azure Information Protection. We're then going to discuss Azure Monitor and Service Health, and we're going to introduce you to Azure Key Vault. We're then going to introduce you to Azure Sentinel before introducing you to and demonstrating Azure Security Center. By the end, you'll understand the core monitoring tools available in Azure, and you will understand the benefits of these tools to your organization. Let's start off then with Azure Information Protection and security monitoring tools. Azure Information Protection is a pretty useful tool. We use Azure Information Protection to classify documents and emails. Azure gives us some built-in classifications that we can use, and you and the stakeholders in your organization will create classifications relevant for you. Classifications are labels that are attached to documents Think of security levels like open, secret, top-secret, these can all be classifications that your company uses. Each classification can be added as a label to a document. Once documents are labeled, they can be protected. This protection comes in the form of encryption, and in order to gain access to the documents in the future, you must be assigned the appropriate rights. These labels go beyond standard permissions because these labels will stay with the document no matter where it is, whether that document is on your SharePoint service in Azure Storage, or even if that document is downloaded onto removable media, the labels and its protection stay with the document. Azure Information Protection labels can be applied automatically, can be applied manually, and we can

320

recommend the use of different labels to our users based on the content that they are creating. There are two sides to Azure Information Protection. First of all, the classification of documents. These classifications come in the form of metadata that can be attached to the header or added as watermarks to the documents you're trying to protect. Once classified, then the documents can be protected. Azure uses Azure Rights Management to encrypt the documents using Rights Management templates. Then when a user wants to again access to a document, they can apply for a certificate that will grant them the appropriate rights. This process tends to be automatic and performed by the applications that the user is using. Ideally, documents and emails will be classified when they're created. But you'll probably have a load of existing documents, even Azure or on-premise that need to be protected. For on-premise data stores, you can use Azure Information Protection scanner to scan those data stores and apply labels, and then those documents can be protected. For cloud-based data stores, we can use Microsoft Cloud App Security. Just like Azure Information Protection scanner, this tool will scan your cloud stores, classify documents so we can apply protection to them. Azure gives us a lot of security and reporting tools. Three tools that are commonly used include Azure Monitor to collect and analyze metric information, both on-premise and in Azure, Azure Service Health that we can use to see the health status of the Azure services, and Azure Advanced Threat Protection that can be used to detect and investigate attacks against our users. Let's chat about these three tools in a bit more detail. Azure Monitor is used to collect, analyze, and act on telemetry. It acts as a central point where resources both in Azure and on-premise can report information. We can use the information reporting to troubleshoot issues and run in performance. There were two types of data collected by Azure Monitor, metric information from services that we've deployed and logs from services we've deployed. And again, these metrics and logs coming from both Azure deployed resources and on-premise. Azure Service Health is a service that's automatically provided to us by Azure. It notifies us about the status of Azure services around the globe. Through Azure Service Health, we can see the reports of incidents that have occurred, such as downtime to services and downtime to regions and availability zones, and planned maintenance that might affect the services and resources that we're consuming in Azure. Azure Service Health offers personalized dashboards that you can use to view the health status of services that are relevant for you and your organization, configurable alerts so you don't have to be sat in front of a dashboard when a situation occurs. Instead, you can receive emails that will alert you to the changing of a service's status, and guidance and support that will help you navigate through a service issue. Azure Advanced Threat Protection is all about your users. It can be used to monitor and analyze user activity, it's used to identify suspicious activity events that you can then try and protect against. Azure Advanced Threat Protection works with both Azure and your on-premises Active Directory forests. It can be used to identify reconnaissance attacks, compromised credentials, lateral movements, when an attacker gains access to your network and then slowly moves through your network looking for vulnerable systems, and domain dominance where legitimate credentials have been used to gain access to your forest to perform malicious activity.

Chapter 11 Azure Key Vault Basics

A long time ago, it took a lot of effort to encrypt and, especially, decrypt information. Today, most secure operations like that is done in specialist hardware. So particularly in the cloud, we attempt to encrypt everything. The conversation today, then, is about secrets management. Where do we keep the secrets that are used to perform our encryption? Where do we keep the secrets that are used to access Azure secure resources? Azure Key Vault is a service we can use to protect our secrets. Secrets come in many forms like certificates, pre-shared keys, connection strings, passwords, and it's the secure management of the secrets that can be an issue for IT. How do we control access to things like passwords, API keys, and of secrets? Have a little think. How do you control access to passwords and API keys right now? Are they stored securely? How do you create and control encryption keys? Where are they stored and who has access to them? And how do you provision, manage, and deploy digital certificates? You need to answer these questions, and your answer should involve some form of secure storage for your secrets, date audited, and only select people and applications have access to it. And this is where Azure Key Vault comes in. Azure Key Vault can be used to centralize the storage of application secrets. Azure Key Vault uses hardware. It uses hardware security modules. These hardware security modules have been validated to support the latest Federal Information Processing Standards. That means if you want secret storage that can be used while you're working on government contracts, Key Vault can work for you. When using Azure Key Vault, we can enable logging to monitor how and when our secrets are being used. And crucially, Azure Key Vault can just centralize administration of all our secrets. Azure has some recommendations for us when we're using Key Vault. Firstly, we should use a separate Key Vault for each application that requires centralized key management. This makes it easier for us to control access to sets of keys and secrets on an application-by-application basis. We should also make sure that we take regular backups of all our Key Vault That way, if something goes horribly wrong, we can restore from those backups. We should turn on logging and set up alerts to inform us when certain events occur, and we should also enable soft delete and purge protection. This makes it even easier for us to recover secrets if they've been accidentally deleted and protects the Key Vaults themselves from accidental deletion.

Chapter 12 Azure Security Center Basics

Now, we're going to take a look at Azure Security Center and Azure Sentinel. Security is always a challenge, but in the cloud, it's even more of a challenge than on-premise. In part, that's because services in the cloud changed rapidly. How do we know that changes to Azure services meet our security requirements? As security tools improve, attacks are becoming more sophisticated. But how do we keep up to date with new threats? We also have to contend with a skills shortage. We have lots of information available to us in the cloud, but do we have all the stuff we need to digest and act upon that information? Azure Security Center is designed with these challenges in mind. If you are using Platform as a Service services in Azure, like Azure Web Apps, then Azure Security Center is already working for you, monitoring those services and reporting on their security status. There's no need for you to do anything for those services. For non-Azure services, like operating systems you deploy in the cloud, we can deploy monitoring agents to gather security information. As well as monitoring for security threats, Azure Security Center also reports our compliance status against certain standards. It provides continuous assessment of existing and new services that we deploy. It also provides threat protection for both infrastructure and Platforms as a Service services. One of the newer security services provided by Azure is Azure Sentinel. Azure Sentinel is both a cloud-native security information and event management system and a Security Orchestration, Automated, and Response system, so both a SIEM and SOAR solution. Azure Sentinel offers a single solution for collecting data at cloud scale. It can then take that data and help detect previously undetected threats. Azure Sentinel looks for threats using artificial intelligence. It allows us to respond to incidents rapidly, much quicker than traditional monitoring tools would have highlighted the threat. With Azure Sentinel, you connect to your security sources using data connectors. These sources can be storage, virtual machines, security appliances that we want to collect information from. We can then analyze the data collected using Azure Monitor Workbooks and Analytics Workspaces. These are very powerful tools that allow us to search for and display information that's relevant for us. We could then take the information we've gathered and use that to trigger security automation using Orchestration Playbooks. Playbooks are an extension of Azure Logic Apps. Logic Apps are a serverless workflow service that allow us to automate a series of steps. In this example, perhaps a series of steps in response to a security threat that Azure Sentinel detected. With Azure Sentinel, we could perform deep investigation and hunting. This allows us to discover isolated pieces of information that by themselves might seem innocuous, but when brought together, help us discover a security threat.

Chapter 13 Azure Service Trust & Compliance

In this chapter we'll be taking a look at Azure compliance and data protection standards. We will first discuss some of the common industry and compliance standards that Azure supports and your company might be trying to achieve. We'll discuss Microsoft's privacy statement and what that statement means to you and your organization. We'll introduce Azure's Service Trust Portal, and we'll also discuss Azure special regions as well. Understanding compliance will lead to secure Azure deployments, save your company money, and help win contracts you may otherwise have lost. So we'll start off by talking about some of the industry compliance standards that Azure supports. A lot of us work in industries where some form of regulatory compliance is required. Regulatory compliance is the process of ensuring that you follow the standards or laws laid out by a governing body. As a company, we'll employ people and develop processes to help detect and prevent violations of our security regulation requirements. Compliance monitoring can be complex, particularly in today's hybrid world where we have both on-premise and cloud systems to manage. Azure provides several tools to help us assess and maintain our compliance posture. There are lots of compliance standards out there that you might have to adhere to. Here we've got a selection of some of the most common standards. First of all HIPPA, the Health Insurance Portability and Accountability Act. HIPPA is a US standard that lays out data privacy and security provisioning for safeguarding medical information. We have PCI, the Payment Card Industry Standard. PCI lays out standards for securing the handling of credit cards. In the EU, we have GDPR, General Data Protection Regulation. This is an EU standard for data protection and privacy. FedRAMP is the Federal Risk and Authorization Management Program and is an information security standard used by the US government. Any organization working with the US government at any level would have to adhere to FedRAMP. We then have standards laid out by the International Standards Organization, such as ISO 27001, which is part of their information security standard. These five are just examples. There are many more standards that you might have to adhere to. And although we will have to keep our own proofs and documentation proving that we're adhering to these standards, Azure gives a series of tools that we can use to measure our Azure-deployed services against these and many more. Azure supports more than 90 global compliance standards. They provide documentation about their services and which standards their services are certified against. And Azure gives guidance on what areas of these standards are our responsibility and which areas are theirs. Azure supports over 35 industry-specific offerings with documentation to support the rollout and management of compliance features. If our Azure subscriptions have to be deployed to support a particular standard we can use Azure Blueprints to deploy a complete environment configured to our compliance needs. As well as providing tools that allows us to honor our compliance posture, Azure itself is certified against all the standards that it supports. And Azure offers access to third-party reports from orders that gives us proof of their compliance. One powerful compliance tool that we outlined in module 7 is Azure Security Center. As part of Security Center, we can see our current compliance posture measured against some of the most common standards like GDPR and PCI. One of the most important tools for modeling your compliance posture and for viewing information of Azure's compliance status is Azure Service Trust Portal and

Service Trust Center. The Azure Service Trust Portal is probably the first tool you will use on your compliance journey. In this portal you will find details of Microsoft's implementation of controls and processes against Azure and other Microsoft products. Although anyone can access the portal, if you log in as an authenticated user you'll get access to information not visible to everyone. When you log in you need to log in with a Microsoft cloud service account. This could be any user in Azure Active Directory with the correct delegated permissions. In the portal you will find Compliance Manager. This is your section of the portal where you can document the steps you are taking to become compliant against certain standards. You'll find trust documents. These include Microsoft security information, as well as design information that will help you on your compliance journey. You will find compliance information specific to different industries and regions, as well as links to Microsoft's general trust center. You will also find My Library. This is where you can save and access your compliance documents so all your compliance information is in one place. Microsoft Trust Center is accessed through the Trust Portal. Through Trust Center you can view security, privacy, and compliance information, access to Microsoft product compliance information, and you'll find compliance tools such as compliance score, audit reports, and data protection resources. So let's take a look at the Service Trust Portal and Microsoft Trust Center.

Chapter 14 How to use Azure Trust Center & Compliance Manager

In this demonstration, we're going to be working with Azure Compliance Manager and the Azure Service Trust Portal. This is the Service Trust Portal.

Notice the URL, servicetrust.microsoft.com, and the fact that I'm logged in. I've logged in with a user account that's been assigned the compliance role in Azure AD. Through this portal then, we can access Service Trust, Compliance Manager, Trust Documents, and if we click on the drop-down next to More, we can see links, amongst other things, Industries and Region-specific compliance information, Trust Center, and My Library.

If we scroll down on this first page, here we can see links to independent Audit Reports for Microsoft Cloud Services. These provide information about Microsoft's compliance status. Notice here FedRAMP, ISO 27001, and the link where you can View all Audit Reports. Scroll down a bit further, and we get to Documents and Resources.

Through here, we can see the results of penetration tests and security assessments carried out by third parties. We can see information on Azure Blueprints that we can use to rule out compliant subscriptions, as well as access to documentation, including White Papers, FAQs, and Compliance Guides. Let's go back up to the top of this page, and we'll select Compliance Manager.

Compliance Manager Tour

Compliance Manager includes the following capabilities:

At-a-glance summary of the shared responsibility model reflecting both Microsoft's and your organization's data protection and compliance posture for standards and regulations such as ISO 27001:2013, NIST 800-53, the Health Insurance Portability and Accountability Act (HIPAA), the European Union General Data Protection Regulation (GDPR) and others.

Risk assessment workflow and management tools that provide task assignment and verification to help Governance, Risk & Compliance teams and IT departments work together to streamline internal compliance activities.

Intelligent tracking that understands common and similar compliance activities across multiple standards and regulations to reduce your organization's costs and efforts from regulation to audit by applying a single activity to multiple Assessments or controls.

If you're not logged in with your proper credentials, you'll get an error when you try to access Compliance Manager. If you're not familiar with Compliance Manager, you can take a tour. If you are, you can scroll down and get started. Compliance Manager is all about assessing your deployments against certain standards.

So here you can see I'm measuring my Office 365 deployment against GDPR and NIST, I'm measuring Azure against ISO 27001, as well as GDPR, FedRAMP, and the UKNHS standard.

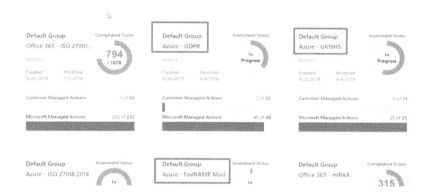

If I select Azure GDPR, at the top here, we could see Assessed Controls, and mine indicates that I'm 36% Assessed, and that would be 47 out of 130 controls.

And the statement of this assessment is In Progress. Let's scroll down and see a few more details about the assessment. We should see three sections, Azure in-Scope Cloud Services, Microsoft Managed Controls, and Custom Managed Controls.

Let's view the Azure in-Scope Cloud Services. There's a long list here.

- API Management
- App Service (API Apps, Logic Apps, Mobile Apps, Web Apps)
- Application Gateway
- Application Insights
- Automation
- Azure Active Directory
- Azure Container Service
- Azure Cosmos DB (formerly DocumentDB)
- Azure DevTest Labs
- Azure DNS
- Azure Information Protection (including Azure Rights Management)
- Azure Machine Learning Studio
- Azure Resource Manager
- Backup
- Batch
- BizTalk Services
- Cloud Services

- Data Catalog
- Data Factory
- Data Lake Analytics
- Data Lake Store
- Event Hubs
- Express Route
- Functions
- HDInsight
- Import/Export
- IoT Hub
- Key Vault
- Load Balancer
- Log Analytics (formerly Operational Insights)
- Media Services
- Microsoft Azure Portal
- Multi-Factor Authentication
- Notification Hubs
- Power BI Embedded

- Redis Cache
- Scheduler
- Security Center
- Service Bus
- Service Fabric
- Site Recovery
- SQL Data Warehouse
- SQL Database
- SQL Server Stretch Database
- Storage
- StorSimple
- Stream Analytics
- Traffic Manager
- Virtual Machine Scale Sets
- Virtual Machines
- Virtual Network
- Visual Studio Team Services
- VPN Gateway

Each one of these services then can be secured against the GDPR standard. You should be able to see a similar list for each of the standards that Compliance Manager supports. Just because of service is on this list, it doesn't mean it's fully compliant. To be fully compliant with standard, we have to break down the responsibility between ourselves and Microsoft. If I minimize this list, we have Microsoft Managed Controls, these have passed the standards that Microsoft is responsible for, and we have Custom Managed Controls, these have passed the standards that you're responsible for implementing.

Azure in-Scope Cloud Services

Microsoft Managed Controls

Conditions for collection and processing	4/5 Assessed
Personal data sharing, transfer, and disclosure	7/7 Assessed
Privacy by design and by default	3/3 Assessed
Rights of individuals	1/1 Assessed
Security	30/32 Assessed

If we view the Microsoft Managed Controls, here we can see a number of assessments in different categories and the number of assessments that have been assessed.

334

If we take a look at Rights of individuals, for example, this contains one control detailed on the left-hand side, we can see a Test date, and the fact that this was tested by a third-party independent auditor. Crucially, we can see the Test result. So Microsoft passed this test. You will be affined the independent audit, which provides proof that Microsoft passed this control. Let's collapse the Microsoft controls, and now take a look of the Customer Managed Controls.

These controls are your responsibility. In order to be GDPR compliant, you would have to make sure that all of these controls are enforced. Let's take a look Right of individuals, for example. So there are 11 controls as part of this section, and none of them have been assessed.

As an organization then, it would be up to you to research the relevant articles and put procedures in place to enforce the article controls ready for assessment. In this section, I can assign this control to an individual by using Assign option. I can also implement status information, and we can provide a date for status changes. Using Manage Documents, we can upload documents that are relevant for this article, that perhaps outline the steps we have taken to fulfill this article. We can also provide dates of tests that have been run to assess adherence to these controls and the results of those tests. Ideally, your tests would also be run by a third-party independent auditor. What Compliance Manager is given us then is a way to visualize our readiness for assessment. Instead of you having to fight your way through all the different controls for a particular standard, and then document your adherence to those controls in a third-party tool, we have all the information we need here in one place. Let's go back to the Service Trust Portal.

If you're trying to find the Microsoft Audit Reports, you can find that from the Trust Documents section, along with data-protected information and information on Azure

336

Security and Compliance Blueprints. If we select More, one useful section is Resources.

Through here, we could see information about Microsoft's Global Datacenters, access Frequently Asked Questions, and access the Security and Compliance Center. The Security and Compliance Center offers more general information around security and compliance, including security information on Office 365. If we select More again, and select My Library, it's in My Library where you could save reports, as well as white papers and other resources that will help you document your compliance posture.

There's one other website that I want to show you in this demo. This website, privacy.microsoft.com, gives us access to Microsoft's Privacy Statement. Here we can find details on the type of personal data Microsoft collects about you.

It gives information on how Microsoft uses that personal data, reasons why they might share your personal data, and how we can access and control our personal data. This statement was last updated in January 2020, and it's well worth you getting to know this statement, so you and your organization have a good idea of how your personal data will be used by Microsoft. As this statement gets updated, it's also somewhere that you should visit on a regular basis.

Chapter 15 Azure Special Regions

When a deployment's launched in Azure, we deploy to Azure regions. Most regions are equal, but some are special. In this section, we're going to cover Azure special regions. Azure services are deployed to multiple data centers around the world. For ease of management, high availability, and disaster recovery, these data centers are grouped into regions such as West US and UK South. You can deploy your resources to a region that matches your requirements. Requirements are based on cost. Some regions are cheaper than others. You might choose regions that are closest to your customer base all because the services that you want are only available in certain regions. Azure special regions exist for compliance and legal reasons. These regions are not generally available, and you have to apply to Microsoft if you want to use one of these special regions. Currently, there are three categories of special regions. US Gov regions support US government agencies. This includes US Gov Virginia and US Gov Iowa. We have the China special regions. This includes China East, China North. The China regions are managed in partnership with 21Vianet. We also have the Germany regions, Germany Central and German Northeast. These regions are managed for a data trustee model. This model means that data in the Germany regions will reside in Germany only and be compliant with German data laws. You must request access to Azure special regions if you want to deploy resources to them. The US Gov regions are for additional compliance certifications such as FedRAMP and DISA Level 5 DoD approval. So if you're working on a federal, state, or local US government project and you need to adhere to the standards, you could apply for access to the US Gov region. Regarding the China regions, it's worth pointing out that Microsoft does not directly maintain these data centers. They are owned in partnership with 21Vianet. China has some very specific rules about how data enters and leaves the China regions, and by partnering with a Chinese organization to manage these data centers, Azure could adhere to these rules. Germany has very specific rules about data residency. To conform with these rules, all data in the Germany region stays under the control of T-Systems. T-Systems is a company owned by Deutsche Telekom.

Chapter 16 Azure Compliance Resources

In this chapter, we're going to be discussing Azure compliance resources. The goal is to introduce additional compliance material that Microsoft makes available online. One of Microsoft's building blocks for their online services is Trusted Cloud. Trusted Cloud is built on a series of foundations, including security, privacy, and compliance. Building on the security foundation, Azure helps keep our customer data secure. Azure provides network and infrastructure security, data encryption, strong authentication and authorization, as well as tools that allow us to audit access to Azure subscriptions so that we can keep track of who is accessing data. One of the principles of the Privacy Foundation is that Azure customers own and control their own data. We get to decide the regions that our data is stored in, we have the ability to access our data from any location at any time, our data is encrypted both at rest and in transit, and there's even rules of how Microsoft will dispose of our data if we cancel our subscriptions. To help us satisfy compliance, Microsoft currently supports integration with over 90 international compliance standards. These include global, national, and industry-specific compliance standards that we can certify against. To help you build secure, compliant architectures in Azure, you should spend time with the Microsoft Cloud Adoption Framework. This framework outlines cloud adoption best practices that have been brought together from Microsoft employees, partners, and customers. The guidance laid out in the Cloud Adoption Framework is not only for IT decisionmakers, but also for business leaders. The Cloud Adoption Framework helps you define a business strategy for cloud adoption. It provides guidance on best practiced governance of Microsoft Cloud

Services. So if you're starting out on your Microsoft Cloud journey, the Cloud Adoption Framework should be one of the first resources that you use. It will keep us away from bad practices and will help all parts of the business, both technical and nontechnical, understand why the cloud is right for them and the best way to adopt cloud services for each department's particular requirements. If you are responsible for compliance for your organization, then I encourage you to seek out the Azure compliance documentation. This documentation is your starting point for learning about compliance in Azure. The Azure compliance documentation is organized into both regional and global compliance offerings, as well as several industry-specific offerings. These include compliance standards aimed at financial services, the automotive industry, media, and energy companies. By using the Azure compliance documentation, you can find out how Microsoft can help you conform to compliance standards such as GDPR, HIPAA, and FedRAMP to name just three of over 90 compliance offerings that Microsoft Online Services supports today. Most organizations are keen to keep personal information private, so understanding what personal information Microsoft collections from us and how it uses that information is very important. The Microsoft Privacy Statement explains how Microsoft collects and processes personal data and for what purposes that personal data is collected. The privacy statement includes product-specific information. This means we can identify the type of personal information that each individual product is collecting from us. This helps understand what information might be exposed when we're using individual products. Microsoft collects and uses our personal data for things like improving and developing products, personalizing products and making recommendations, advertising and marketing, and performance analysis and research. You can find the Microsoft Privacy Statement online, and it's definitely something you and your team should seek out so you can have a clear understanding of what personal information each Microsoft Service collects and how it uses that data. When you start to use any Microsoft online service, such as Microsoft Azure, Microsoft 365 or Microsoft Dynamics, you are agreeing to a set of Microsoft terms and conditions. These terms and conditions are laid out in agreements such as the Microsoft Online Subscription Agreement. Amongst other things, this agreement lays out acceptable use and unacceptable use of Microsoft Online Services. This agreement is an agreement between Microsoft and the organization you're representing or Microsoft knew if you didn't specify an organization when you signed up to an online service like Azure. Depending on the industry you're in or the region you're in, there may be other subscription agreements that you're also agreeing to when you first sign up for Microsoft services. So again, a bit like the privacy statement, seek them out and make sure you're happy with the terms of agreement before you start consuming Microsoft Online Services. Another useful piece of documentation is the Online Service Terms. These lay out the terms by which each Microsoft Online product is offered. It's through the Online Service Terms that you find the licensing agreements for each of Microsoft's online services. One addendum to the Online Service Terms is the Online Service Data Protection Addendum. This addendum lays out how data is protected, what Microsoft's responsibilities are for data protection, and what the customer's responsibilities are. In today's world where data protection is a key aspect of what we do, a good understanding to the addendum is vital. Microsoft also published their service level agreements for each of their services that are bound by an SLA. On a more technical note, when we initially think about cloud, we often think about shared resources, so shared compute, shared storage that our company might be sharing with other companies that are also using Azure. But if the compliance standards that we're hoping to certify against require additional levels of isolation, then we might consider using dedicated hosts. Azure dedicated hosts provide physical servers that we can use to host one or more virtual machines. Each dedicated host is dedicated to a single organization. This gives you host-level isolation that can help you address certain compliance requirements. Dedicated hosts also give you visibility of the underlying cause, and this can help you meet server-based software licensing requirements, which can help you bring your own licenses into the cloud. Dedicated hosts may not be the first thing we think about when we think about compliance in Azure, but by giving us our own dedicated servers that allow us to isolate our virtual machines from the virtual machines of all the other customers in Azure, dedicated hosts can be an important part of our compliance tool set. In summary we started off by looking at Identity and Access Management. We looked at Azure AD and discussed how important Azure AD is for Azure cloud security. But not only Azure, Azure AD underpins security of all Microsoft cloud platforms. We mentioned Azure AD Domain Services, Microsoft's managed directory service in the cloud, we discussed role-based access control and how it can be used to provide granular access to Microsoft cloud services, such as Azure and Office 365. We discussed the use of built-in and custom roles in RBAC, as well as the three most commonly used roles, Owner, Contributor, and Reader. We also demoed how we could use these roles to provide access to resource groups. We then moved on to discuss governance tools and secure virtual networks. We discussed governance tools like Azure

Policy, Azure Initiatives, and Azure Blueprint, and we saw how each one of these builds upon the other with Azure Policy enforcing controls during deployment and Azure Initiatives that we can use combine a group of policies so they can all be applied in one go. We then discussed Azure Blueprints and saw how they can be used to deploy a secure and compliant subscription. We looked at security and virtual networks. We have network security groups and application security groups, and we discussed how application security groups can simplify our network security group deployment. Next we focused on Azure firewalls and user-defined routes. We discussed Azure Firewall and its capabilities, we discussed Azure DDoS protection for our virtual networks, and then we discussed user-defined routes and how we can use user-defined routes to control the flow of traffic. We also showed you a selection of Azure security solutions and identified different use cases for those solutions. Finally, we discussed security and compliance. We talked about Azure Information Protection, we discussed and demonstrated Azure Key Vault, we discussed Azure Monitor, and we discussed and demonstrated Azure Security Center. We then moved on to discuss compliance. We discussed some of the common compliance standards, we discussed Azure special regions, and we had a look at Azure Trust Center and the Azure Trust Portal along with Compliance Manager and Microsoft's Privacy Statement. Next, you have learned about some of the common industry compliance standards. We discussed the Azure Service Trust Portal and how we interact with it, and you learned about Azure special regions.

BOOK 3

**MICROSOFT AZURE
PRICING & SUPPORT OPTIONS**

**AZURE SUBSCRIPTIONS, MANAGEMENT
GROUPS & COST MANAGEMENT**

RICHIE MILLER

Introduction to Azure Subscriptions

Azure subscriptions are the first construct of Azure, and in the following chapters, we're going to learn all about Azure subscriptions, how to use them, why they're there, and other aspects of Azure subscriptions. We're also going to learn about management groups and how those work with Azure subscriptions. The first thing is we're going to describe an Azure subscription and understanding what it is, understanding the different uses and options with Azure subscriptions, and then we're going to understand management groups, when you would use them, why you would use them, and how they fit with subscriptions. Let's look at the scenario first that we'll be covered and you'll see throughout the duration of this entire book. The scenario is that we work for a company that has decided to adopt cloud. The company is exploring different cloud providers, not just Azure, but Azure is one of those cloud providers. One of the very first steps of adopting Azure is to understand how the pricing and the support options work to make sure they fit your organization's needs. You have been tasked with learning the fundamentals about the pricing and support options. You need to document these and bring these back to the team and report on these to help the team make the decision on if they're going to go with Azure or if they're going to go with another cloud provider.

Chapter 1 How to create an Azure Subscription

The first thing with adopting Azure is creating a new subscription and then tying that subscription to an account and deploying your cloud resources that you will consume into the subscription. At the top level, you have the subscription, and then you have what's called a resource group and a resource group is used to group your resources that share a lifecycle. Each resource is going to belong to a resource group, and then the resource group is going to belong to a subscription. So regardless if your resources are web apps, databases, virtual machines, maybe a Kubernetes cluster, they're all going to be associated with some sort of resource group, and that resource group has to be associated with a subscription. An Azure account is used for contact information and billing details for an Azure subscription. Every time you spin up a new subscription, it has to be associated with an Azure account. There's an email tied to an Azure account, and the person that owns that email is responsible for the monthly cost of the Azure consumption that happens in that subscription. An Azure subscription is just a logical container and grouping of Azure resources and administration. The different elements of an Azure subscription are it's a legal agreement, it's a billing unit, it's a logical boundary of scale, and it's also the very first container that's created, and it's an administrative boundary. So let's walk back through these. So it is a legal agreement, so if you have charges against a subscription, you are legally bound to paying for those and also the use of the subscription and the things that are done within that subscription. It's a billing unit, so you can have many subscriptions, and you can have different billing tied to different accounts and go to different, let's say, like departments or people. So if you need to separate billing for any reason, a subscription might be a way to do that. It's also a logical boundary of scale, so you can only have a certain amount of VNets deployed into a subscription, or you could only have a certain amount of web apps deployed into a subscription. Microsoft has soft limits around different amounts of resources that can be deployed in a subscription. If you need a higher amount, you can reach out to Microsoft and ask to have that increased. But just keep in mind that the subscription can be a logical boundary of scale. Then the first container created is you create this subscription before you create any resource groups or before you create any resources. You have to have that subscription there. But let's talk about the relationship between Azure Active Directory and subscriptions. This is key, and this is important to understand. What is Azure Active Directory? It's Microsoft's identity and access management service that runs in Azure itself. It's used for being able to sign in and access cloud resources. A subscription is going to have a trust relationship with at least one Azure Active Directory. An Azure Active Directory can have trust with multiple subscriptions, but each subscription could only trust one single Azure Active Directory, and this is something important to keep in mind as you're working with subscriptions and you're deploying more subscriptions. In your Azure Active Directory is where your accounts will live, like your user accounts and your different groups. So when you're assigning permissions to subscriptions, you're assigning permissions to resource groups, etc., keep in mind the relationship between Azure Active Directory and your subscriptions, and that will help you understand how things work as you go to assign permissions.

Chapter 2 How to Add and Name Azure Subscriptions

But when should I add a new subscription? The first question that you'll ask when you want to know, should I add another subscription here or not is going to be do you have concerns of exceeding limits within a subscription? Are you going to add more VNets than Microsoft allows in a subscription? If the answer is yes, then you'll add a subscription. If the answer is no, then you'll move to the next question. Do I trust the subscription owners? When you spin up a subscription, you will be a subscription owner, but you can also assign that permission to someone else. That could be another department head or just another person on your team. Maybe you need to separate that security. Maybe you don't want that person having owner-level access to the resource groups and resources in your subscription. If the answer is no and you don't trust the subscription owners, then add another subscription, and you will add that person to that additional subscription. If the answer is yes, then move on to the next question. This question is, do you need to constrain or scope resource providers within a subscription? A resource provider is there in Azure behind all of the services. For example, virtual machines in Azure have their own resource provider, SQL databases for the PaaS SQL offering have their own resource provider. So maybe you want to have a subscription and you want to allow folks that will be consuming from that subscription to deploy VMs, but maybe you don't want them deploying Azure App Services to run web apps. Maybe you want to have that capability in a totally separate subscription. You could certainly do that, and you could scope the resource providers at a subscription level. So if the answer is yes, that you need to scope a subscription based on resource providers, then you'll add an additional subscription. If the answer is no, then you move on to the last question, and that is can administration be delegated through RBAC controls? If the answer is no on that, then you'll add an additional subscription. If it's yes, that's usually the criteria that we look at when deciding, do I need another subscription or not? Naming of your subscriptions is absolutely critical. This should be done as a part of your planning and really as the first step. This can help with things like chargeback, help IT teams find and managed resources, and just overall be an aid in the operations of your Azure environments. There's many ways to name subscriptions, and you may come up with your own method. At the top level we have the company name, and then we're going to add a department to the name, and then we're going to add a location to the name, and then we're going to tag it with an environment. We'll have that be a part of the name, and then we'll increment the instances with a number. So if we have several of the same names, we'll add an additional number, like 1, 2, 3. The pattern starts with company, department, location, environment, and then instance.

Chapter 3 How to Provision a New Azure Subscription

As far as provisioning a new Azure subscription, you have a couple of options. The first option is you could come out to this azure.microsoft.com/ site:

You can click on this Start free or you could click on the Or buy now below. I'm going to go ahead and click on the Start free. This is kind of the first way that you could sign up for a subscription. The other way is you could add a subscription from an existing account.

Here you would need to put in either an email account, or you would need to go ahead and create one, or you could sign up with your GitHub account. We're not going to go all the way through the process here, but we're going to take you partway through the process so you can see what it looks like. So I'm going to go New, and I'm just going to paste in just an example account, and then we'll go Next. Then it wants a password, so we'll give it a password, and we'll click Next. We put in our information, and then we verify our identity. The next step would be to identify by a credit card.

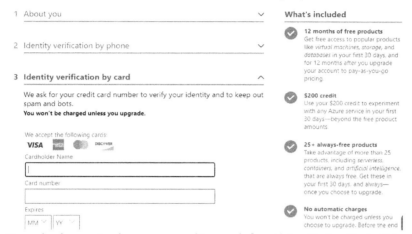

You do have to have a credit card for this. Note that this would be the free account, so you would have the $200 credit and you could use only free services on here, so you won't be charged. Then the last step would be to go ahead and accept the agreement, and then you would have your new free Azure account. We're going to switch gears, and we're going to go ahead and look at provisioning a new Azure subscription from an existing account. I'm going to click on Pay-As-You-Go.

That's the offer that we're going to go with here and then it asks for payment information.

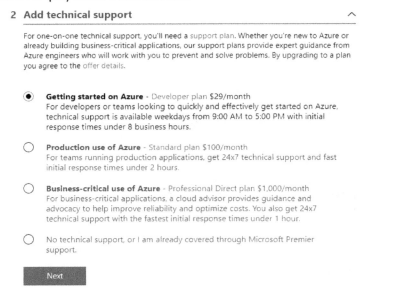

Then it's going to ask you what type of technical support do you need on this new subscription? I'm going to say no for none. Then you accept the agreement and then go ahead and click on Sign up, and it will provision your new subscription.

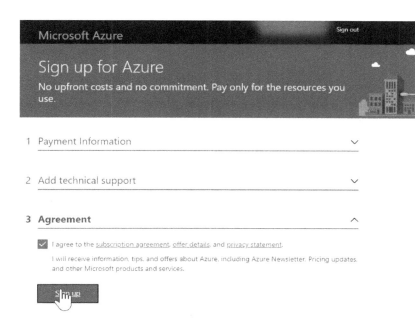

Setting up the account sometimes can take a few minutes. Then when it's done, it brings you into the Azure portal right into this Quickstart Center.

We can go ahead and click on Subscriptions, and it will bring us to the list of subscriptions. That was the process of provisioning a new subscription, to an existing account.

Chapter 4 Azure Management Groups

Management groups allow you to apply governance conditions a level above subscriptions. The governance conditions are talking about access, so RBAC and Azure policies. Azure policies are a way to either audit or enforce conditions on a subscription, resource groups, or resources in a subscription. For example, maybe you want to only allow people that have access to your subscription to deploy in a certain region. An Azure policy can be used to do that. So if you have many Azure subscriptions, you can use management groups to help make the management of those subscriptions easier. Let's look at the container hierarchy in Azure, and this is not to be confused with Docker containers. At the top level, you have your management group, and then you have your subscription that rolls into that, or you could have multiple subscriptions. Then you have a resource group that rolls into the subscription, and then you have resources that roll into a resource group. This is a breakdown of the overall container hierarchy from top to bottom. How to use management groups with Azure subscriptions. So when we deploy our first management group, that's what's known as the root management group. We have access and Azure policies applied to that. We can have additional management groups roll up to this root management group. Let's say for example we have a marketing management group, and we have separate access controls and we have separate Azure policies apply to that management group and we have a subscription there, and then resources inside of that. We also have an IT management group, but we have sub-management groups under the IT management group. In there, we have one for development and one for an infrastructure team. The development management group and the infrastructure management group both have multiple subscriptions. Something to note is we're applying the access and the Azure policies at the IT management group level, and the development and the infrastructure management groups are inheriting those permissions and Azure policies and so are the subscriptions underneath those and the resources as long as we didn't break the inheritance. This is a visual of how management groups fit into the overall picture of your Azure container hierarchy and how subscriptions fit into that picture as well.

Chapter 5 Azure Planning & Management Costs

A key component of adopting Azure Cloud is knowing cost. It is important to map out the Azure products and services that will be used and their initial and long-term costs. In the following chapters we will explore the various pricing options and calculators that are available to assist us when estimating cloud. Understanding options for purchasing Azure products and services will be the first topic and then we'll learn about the Azure free account and what that means and what that comes with. We'll look at different factors that can impact your cost in Azure. We'll learn about zones for billing purposes and then best practices for minimizing Azure costs. Then we'll take a look at the different Azure pricing calculators and how you can use those for estimating. The first one here is the Azure free account. With this account, you get $200 in Azure credit that can be used within 30 days. You also get access to free Azure services. The second type is the pay-as-you-go. So you will be charged monthly for the services that you use in a billing period, which is the monthly billing period. The next one is the student account, and you get $100 in Azure credits that can be used in a 12-month period. No credit card is required to sign up or use this type of Azure subscription. The final one is the enterprise agreement, and this is where you purchase Azure services and Microsoft software under a single agreement, and this is usually used for organizations to purchase their Azure credit from Microsoft.

Chapter 6 Azure Free Subscription & Free Services Options

What are the options for purchasing Azure products and services? Well, let's go through the list. First, you have your enterprise agreement, which we just touched on, and these are usually designed for very large organizations. This comes with the premier support and dedicated Azure resources. There's generally an annual commit for spend with the Enterprise Agreement. What that means is that you have committed to spending a certain amount on Azure on an annual basis. This happens at your organizational level, and usually with this, you can get deep discounts on your Azure cost. The second is the Direct - from Microsoft. So you'll get a bill for Microsoft, you'll have a support plan through Microsoft, and you self-manage or you can use a partner to help you with your Azure provisioning, your deployment, and basically building out your cloud environment. The last is the Indirect - Cloud Solution Provider or also known as CSP. You will receive a bill from the CSP, not for Microsoft, and you will get your support through the CSP, not directly through Microsoft. And you'll work with the CSP for any Azure provisioning, deployment, and uses management. There are some benefits to working with the CSP. For example, a lot of times CSPs will have very talented folks as a part of their organization that you will be able to work with. Now, let's talk about the Azure free account. You can go and sign up for this and you will have access to many popular services for free for 12 months. Again, you also get that $200 credit for 30 days. Then you'll have access to 25+ services free forever. What are some of the popular services that are free for 12 months? You have Linux VMs, you have Windows VMs, and you have 750 hours for each one of those. You have other things like managed disks. You have access to 5GB of file and blob storage. You can deploy SQL Database, Cosmos DB, and also egress bandwidth. In regards to the free services that are free forever, here's a list. Keep in mind that this always changes. Microsoft is always releasing new services to Azure, and they often make services free and include them on this list. Let's go through some of the popular ones. You can have like Azure App Service where you can have up to 10 of web, mobile, or API apps. Azure Functions is another popular one where you can have up to a million requests per month. So you can get some good use out of that one. DevTest Labs, so if you're running like lab environments and you want some of the capabilities that come with DevTest Labs, that's a free service. If you're running VMs, if you're running other things in those labs, you will be charged for that. But you won't be charged for the DevTest Lab service itself. Also like AKS, so Azure Kubernetes Service. You've probably heard of Kubernetes. This is a managed Kubernetes service from Microsoft. The service itself is free, but keep in mind you will pay for any VMs that are run, any underlying storage that's consumed, you'll pay for those things, but you won't pay for the AKS service itself. Other valuable services are like Security Center. There's a free tier. So as you're deploying things on Azure, you definitely want to turn that on to give you insight into your security posture on your cloud environment. Event Grid, you can get up to 100,000 operations per month. There's some Active Directory B2C, authentications that you can you can leverage. Azure automation is another big one where you can get up to 500 minutes per month and then networking. The networking is usually free, so VNets, subnets, load balancers, that stuff is free, which is great. Keep in mind you'll usually be using VMs with your networking or PaaS services, and so you will be paying for those things, but you won't be paying for the underlying networking itself. Then another big one is App Insights and Azure Monitor. You get up to 1GB free per month of storage, but the services, you can just turn on and start using them. Then the one that I really like is the Azure DevOps where you can get up to five users with private repos with that Azure DevOps.

Chapter 7 What's Affecting Azure Costs?

Let's now cover the factors that can affect your costs in Azure. Location is a big one. Azure is global with regions all over the world, and it does matter where you deploy your resources and what regions you select. Regions are going to have different pricing. For example, North Central US is going to have a lower cost than West US or even East US. South Central US is going to have a lower cost than US East or US West. Part of the reason is there's local factors that are impacting the costs such as staffing in those local areas, in those data centers, connectivity costs, cooling costs, things like that. That is all factored into the actual price that you receive as an Azure customer. The next item is the resource type. Costs are specific to each resource and the usage that the meter tracks, and the amount the meter has associated to the resource will depend on the resource type. So keep that in mind as well as you're consuming and the different types of resources. The next one is service. As your usage rates and building periods can be different if you're using, let's say, an enterprise agreement versus a direct or even a CSP. So, for example, with the enterprise agreement, you will probably have discounted services. As you're consuming services from Azure, you'll be receiving those discounts, so you'll have a lower cost because of your enterprise agreement and what you've negotiated with Microsoft. The last one is egress traffic. Sending data into Azure, aka ingress, also known as inbound, is always free. It's always free to get your data into the cloud. Pulling data out of the cloud, known as egress or outbound, has a cost. Bringing data into the cloud, ingress, is free. Sending data out of the cloud, egress, is going to have a cost. You really need to understand the traffic flow for your environment or the solution that you're running in Azure, and that will help you estimate the cost that you will be paying for any egress traffic. An Azure zone is a geographical grouping of Azure regions for billing purposes. Data transfer pricing is based on the zones. But what are the zones? Zone 1 is the United States, US Government, Europe, Canada, UK, France, Switzerland. Zone 2 is APAC, so it's East Asia, Southeast Asia, Japan, Australia, India, Korea. Zone 3 is Brazil, South Africa, and UAE. Then there's something called DE zone 1, which includes Germany. Keep in mind that these change over time, and Microsoft is adding new regions, new countries, to Azure all the time. So the zones will update and will expand. So make sure you check the Microsoft documentation on these for the latest and greatest.

Chapter 8 Best Practices for Minimizing Azure Costs

The first one is reserved instances. Let's say, for example, you know, as an organization, you're going to run X amount of VMs for the year. You just know that. What you can do is you can pre-pay for those virtual machines and get a discounted rate. It's a really great way to save money and minimize your cost when you know what you're going to consume. The next is Azure cost management. Once you're running workloads in Azure, you could take a look at the Azure cost management tools inside of Azure and start to drill-down and see what things are costing you, what resources are costing you, on a monthly basis, on a daily basis. There's a great breakdown. There is also some forecasting that could be done in the Azure cost management so you can predict what it's going to cost you for the next 30 days or into the future. This is a great way to go and analyze your spend and start to minimize your cost and make adjustments. The next is quotas. You can put quotas in place around the resources and the amount of resources that you're using. The next one is spending limits. You can actually put spending limits in place. If you are approaching that spending limit, you won't be able to deploy like more resources, and you can ensure you're not going to go over a budget. There's also Azure Hybrid Benefit. What this is if you have software assurance and you're bringing, let's say, servers from on premises, whether it's Windows servers or maybe even SQL servers up to Azure, you get deep discounts on the licensing for running in Azure. I've seen this change a little bit over time, so make sure you go out to the documentation to understand the latest and greatest with the Azure Hybrid Benefit and/or talk to your Microsoft representative, and they'll be able to give you the insight and the latest information on the Azure Hybrid Benefit and how it can apply to your specific scenario. The final item on this list is tags. When you're deploying resources in Azure, you will want to tag your resources. You can use this as a tool for showback or chargeback in your organization, and it's also useful just to identify and know what things are and what they're for. For example, I usually like to put tags in place to ask the question of when will this expire? Do we need this resource indefinitely? Can we spend this resource down in 60 days? It's good to ask that question, and having a policy for tagging is going to help you enforce that. Also, it's good to identify what things are for. If you have a resource that's costing you a lot of money per month, and it's tagged so you can identify it, identify who the application owner is, maybe who the team is, then you can go talk to that individual and find out do they really need that? Do they know it's costing that much money per month?

Chapter 9 Azure Pricing Calculator Basics

There's two calculators that you can use to help you estimate costs. The first one is known as the Azure pricing calculator, and you can use this to estimate cost of Azure products. The second is the total cost of ownership or TCO calculator, and this is good for estimating the cost of migration and the cost of ownership. The Azure pricing calculator is web-based, and you can use this to estimate the cost of Azure services and really go down to a granular level. If you're putting together a solution and you want to know how much that solution is going to cost to you, this is a great tool to help you get that cost. You can add services, you can add tiers, and you can get your estimated consumption out of this calculator. For example, let's say you are designing a solution that consists of maybe three web front ends, and you need to run them on Azure App Service. Maybe you need to run SQL Server, and you need to run that on an IaaS VM for whatever reason, and you need some storage, and maybe you need something like Event Hub. Well, you can go and add all of those individual components to this calculator, and then you can see a breakdown of the cost per service, and you can see the breakdown or the summary of the cost of all of these services together, and you can see the cost on a monthly basis and the cost on an annual basis. You also can add different levels of support to the calculator. You can see that right in the cost as well. Then you can save an estimate to come back to it later, or you could even share it with colleagues if you need to. You can export the estimate from a calculation on this calculator to Excel and then work with it from there. It's pretty flexible, and it's really easy to use. The TCO calculator is good when you're planning a migration to Azure from your on-premises data center. This is very helpful when you need to see what it's going to cost to run X amount of workloads in Azure over a period of 5 years. This helps you understand and estimate your operations costs or your run costs. You can use that data to compare and contrast with your cost for running the same workloads on premises. This is good to see how much things are going to cost you in Azure for the same type of workloads and help you understand if you have a savings there.

Chapter 10 How to use the Azure Price Calculator

In this demonstration, we're going to go ahead and price an IaaS-based solution using the Azure pricing calculator, and then we're going to go into the total cost of ownership calculator, and we're going to calculate how much it's going to cost us to run this solution over a period of 5 years. We are out on the Microsoft Azure site at Azure Pricing.

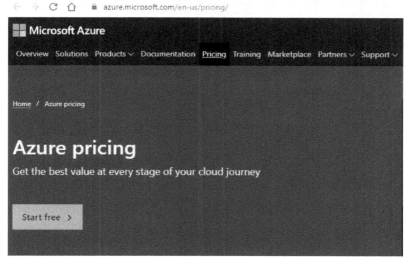

This is where it's easy to find both calculators. On the pricing calculator, you'll notice several things. The first thing is you will want to log in with your Windows Live account. You'll know that by looking in the upper right-hand corner, you'll see that you're actually logged in. The reason we want to log in is because we're able to save estimates, and were able to share estimates. So if you want to get back to your estimate, you'll need to be logged in so it can be saved to your account. At the top of the pricing calculator, we have several tabs that we could work through.

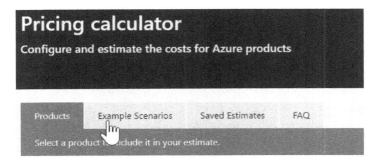

We have products here, and this is where we would actually add products to our estimate so we could flip through the different products in Azure Services like so. We could actually click on a product here, and it would add it to our estimate. Here we have Example Scenarios and under Example Scenarios, you could create an entire estimate from a pattern that Microsoft has developed and that they have out there on the Microsoft documentation on their docs site.

There's several patterns here, and it doesn't cover all the patterns that Microsoft has created, but there's a lot of them here. So if we wanted to do CI/CD for containers, we could see the solution, which is the pattern.

We could see the products that are involved in that. Then we could go ahead and add this to an estimate. What that will do is create a brand new estimate, and it will actually add all of these products to that estimate. Then you could go and tweak the cost for each of those products for your specific needs. Then you would have an estimate that goes along with this pattern. You could also go and click on this and that would bring you out to the Microsoft docs site where it has full information about this specific pattern. We could also click on Saved Estimates too and this will show any estimates that you have that you've done in the past that you saved. You could actually open them from here, you could delete them or you can export them. You could even copy and then work from there and then there's an FAQs tab that just kind of gives you information on how to use the calculator. You can add the amount of hours you will require and it's going to reflect the actual cost. You can change some other things too, like you could say, you could go to months, you could go to days as far as how often you think you're going to be running this service in Azure. You can also do some things like change the tier, and that's also going to impact the price. You really need to understand the services that you're planning to use and then come in here and modify accordingly and tweak so that you can get the accurate pricing. You'll have different options for different services and products that you have added. We could also change the operating system. For example when I switch the requirements to Linux look the pricing will decrease because there is no licensing cost. So keep in mind if you're going to run Windows servers on Azure in your environment, you will want to look at the hybrid benefit to see if you can save some money there or even your enterprise agreement. Then we can change the instance types. So you see all of the different virtual machine types, so you could change that. You could make it a bigger one, and it's going to increase the cost. Then under OS, we could say that we have the hybrid benefit, and that brings the cost down as well.

Or if you don't have a license for this server yet, you can say license included, and then when you deploy that server, you get the license with your Azure subscription. You also have an option of reserved instances. You could also configure some other options, like managed disks and etc. So in our solution, we have virtual machines, and then we have App Service. App Service is actually PaaS, so Platform as a Service. And let's say we wanted to add that because we're running some web servers and we're running SQL Server so we want to keep that server in this solution. We're going to have three instances of the App Service because we're running three servers on premises, and we want to continue to have three web servers so we can do load balancing. You have some options to configure this App Service, which will impact your pricing. And you have different options, so things like SSL and IP for the App Service that you don't have with the virtual machines. If we keep going, I have virtual network added here. We can calculate our inbound and outbound, so our egress and our ingress. I've also added an application gateway with WAF, or web application firewall.

That is just to protect my traffic coming into these app services, or my web servers. It's there to protect it, and there's a cost with this as well. You can go ahead and estimate this is well, and there's options to configure that. As you tweak and move the dials up and down, you'll impact the hours. If we keep going, we have some storage accounts.

Then as we keep moving down to the bottom, we have support added.

With support, we have the option to check different levels of support. I have it on Professional Direct but look at what happens to the price as I change it to Developer.

So it decreased the price by a lot. We've gone over the pricing and support options, so keep in mind the proper level of support that you need for your solution that you're going to deploy on Azure. At the very bottom of your estimate, you have several options.

You can export this out to Excel or you could save this. When you save this, it will save it to the Azure site under your account and that's why it's important to make sure that you're logged in. You could also do a save as if you want to change the name instead of having a generic name. Then you can also share the link. What this does, is that it generates a custom link for this estimate, and you could go ahead and share this with the rest of your IT team or someone else if they need to look at the cost, and they would be able to come in and adjust the resources as well so that the cost could go up or go down and you could collaborate on a calculation on an estimate. Then you have some options to display SKUs and/or display resources which you could turn on or off.

Chapter 11 Azure Support Options

Another part of adopting Azure is to understand all of the available support options and channels so in the following chapters we will explore the various support channels and leave with an understanding of where to go for help when needed. First, we'll look at understanding the support plans that are available in Azure. Then, we'll understand how to open a support ticket and what that process looks like. Then we'll look at the available support channels that are outside of the standard support plan channels in the Azure portal. Then we'll take a look at the Azure Knowledge Center and how to use that. The first one we have to cover is the basic support plan. This comes with all Azure subscriptions, and it's a basic support plan that includes the following: 24/7 access to billing and subscription support, so that's billing and subscription support. It doesn't necessarily mean you get support if you're having issues with a virtual network or a network security group or some other service. It does include online self-help, Azure products and services, documentation and whitepapers around those, and support forums. Other Azure support plans include the following. There's a developer plan. There's a standard plan. There's the professional direct. Then finally, there's the premier. What are the details of all of these plans? These consist of the following. The developer plan is really for non-prod. From a tech support perspective, it's email only and it goes up to a severity C, and you can get a response within 8 business hours. From an architecture standpoint, Microsoft will give you some general guidance. The standard plan is really meant for production subscriptions, so if you're running production workloads, you'll want to have the standard plan at a minimum. This gives you tech support access 24 x 7 via email or phone. This can go anywhere from severity C up to severity A, and you can get a response within a 1-hour timeframe. From an architecture standpoint, Microsoft will give you some guidance based on best practices. From an operation standpoint, they'll give you some support for onboarding services, service reviews, Azure Advisor, consultations, and such. From a training perspective, you'll have access to some web seminars that are led by Azure engineering. Then you do get some proactive guidance with this as well from a ProDirect delivery manager. The next one up is the professional direct, and this is for those business-critical workloads or business-critical subscriptions in Azure. The tech support and the response times are going to be identical to what you get with standard - same thing with the architecture, operations, training, and the proactive guidance. With the premier, that's kind of the top tier that you have available for you, and this gives you some extra things. The tech support and the response times are going to look the same. When you get to architecture, you'll have customer-specific architectural guidance. Microsoft will actually help you with your design. They'll help you with some reviews there and give you tips, best practices. They'll help you with some performance tuning if you need it around certain services. Think about like databases, web apps, etc., and some help with configuration. From an operations perspective, there's a TAM, that's a technical account manager, that's dedicated to you and will help lead service reviews and if you have support tickets in and you need to know what's happening with those, you can reach out to that dedicated person for those things. The TAM is very, very helpful is what I've found. From a training perspective, you've got access to the online web seminars, but you also have access to some on-demand training. Then from the proactive guidance, you also have the ProDirect delivery manager, but you also have your TAM that you can reach out to for help there if you need some guidance there. Then you also have access to launch support. That's for an additional fee though. That covers the comparison and the details of all the different plans that you have available with your Azure subscription. But how do you open a ticket in Azure? The first step is you need to go to the Azure portal. The second step is you need to click on the help and support. The third step is click on a new support request. When you click on the support request, you will be presented with a form, and go ahead and fill out the form with the details like what is the service that you're having an issue with or you need help with, what are the details, what's the severity level of the support request. Once you have that all completed, you go ahead and submit it, and then Microsoft will get back to you within the designated response time. It's pretty straightforward.

Chapter 12 Azure Knowledge Center

Now let's talk about the different support channels that are available outside of the support plan, the typical standard support plan. The first few are actually forums. You have the MSDN forum, you have the StackOverflow forum, and you also have the Serverfault forum. You will find Microsoft MVPs out on these forums, answering questions, other community folks, and you may find Microsoft employees from time to time out on these forums answering questions as well. So they are a really great resource. But keep in mind, there's no official SLA around response times, but they're still very, very helpful. With the StackOverflow, that's more geared towards developers. And the Serverfault is more geared towards the IT pro. And MSDN is kind of a mix of all. The last one here is Azure Support on Twitter. So you can actually tweet @AzureSupport, and Microsoft will respond to you. I've found this to be very, very useful as well, and they're very responsive. Again, there's no guaranteed response time or SLA on this. It's just kind of like you tweet at this, and Microsoft will get back to you. These are the support channels that are outside of the standard support channels that you can leverage when you're looking for support on Azure. Let's now look into the Knowledge Center. This is an online website where you can go for general questions and get those answers and get them quickly. The knowledge is comprised from community, Azure experts, developers, and customers all brought into a single place. You can search in this Knowledge Center, you can browse, or you can filter by products. You can scope it down to what you need to get to quickly. So if you're looking for something around networking or maybe DNS in Azure or websites or whatever, you can filter down and get to the answers very quickly and this will link out to documentation or other resources. The Knowledge Center is very helpful and a great resource for you to use as you're looking for support around your Azure subscription in your Azure environment.

Chapter 13 How to open a Support Ticket on Azure Knowledge Center

In this demo we're going to cover how to search the Knowledge Center, and how to open a support ticket within the Azure portal. You can get to the Azure Knowledge Center website on the URL; azure.microsoft.com/en-us/resources/knowledge-center.

From here, you can scroll down and you can see the Popular questions, and you can click on any one of these.

What I want to do is target a specific scenario just to kind of give you an idea on how this works. I could search, but what I'm going to do is use the filter here, and I'm going to click on Browse and then I want to check on something in regards to networking.

I'm going to click on Networking, and then it gives me this additional flyout where I want to click on Virtual Network. When I click on Virtual Network, it gives me options at the bottom of the screen but I'm going to scroll down again and you'll see the options here, and maybe you don't see what you're looking for yet, so you can click on the View more button, and that's going to expand.

v

What I'm actually looking for is that I need to increase the number of network security groups in my subscription. When I click on that, that's going to bring me to another page, and from here what it gives me is this Learn More, and if I click on this, I'll open it in another tab, this is going to link me out to the Microsoft documentation on how to do this and give me more information on my network security group limits and my subscription.

Networking limits

Networking limits - Azure Resource Manager

The following limits apply only for networking resources managed through **Azure Resource Manager** per region per subscription. Learn how to view your current resource usage against your subscription limits.

> ⓘ **Note**
>
> We recently increased all default limits to their maximum limits. If there's no maximum limit column, the resource doesn't have adjustable limits. If you had these limits increased by support in the past and don't see updated limits in the following tables, open an online customer support request at no charge

On the documentation and I can scroll through and you would see the different limits for your network security groups and you would be able to go from there and get the information you need.

Allow **X** attempts during MFA call	1	99
Two-way text message timeout seconds	60	600
Default one-time bypass seconds	300	1,800
Lock user account after **X** consecutive MFA denials	Not set	99
Reset account lockout counter after **X** minutes	Not set	9,999
Unlock account after **X** minutes	Not set	9,999

Back in the Azure portal, I went ahead and I clicked on Help + support, and it brought me to the dashboard.

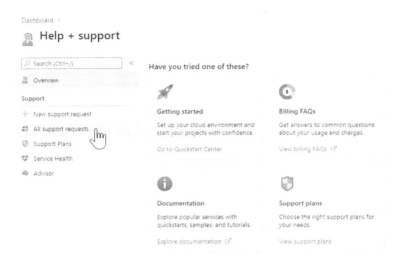

I have a few options here. I can look at Support Plans, Service Health, Advisor, All support request that maybe I have something that I've already submitted and I want to see what the status of those are. But what I want to do here in this scenario is just open a new support request, so we'll go ahead and click on that, and it's going to go ahead and open up and ask what's my issue type?

What I want to do is increase the limit of network security groups on my subscription. That's my goal. So I need to go ahead and select a subscription here, and the quota type and then I'm going to click Next on Solutions and this will give us our details that we need to fill out for the form.

+ Help + support | New support request

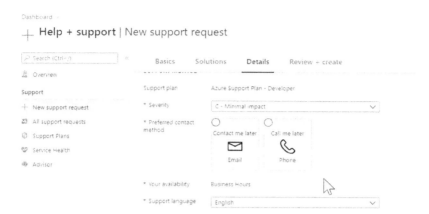

It's a severity C, so it's not a big deal. I'm going to do email for my contact, and I'm going to leave everything default there. If you needed to describe the issue if you were putting in a support ticket for something else, you would be able to describe the details there. I'm actually going to select the resource that I want to increase the limit on. We're looking for Network Security Groups, so we select that and we can see the current limit is 5000, so let's just say we want to request this to increase to 7000.

We're going to save this and continue, and then we'll go ahead and click on Next for the review and create.

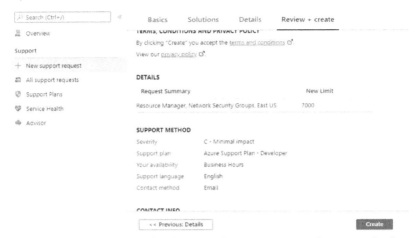

Help + support | New support request

Basics	Solutions	Details	**Review + create**

TERMS, CONDITIONS AND PRIVACY POLICY

By clicking "Create" you accept the terms and conditions ⌕.

View our privacy policy ⌕.

DETAILS

Request Summary		New Limit
Resource Manager, Network Security Groups, East US		7000

SUPPORT METHOD

Severity	C - Minimal impact
Support plan	Azure Support Plan - Developer
Your availability	Business Hours
Support language	English
Contact method	Email

CONTACT INFO

[<< Previous: Details]   [Create]

Here is a summary of what you're going to submit with this ticket, and then you would go ahead and click Create to go ahead and submit the ticket.

Chapter 14 Azure Service Level Agreements

A part of planning and supporting cloud environments is understanding the available service level agreements and it's important to understand the SLAs and how they apply to the cloud services that you will consume. So, in this chapter, we're going to take you through the ins and outs of SLAs and how they apply in Azure specifically. Let's look at the topics we're going to cover specifically. The first topic is we're going to dive into what an SLA is and make sure we have a clear understanding of SLAs. Then, we're going to talk about something called composite SLAs and how they work and how you would figure out a composite SLA for a solution that you have in Azure. Then finally, we'll finish off with understanding how you can determine the appropriate SLA for the services you plan to consume and/or the solution that you plan to spin up in Azure. SLA stands for service level agreement, and a service level agreement really comes from ITIL, which is a framework for managing IT that's been around for quite some time. An SLA is a commitment between a service provider, so think of Azure, think of Microsoft as that service provider, and its internal or external customers. You, as someone that's consuming cloud services, would be that external customer. Microsoft is the service provider, and they're providing you an SLA as an external customer. The SLA itself outlines what the service provider, in this case Microsoft, will provide to its customers and the standards that the provider will meet. Azure SLAs are a little bit different, so let's talk about this. In the context of Azure, an SLA is going to detail the commitments for uptime and connectivity, and this is what Microsoft is going to guarantee around its various services. The different services within Azure are going to have different SLAs, and so it's important for you to know what the SLAs are of those services before you just go ahead and consume it and to make sure that those SLAs fit with your business and meet the needs of the business. Before you're consuming a service within Azure, make sure you go out and look at the SLAs that are available and what they are and what the connectivity and uptime commitments are for Microsoft around those services and make sure they align with your business needs. Now let's talk about a composite SLA. What is a composite SLA? Well, in Azure, this is when it involves more than one service that's really supporting an application. It's rare that you will have one service that you're consuming in Azure, and you need that SLA around that service. Chances are in cloud, in Azure, you're going to have multiple services that you're consuming from Azure that are powering an application. This is where the composite SLA comes into play because each of those services are going to have their own SLA, and those together make up the composite SLA that's supporting that application. This is going to be centered around availability and connectivity of those services. Let's look a little bit more at a composite SLA, and let's look at an example here. So let's say, for example, a company is planning to have a web app as the front end of an application and planning to have some databases or a database as the back end of an application. Within Azure, we'll have a web app, and it has 99.95% for it's SLA. That's what's guaranteed from Microsoft around that service. That would be a web app running on Azure App Service. For the database, let's just go with a SQL database, and this is managed SQL, so it's PaaS SQL database, and that's going to have 99.99% for the SLA. What you have to do for the composite SLA is basically calculate these two together to come up with the composite SLA percentage, and this is what that would look like; your web app and your database together. So we have 99.95% guaranteed for the SLA for the web app and 99.99% for the database. We multiply those two together, and we get 99.94% for the composite SLA. For your business needs, that 99.94% SLA might be good enough. Maybe it's not. There are methods to increase that SLA. You can do things like replication with the SQL back end. You could look at replicating the front end. That all goes into the architecture and the design and the way you design your application, and that will enhance or modify that SLA to meet those business needs.

Chapter 15 How to Determine the Appropriate SLA

Now let's talk about things you should look at to help you determine the appropriate SLA for your business. Let's kind of start from the bottom up because we just got done talking about a composite SLA. What you want to do is look at the included services and their SLAs and how that's going to make up the entire overall SLA of the application that you're planning to run. As your architecting or designing an application, you'll map out what services you're planning to use. You need to go look up those SLAs. Then just like we just went through, you start to calculate, what is the composite SLA, and does that really meet my business needs or not? The next thing is you want to look at the availability metrics, so your mean time to recover, your mean time between failures, and we have the definition of what those are there. Just make sure that you understand what those are against the services and make sure those meet your business needs. Same thing with your recovery metrics; those are critical as well, so your RTO and your RPO. So your RTO, your recovery time objective, and that's what is the maximum that's acceptable, for an application to be unavailable after an incident. Then your RPO, the duration of data that you can afford to lose if there's a disaster. You want to take all of this into consideration when you're designing your application and when you're looking at services within Azure, and you're looking at the SLAs. You want to look at the SLAs and see if the SLAs meet your objectives and your goals of that application and the business needs. If they don't, what adjustments do you need to maybe make in regards to replication or disaster recovery technologies there to help meet that? The next one is dependencies. It's critical to understand all internal and external dependencies of the application, and then you can understand any SLAs that are around any of those dependencies. Chances are your dependencies are all going to live in Azure. You have the URL to go look up the SLAs, but there may be dependencies on other services that are outside of Azure, and it's important to understand those SLAs as well. You can take the same steps that you took to calculate the composite SLA even with external dependencies and use that formula to figure out the composite SLA with external dependencies as well. The last one is really critical, and it's cost and complexity. We can get better SLAs if we need to, but chances are that's going to come at a cost. Is the better SLA really worth the increased costs that you may incur by increasing that SLA? Or does it make sense to go with what you get out of the box from Azure, and can the business live with that? This warrants really understanding the SLAs that are there around the services, understanding the composite SLA, understanding the business needs, and understanding the cost. You may need to go have a conversation with the business to understand if the out-of-the-box SLAs are good enough, and maybe they are. Maybe they meet what has already been determined in regards to SLA needs. If not, go have that cost and find out if the business is willing to pay a higher cost to get increased SLAs.

Chapter 16 Azure Service Lifecycle

Azure is constantly changing at a very, very fast rate. It's important to be able to identify what features and services are production-ready and plan around the future roadmap of Azure. In this chapter, we're going to dive into how you do that, how you plan for the services and the feature updates. We're going to talk about preview for public and private, as well as general availability, and what all of that means and how you can stay up to date with services in Azure and how you can know when services are ready for production use. First we are going to cover public and private preview features, what that is, what that means, how you can identify those. Then we are going to look at understanding the term general availability and then, understanding how to monitor feature updates and product changes. But what are Azure previews? Microsoft has Azure feature previews, and these previews are for eval features, products, services in Azure are still in a beta or pre-release stage. This is when you can get early access to the services that Microsoft is still working on, and you can start to provide feedback. You can start to consume the service, try it out, see if it's going to fit for the use for what you need, and really just get that early access. These previews are also a way for Microsoft to get services to customers early on and start to get feedback so they can improve the products as they're still developing on those products and start to interact with the customers to make sure the use cases for the services in Azure are good to go. What is public and private preview? Well, Public is when any customer that's consuming Azure can go out and sign up for the preview of a service and start using that service and start getting that feedback to Microsoft and just start using and consuming that service. Keep in mind that with a public preview, you may not have SLAs around the service, and you may not have official support around the service. Also, you may see things changing rapidly in the UI or the way that service works, and you might see some bugs here and there. Private preview is like a public preview in that it's a way for Microsoft to get early access to you to a service, but this is usually by invite only, or you might have a form in the Azure portal or outside of Azure that you have to sign up for to get access to the preview of that service or product feature, etc. An example I can give here is that the Azure Kubernetes Service has been out for a while, but it's rapidly changing, and Microsoft is rapidly adding updates to that service. Some of the updates you've been able to get access to through private preview, like when Microsoft started working on the Azure policies for the Azure Kubernetes Service, you couldn't just go into the portal and sign up for that, and it would be turned on, and it would start working. You had to fill out a form and then get approval on the back end to start using the Azure Policy services for that Azure Kubernetes Service. So the public preview is available to anyone, where the private preview is limited and you have to sign up for it whether it's directly or whether you have a link to a form from Microsoft. Now let's talk about access to the public previews. Within the Azure portal, there's really two ways where you can get to the public previews. You can create a resource, or you can go to All Services. You will see a label on the service preview, and that's how you'll know that the service is in a preview state. Then you can go ahead and just click on the service, go ahead and create the service and start consuming it. Or if you go to All Services, you'll just see it and you'll know that it's in preview, and you might already be using it, or you could create it from there and start to consume it as well. The term general availability - what does this mean? Well, after Microsoft is done with the preview stage of a service or product feature, once they've had it out there in the market for a while with Azure customers, it's been successfully tested, it's finally released to Azure customers, generally it becomes a part of Azure's default product set. This is when it moves to becoming generally available or often referred to you as GA. And when a service goes into a GA state, it will basically have SLAs on it. It will officially be supported so you could call tech support and get help with that service. You won't have to work with a special group that's actually working on that service. And it will be ready for production use. But how do we monitor feature updates and product changes in Azure? There's three main areas to do this. The first one is the What's New page in the Azure portal. The second one is the official site for important updates, roadmap, and announcements to Azure products. This is great because it has the roadmap there as well. So you can go out there, and if you want to see what Microsoft is planning for the future, what's coming to Azure even before it hits a preview state, you can go to this updates site. Then the last one is the official announcements from the Azure blog. As Microsoft releases stuff to general availability or even if they announce something new in a preview or a feature add to a service in preview, they'll announce it on this Azure blog as well. This is just generally a good place to follow for good information around Azure, and you'll find other Azure blogs out there under the azure.microsoft.com/language of your company/blog. I highly recommend that you go out and you follow this blog, subscribe to it. because it has a lot of good updates. These are the three main areas where you can go and get updates around what's coming in Azure. Now, we're going to take you through some of the links so you can see preview services in Azure, and you can learn about upcoming previews and updates to Azure. We're in the Azure portal, and we're on All Services and I just wanted to show you that you can scroll through here and you can see the services that are in preview.

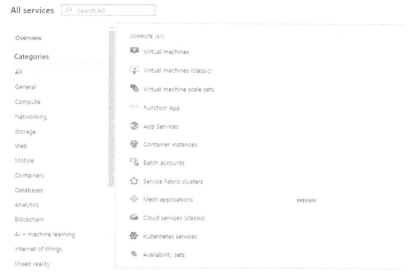

If we keep scrolling down, you can easily identify the services within Azure that are in preview and the ones that are not. So we can see Mesh applications there is in preview. We can also see SAP HANA on Azure is in preview and then Azure Spring Cloud.

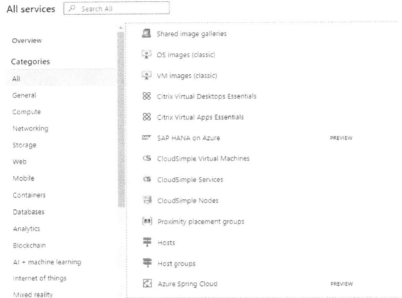

It's really easy to go through here and identify the services that are in preview. We're on the What's New page in the Azure portal now, and you can see updates around all Azure services from this What's New page.

You can click on the link for any of these updates, and it's going to bring you out to the Microsoft update site for Azure.

Also, while you're in here, you can change the timespan for these updates. You can see what's new in the last month, what's new in the last 6 hours. You also can change the tag here to scope it down to a specific service that you want to see what's new about this service.

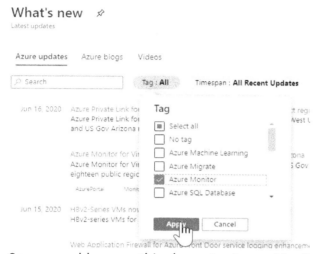

So we could scope this down to Azure Monitor, click Apply here, and we'll see the latest update there for this service. A couple of other things to note here is you could go to the Azure blogs, so you could see updates right here, or you could see updates from the Azure blogs and link right out to the latest blogs. And you could go to Videos here and see updates from here as well. Now we're on the Azure updates site, and on this site, you'll see that you can search for the service that you care about.

You could type in Azure Monitor or any other service, like Network, and then it will give you the list of updates and preview features for that service. You also could just do the browse, and you could scope it down to get a narrowed list. When you scroll through here, you'll see links, and you can click on the link to get to the specific page for that update with more information around that update. It's very useful and good information to understand what things are in preview, what updates are coming, what's happening with Azure overall. Back on the homepage of the Azure updates site, you also can scope things down just to preview services by checking the box and go ahead and filter the results. Or you could see things that are in a GA status by clicking on Now Available and filter the results. Then you would scroll down and you would only see services that are in GA, or, in comparison, you could do the same thing for the preview. This is a good way to come and quickly see what's what from a GA and a preview status on the Azure updates page. The last site here is the Azure announcements blog.

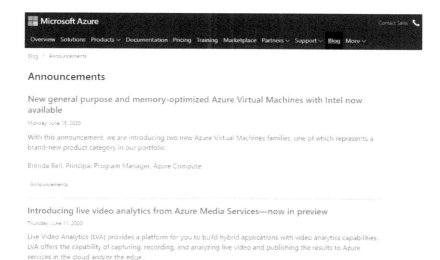

Blog / Announcements

Announcements

New general purpose and memory-optimized Azure Virtual Machines with Intel now available

Monday June 15, 2020

With this announcement, we are introducing two new Azure Virtual Machines families, one of which represents a brand-new product category in our portfolio.

Brenda Bell, Principal Program Manager, Azure Compute

Announcements

Introducing live video analytics from Azure Media Services—now in preview

Thursday, June 11, 2020

Live Video Analytics (LVA) provides a platform for you to build hybrid applications with video analytics capabilities. LVA offers the capability of capturing, recording, and analyzing live video and publishing the results to Azure services in the cloud and/or the edge.

Again, you can see that Microsoft is making full blogs about announcements. Here's one that's the general availability of Azure files on premises with Active Directory Domain Services authentication. If you click on that, it just links out to a full blog with a lot of information about the release of this service and links to getting started, who to contact. It links out to the Azure Storage forum. So it's very useful and a great way to understand what Microsoft's done with services or doing with services. They'll often write blogs when they're announcing previews, and you'll have links out there to get in contact with Microsoft or go to forums or different special places to understand more about that service.

BOOK 4

MICROSOFT AZURE
AZ-900 EXAM PREPARATION GUIDE

HOW TO PREPARE, REGISTER
AND PASS YOUR EXAM

RICHIE MILLER

Chapter 1How to Register for the AZ-900 Exam

In the following chapters, we're going to learn how to register for the AZ-900 Certification exam. We will first learn how to register for the AZ-900 Certification exam, learn about the different certification providers, as well as the different steps in the registration process. We will then look at the flow and really some tips and tricks whether you decide to take your exam at a testing center or take your exam at home or in your office. By the end, you will be able to register for the AZ-900 exam, as well as have an overall idea on how the examination process will work. Let's start by learning how to register for the AZ-900 Certification exam. First things first, in order to register, you need to have a Microsoft account. It's very important that if you have done a Microsoft certification before, make sure to use the same account all the time. If not, you'll have two different MCP, or Microsoft Certified Professional, IDs and your transcript will be split. To be honest, it's a bit of a mess to actually merge them afterwards. It's doable through support if it ever happens by accident, but let's hope we don't have to use the support. So try to always use the same Microsoft account every single time. If this is your first ever Microsoft certification, make sure to choose a Microsoft account that you want to use for the long term, and you will create your certification profile. As a tip, make sure to enter your name exactly as it appears on your government issued identification. For example, a lot of us have middle names or really names we don't use all the time, so make sure your certification profile matches exactly what you have on your ID. There are two exam providers for the AZ-900 exam. The first one is Pearson VUE, and the second one is Certiport, which is for students or instructors. Certiport is actually a

Pearson VUE business, but it's still shown as two different options on the site. Even if you're a student, unless you have a very specific reason to go use Certiport, such as a class requirement, I would personally go with Pearson VUE since all of the other exams above Associate level, so Associate, Expert, Specialty, are only provided by Pearson VUE. This way, if you decide to pursue your certification journey further, you will already have the experience with the certification provider and it will be one less thing to worry about rather than switching providers between your Fundamental exam and then your Associate exams and higher. To start the registration, you need to go to the exam page, and you will have the schedule exam option with either Pearson VUE or Certiport. So, let's go through the process. First, it will ask you to sign with your Microsoft account, and if you have done certifications before, you will need to validate your certification profile.

Certification Profile ✎

Exam AZ-900 Microsoft Azure Fundamentals | Change

Profile   Linked account ❶

ⓘ Please verify that your information is up-to-date. Edit Profile

*Required fields

If this is your first certification, you will need to fill it up, but it should only take you 2 to 3 minutes. You will see your email, as well as your MCP ID so you can make sure that you're logged in with the right account. If you have participated in various Microsoft promotions or conferences, you might have a discount on your exam, which will be presented to you on the Exam Discounts tab. After you validate your information and choose a discount if you have any, we need to choose where will we take the exam. The two choices are either at a test center or online at your home or office.

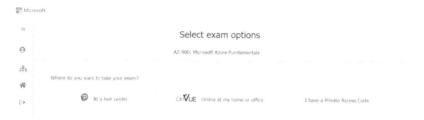

Depending on what option you choose, you will actually be presented right away with some extra interesting information and links to resources. Remember that even if you take the exam at home, it's still a proctored exam, so a proctor will be watching you on camera and hearing everything through your microphone, so whether you take it at a test center or at your home or office, still the same security standards apply. The next step will be to select the exam language.

As the AZ-900 is a very popular exam, it actually exists in multiple languages, but not all Microsoft certifications have as many options. If you have selected to do it in person, the next step will be to choose the location where you want to do the exam. You will be presented with choices based on the address in your certification profile, and you can also choose multiple test centers if you want to compare availability. Next, you will need to select the date, as well as the time you want to do your exam at. Make sure you check your calendar and block that time off. This way, nobody schedules meetings or anything during that time and I would block off extra time before and after because you really don't want anything, a meeting, a presentation, to stress you while you take the exam. Something to consider as you select your date and time is if you need an accommodation, both Pearson VUE and Certiport can provide appropriate arrangements for individuals that demonstrate a documented need. It can be things such as extra testing time, a separate testing room, or even breaks. Special accommodations can take up to 10 business days to be approved, so if you need to request a special accommodation, try to schedule your exam a bit more in advance. This way, you can go through the request process without being stressed for time. After you've selected everything, our next step is to review and confirm the exam in your cart. It will show us the exam name, language, the appointment location, as well as the price, and finally, we have to put our credit card number in and pay for the exam.

After this, your exam registration is complete. Before we finish off the registration part, I just want to share a quick reminder to verify the reschedule and cancellation policies in case you need it. Traditionally, it has been six business days before the exam date in order to change or cancel without paying a fee; however, make sure to double check it. This information will be available in the confirmation email, as well as on Microsoft Docs.

Chapter 2 How to Take your Exam at the Testing Center

Now that we know how to register, let's look at how it works when we take an exam at a testing center. First of all, try to arrive early. You have probably heard this about every important appointment in life, but planning to arrive early will make you so much less stressed in case there's traffic, the subway breaks down, or anything else. An exam is stressful enough, we don't want to add arriving late to the list of things that can stress us out before the exam. Very important: don't forget to bring the required piece of ID with you. According to my last exam confirmation, you need to bring one valid, unexpired, government issued ID with a signature and a photo and the name must match the name on the registration exactly. Always double check your confirmation email for the requirements. I always bring two pieces of government-issued ID with me just in case. Also, don't forget to go to the restroom before starting the exam. Microsoft exams do not have scheduled breaks, and while I'm sure that the proctors can find a way if needed, let's not add more stress to our exam. Let's now look at the overall process and how it works. First, you will arrive at the testing center a bit early and at the reception, give them your name, as well as your appointment details. If they ask you for your exam sponsor or provider, just say Microsoft as Pearson VUE does exams for a lot of different organizations and sometimes they have a lot of different sheets for different exam providers and by knowing to look in the Microsoft pile, it can help them find your appointment a lot easier. They will ask for your government-issued ID, as well as to assign the exam rules, and they will probably mark the check-in time on there. After that, the procedure can vary a bit by testing center but they generally take a picture of you and then they will compare it with the last picture of you taking an exam so they can make sure that you're the same person. Some other testing centers might use different forms of biometrics, but just so you know, there might be an extra form of identification depending on the testing center. After that, you will be provided a locker for all of your personal effects, and you have to put everything in there, and don't forget to turn off your cell phone. I generally like to fully turn it off and not just put it on vibration or silent mode to make sure it doesn't ring or annoy other people as I get a ton of notifications. Remember, you cannot bring anything with you in the exam room except something to take notes on, generally like an erasable whiteboard sheet that the testing center will provide to you. So you don't have to bring anything, the testing center will provide you everything that you are allowed to take in the examination room. After that, you will take the exam and receive your score at the end. Finally, as you leave, make sure you don't forget anything in the locker or your coat before going back home. Adrenaline is generally high after taking the exam and we often forget things. Something to remember is that one of the advantages of doing an exam in person is that you have plenty of people working at the testing center who you can ask for questions. They are nice people, and don't hesitate to tell them this is your first exam if it is so they can really help explain it to you step by step.

Chapter 3 How to Take your Exam at Home

Now that we know what it's like to take an exam at the testing center, what about taking an exam at home? First of all, a few days before the exam I highly encourage you to go perform a system test on the device you intend to take the exam with. This way, if anything is not working, you have a few days to find another machine. Before you actually start the exam, you need to clean up your desk space and room. You need to make absolutely sure there are no papers, electronics, or anything within arm's length of your device. Make sure that you tell your family or coworkers to not interrupt you during the exam. This is very important as if the proctor hears anything or sees anybody else in your camera, it's an automatic failure. Something I didn't realize the first time I took an exam at home, make sure you have your smartphone and a piece of ID nearby because you will need them during the check-in process. When I first did an exam online, I had my phone turned off and in another room, and then during the check-in process it asked me to use my phone to submit a piece of my ID. So it took me a bit of extra time to go get the phone, turn it on, so make sure you have them by you. Also, make sure to close all of the apps and unnecessary services on your machine. The testing system will provide the proctor with a list of everything running, so try to close everything in advance. It makes the process a lot smoother. The last thing is that if you're doing the exam on a laptop, make sure to plug in your laptop or at least have a full battery. To share with you a bit of what has worked for me personally, I prefer to do my exams on the dining table instead of my office. I have too many gadgets in my office and things everywhere, so doing the exam at the dining table means there is less things for me to clean up, and also I don't have to worry about things such as the whiteboard as there is a lot more space around me on the dining table. So I have less things for the proctor to check out before the exam. Also from a device perspective, I use an old laptop with a base Windows install. This way, there's less apps, notifications, services, and things to worry about during the exam. This is not possible for everyone, but I just wanted to share with you what has worked for me personally. Now that we have our pre-exam preparations, you can actually begin online check in and system check for the exam 30 minutes before the exam start time. This gives you more time in case anything doesn't work with your system and allows you to go through the process more calmly knowing that you've got the time. If everything goes smoothly, you'll probably be able to start your exam even before the scheduled time. As soon as your system checks are ready, you'll be put in a queue and when a proctor is ready you will be able to start the exam. But where do we start the exam from? You need to go to the Microsoft Learning dashboard, and from there you will see your appointments and, if you have an online exam, you'll have a button that says Start online exam, right there. If we take a look at an overview of how it works, at a very high-level view, you will first start the exam from the Learning dashboard, and then it will ask you to download the OnVUE proctored exam app in which you will first start by doing a system test. If everything is good, you will provide your phone number where you will get a text message with a link where you can submit your information. You'll be asked to take pictures of you, your ID, as well as your surroundings. After all of that is submitted, you will be connected with a proctor, and depending on the proctor you get, they might talk to you through the device speakers or they might write to you on the chat. Some of them are okay with only the pictures you provided, some of them might ask you to move your device camera around as they might want to see some more things in detail. After all of those checks by the proctor are good, you're ready to take the exam. Remember, the proctor will always see you and hear everything through your device camera and microphone, and you are not allowed to mute it, stop it, block the camera. If not, it's an automatic disqualification. Pearson VUE also has their own nice preparation video on how to take an exam at home and it's about 5 minutes long, so if you want to watch it, it's a nice introduction video if you are taking the exam for the first time. In summary, we have first covered how to register for the AZ-900 exam, the different exam providers, either Pearson VUE or Certiport, as well as how the registration process works. We have then looked at the process, as well as tips and tricks whether you decide to take your exam at a testing center or take your exam at home. Next, we will learn about the AZ-900 exam structure and question types.

Chapter 4 Azure AZ-900 Exam Structure

Now, we're going to talk about the AZ-900 exam structure and question types. We will first talk about the basics of the AZ-900, such as how many questions you should expect, how much time you have, and the overall structure of the exam. We will then talk about the different question types you can expect in the AZ-900 exam. Let's first cover the basics of the AZ-900 exam. Microsoft does not share the exact information about each exam, like other certification authorities might do. Also the number of questions for the same exam might even be different from person to person again on the same exam. Microsoft does provide guidelines for each exam category, which is what I will share, but don't worry if it's not exactly the same when you take the exam. With that in mind, for a fundamental-level exam such as the AZ-900, you should expect to have between 45 and 60 minutes to do the exam, but in your schedule, plan for around 80 minutes of time, which includes the time to set up, sign the non-disclosure agreement, comment the questions, so make sure you block 80 minutes on your calendar in total, but only for the questions or exam part, you'll have somewhere between 45 and 60 minutes. For the number of questions, you should expect anywhere from 40 to 60 questions for this exam. But isn't this almost saying like I only have 1 minute to answer each question, and the answer is yes, for fundamentals exams, you will have somewhere between a minute and a minute and a half for each question, if we look at it from a purely mathematical perspective; however, you should expect short questions. We will talk about the types of questions later more in detail, but really for fundamental exams, I like to describe them as fairly straightforward questions, whether if you know to answer, you should be able to answer it in no time. I do, however, understand that taking an exam is stressful, and adding a time constraint adds even more stress, so my advice is that Microsoft actually offers a feature allowing you to mark questions for review later. So if you read a question, and you're not sure about the answer, you can mark it for review later. This way, you quickly answer all of the questions that you know you've got the answer for, and at the end, you can use the time left to spend more time thinking at the questions you're not 100% sure about. To give you an idea of what it looks like, at the top of the screen, you will have two options, Review later or Comment later.

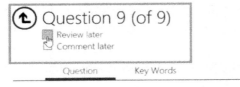

Question   Key Words
_____

You need to choose all the rows from the addresses table according to the following requirements.

- Choose the first three fields from this list: A, B, C, D, E, F, G, H, I.
- Fields F and G must be equal.
- Order the results by the last field in the table.

What should your SQL statement look like?

To answer, type the correct code in the answer area.

Review later is for yourself to tell yourself that at the end, come back and recheck this question, and the commenting is for after the exam, if you want to give feedback to Microsoft that maybe there's a typo in the question, or that it doesn't make sense, or maybe that is outdated. The commenting is not included in the exam time, but it's included in the 80 minutes that we have talked about earlier. After you get to the end of the exam, you will get a review screen like this one where you will see how many questions you have answered and how many you didn't.

You will also see all of the questions you marked for review and for comment, as well as the time remaining. You can then click on the tiles to see the ones you marked for review, and then now did you know how much time you've got left and how many you marked for review, you can really more calmly review them so you can feel 100% confident in your answers. Before we end this chapter, here is the general exam flow that you should be prepared for. After you check in for the exam and all of the prerequisites are done, the first thing you will have to do is read the instructions and accept the Microsoft nondisclosure agreement in regard to certifications. You can also read it before the exam so you have one listing to worry about reading on the exam day. You will also probably have some optional questions about your level of proficiency around the different exam sections. This is for Microsoft to better balance the exams in the future and has no impact in the level of difficulty of the questions you will actually get. After that, it's exam time where you will have all of the different questions for the exam, and after you're done with the exam, you'll have dedicated time to provide comments to Microsoft on questions. This is optional, and it's for you to give your feedback if you found questions were confusing, outdated, had typos, and so on. Again, this is optional. You don't have to do it if you don't want to, but if you see something that's wrong, please do it because it can help Microsoft fix any mistakes, and by providing comments, we make sure the certification experience is better for everyone.

Chapter 5 AZ-900 Exam Question Types

Now that we know the overall structure, let's talk about the types of questions you should expect in the AZ-900 exam. Microsoft will not specifically say which types of questions you will get on a specific exam, but they do share the types of questions for all exams. There are actually 10 types of questions you can expect on any Microsoft exam. They are called active screen, best answer, build list, case studies, drag and drop, hot area, multiple choice, repeated answer choices, short answers, and labs. Given the time constraints, you can really rule out some of them, such as short answer, labs, case studies, as those, in theory, should not show up on the Fundamentals exam. But Microsoft can never confirm the types of questions you can expect, so better be prepared. Let's take a look at what those types of questions actually look like. The one that you're probably the most familiar with is the best answer. You have a question, a list of answers, and you can only select one answer. A very similar one, but slightly different is the multiple choice where you have a question and multiple answers, and you need to select all of them that apply. Microsoft has been fairly good at giving a bit more information on those questions, such as select the three answers that apply and not simply all that apply, but that is not a guarantee. The next one, which is very popular, is the drag and drop. You have a question, you have possible answers on the left, and then you need to drag and drop them to the answer areas on the right. You can often expect questions that are scenario based and they would question you on what Azure products would fit that particular use case. Most times, you will actually have more answer options on the left than possibilities on the right. So you might have like say five possible answers, but only three drag and drop spots, so it doesn't mean that everything on the left will actually be used. Another very popular one is the build list type of question in which you are given a task, and then you need to put the actions from the left in the correct order on the right. This is a bit more complicated because not only do you need to know the appropriate choices because not all of the options on the left are needed, but also put them in the right order. Microsoft does offer some amazing short videos for each type of question and what I like about their videos is that they are filmed in the actual exam interface, so it can give you a good idea on what the actual interface looks like.

Once you go to the page, you'll see a bunch of short videos for each exam in the actual interface. It will either play in line, or you can go to YouTube to watch it in full screen. In summary we have first looked at the AZ-900 exam basics. You have between 45 and 60 minutes to do the exam, but you should plan for about 80 minutes, which includes the NDA, instructions, and comments at the end. You should also expect anywhere between 40 to 60 questions for this exam. To better manage time, if you're not sure about a question, use the Review later option. This way, you can answer all of the questions that you know first and at the end spend the time you have left on those that you are not sure about and maximize the time you have. We have also looked at plenty of question types, such as best answer, multiple choice, drag and drop, build list, and you can go watch short videos for all of the rest of them. Next, we will coever what happens after the exam.

Chapter 6 What Happens After the Exam

Now we will cover about what happens after the exam. There are actually two things that can happen after the exam. You pass the exam or you fail the exam, which can happen as well, and it's okay. I have failed a few Microsoft certifications as well, so we have to talk about that option as well. If you pass the exam, we will learn about the different digital assets that you get and the different steps that you can take afterwards. We will also cover what happens if you fail the exam, who you can see and what are required before you can reattempt this exam. As soon as you click the end exam button, you'll get your score right away. The max score you can get is 1000, but the passing score, or the minimum you need to pass, is 700. A pass is a pass, meaning that only you can see the score on the official transcript. You will not see the score, only if it's a pass. So whether you pass with 701 or 1000, a pass is a pass. If you did your exam at a testing center, you will get a printed version of the score report right away, which you'll not get if you do your exam at home, but you could always print your own score report if you wanted to. Something that is really interesting, the score report will show you how well you did for each high-level exam objective. I personally find the Performance by exam section to be very important. Whether you pass or fail the exam, it will show you the areas that you did great or not so great in. It's important to remember that not each section of the exam will get an equal number of questions. The score report will cover things such as Understand Cloud Concepts, Understand Core Azure Services, Understand Security, Privacy, Compliance and Trust and Understand Azure pricing and Support. But you won't be able to directly find out how many questions you got wrong.

Chapter 7 What if You Pass the Exam

Once you got your score report, let's take a look at what happens if you passed the exam. Once you pass the exam, you'll get three types of digital assets to help you promote your achievement. First of all, you will get a Credly badge, which you might know under the name Your Acclaim, but it has recently rebranded to Credly. You will also get a digital certificate, as well as the exam will show up on your official Microsoft transcript. But with all of those options, what's the goal or how should you use them? Well, the Credly badge is built for sharing on social media or professional sites such as LinkedIn, for example, to show your achievement. As for the digital certificate, you can print it and showcase it in your office, for example. A few years ago, Microsoft used to allow you to order printed copies, but that's not possible anymore. But with a good quality printer, you will get similar results. Lastly, the Microsoft official transcript is very useful when a potential employer or client needs an official document to validate your certifications. If we dive a bit deeper about the Credly badge, they actually made it very easy to click the Share button, and then you can both share it as an update on LinkedIn, as well as add it to your LinkedIn profile as an active certification. If you prefer to not use the Credly built-in mechanism, you can also manually add the certification on your LinkedIn profile. I strongly encourage you to add the certifications to your LinkedIn profile or any other professional social network that you use in order to showcase your continuous learning. Lastly, let's talk about the Microsoft certification official transcript. When you share the transcript, you have an ID, which you cannot change, but you can customize your password, as well as decide if you want to include your address details or not.

After that, a prospective employer can go to the transcript validation tool, enter your ID and password, and then validate your certifications directly on the Microsoft site. This makes sure that no one tampered with the transcript or faked anything in the PDF. The information comes directly from Microsoft, so it's more official. Now that we have talked about all of the ways to share your achievement, don't forget to celebrate your accomplishment. It's important to celebrate when we succeed. However big or small you decide to do it, don't forget to celebrate what you have just achieved. Also, don't forget to take a break, sit down, and enjoy the moment. Whether it's for a day or a week, take some time after the certification to just enjoy. And after that, start looking into your next certification, whether it's another fundamental-level exams or so on or a more advanced certification such as an associate-level AZ-104 or AZ-204. The cloud is always evolving, and it's important to always keep learning more and staying up to date, and I personally find that certifications are a great way to motivate me to keep learning.

Chapter 8 What if You Fail the Exam

Now that we have covered what to do if you pass the exam, what happens if the exam score report comes out and it's a fail? First of all, don't put yourself down too much. It's never fun to fail an exam, but it happens. I have failed certification exams myself, and it's important to see them as a learning opportunity to get better rather than a failure. Also, it's important to know that if you fail, it will not show up on your transcript. So you're the only one that has access to this information that you did not pass an exam. Remember the score report that we have talked about previously? This shows you how well you did for each exam section. That information is even more useful now, because it can help you understand what to focus on as you review the material again for the next time you attempt the exam. Talking about retaking the exam, let's talk a bit about Microsoft's exam retake policy. If you fail the exam for the first time, you need to wait at least 24 hours before being able to retake the exam. If you fail a second time, however, you will need to wait 14 days before taking the exam a third time, and there is also a 14-day delay between twice for the third, fourth, and fifth attempts as well. Microsoft does have a restriction where you cannot attempt an exam more than 5 times in a 12-month period, starting from your first attempt. I hope that it never happens to you but I still wanted to share the information so you know about it. In summary, we have covered what happens right after the exam, and we have talked about the score report and the information it provides. We have also learned what to do if you pass the exam and I think you share it with the world and celebrate. Next we have covered the different digital assets you'll receive, such as the Credly badge, the digital certificate, as well as the Microsoft Official Transcript. After that, don't forget to take a break and then start looking at what your next certification might be, so you always keep learning and keep your skills up to date. We have also covered what happens if you fail, which can happen to all of us, and don't forget, failed attempts do not show up on your transcript, so really only you know. Remember to use the score report to identify which areas you need to improve on. This way, when you go back, you will feel more confident. This is it - you are now ready to go schedule your AZ-900 exam. Good luck and I hope you are going to pass it for the first attempt.

Conclusion

Congratulations on completing this book! I am sure you have plenty on your belt, but please don't forget to leave an honest review. Furthermore, if you think this information was helpful to you, please share anyone who you think would be interested of IT as well.

About Richie Miller

Richie Miller has always loved teaching people Technology. He graduated with a degree in radio production with a minor in theatre in order to be a better communicator. While teaching at the Miami Radio and Television Broadcasting Academy, Richie was able to do voiceover work at a technical training company specializing in live online classes in Microsoft, Cisco, and CompTia technologies. Over the years, he became one of the top virtual instructors at several training companies, while also speaking at many tech and training conferences. Richie specializes in Project Management and ITIL these days, while also doing his best to be a good husband and father.

www.ingramcontent.com/pod-product-compliance
Lightning Source LLC
Chambersburg PA
CBHW071100050326
40690CB00008B/1070